Child and Adolescent Psychoanalysis in a Changing World

This book applies psychoanalytic insight to work with children and adolescents in a changing, often traumatic, world.

Each chapter considers how psychoanalysis can develop and be developed, assessing how in the modern world, psychological disturbance and psychological trauma is manifest in new, unfamiliar ways. From new and different social and technological realities, to the internet, and new sexual discourse, each chapter explores how the analyst can hold onto fundamental psychoanalytic understandings of mental functioning, address the young patient's or family's need for containment, while respecting the importance of drives, the varieties of psychosexuality, and the powerful impact of anxiety on psychological development. In relation to children, these authors disclose the potential destructiveness of impingements from adults on a precious, vulnerable development.

This collection is essential reading for all psychoanalysts and psychoanalytic psychotherapists, as well as other health and educational professionals working with children and adolescents.

Catalina Bronstein is a training and supervising analyst of the British Psychoanalytical Society, and a former president of the British Psychoanalytical Society. She is a child and adolescent and adult psychoanalyst and works at the Brent Adolescent Centre in London and in private practice. Bronstein is also Visiting Professor at the Psychoanalysis Unit, University College London.

Sara Flanders is a training and supervising psychoanalyst of the British Psychoanalytical Society. She works at the Brent Adolescent Centre in London and is Co-Chair of the Child and Adolescent Forum of the European Psychoanalytical Federation.

Child and Adolescent Psychoanalysis in a Changing World

Children on the Edge

Edited by
Catalina Bronstein and Sara Flanders

Routledge
Taylor & Francis Group

LONDON AND NEW YORK

Designed cover image: Norman Miller, Children in the City II, 65.5 x 61, Oil and Mixed Media on Board, 1963, c Norman Miller Estate

First published 2023
by Routledge
4 Park Square, Milton Park, Abingdon, Oxon OX14 4RN

and by Routledge
605 Third Avenue, New York, NY 10158

Routledge is an imprint of the Taylor & Francis Group, an informa business

© 2023 selection and editorial matter, Catalina Bronstein and Sara Flanders; individual chapters, the contributors

The right of Catalina Bronstein and Sara Flanders to be identified as the authors of the editorial material, and of the authors for their individual chapters, has been asserted in accordance with sections 77 and 78 of the Copyright, Designs and Patents Act 1988.

"From March 1979" By Tomas Tranströmer, translated by Robin Fulton, from THE GREAT ENIGMA, copyright © 2006 by Tomas Tranströmer. Translation © 2006 by Robin Fulton. Reprinted by permission of New Directions Publishing Corp.

British Library Cataloguing-in-Publication Data
A catalogue record for this book is available from the British Library

Library of Congress Cataloging-in-Publication Data
Names: Bronstein, Catalina, editor.
Title: Child and adolescent psychoanalysis in a changing world : children on the edge / edited by Catalina Bronstein and Sara Flanders.
Description: Abingdon, Oxon ; New York, NY : Routledge, 2023. | Includes bibliographical references and index. |
Identifiers: LCCN 2022056624 (print) | LCCN 2022056625 (ebook) | ISBN 9781032106458 (pbk) | ISBN 9781032106441 (hbk) | ISBN 9781003216360 (ebk)
Subjects: LCSH: Adolescent psychology. | Child psychology. | Adolescent analysis. | Child analysis.
Classification: LCC BF724 .C435 2023 (print) | LCC BF724 (ebook) | DDC 155.5—dc23/eng/20230309
LC record available at https://lccn.loc.gov/2022056624
LC ebook record available at https://lccn.loc.gov/2022056625

ISBN: 978-1-032–10644-1 (hbk)
ISBN: 978-1-032–10645-8 (pbk)
ISBN: 978-1-003–21636-0 (ebk)

DOI: 10.4324/9781003216360

Typeset in Times New Roman
by codeMantra

Contents

Contributors

Editors

Catalina Bronstein, MD, is a Training and Supervising Analyst of the British Psychoanalytical Society. She is Visiting Professor in the Psychoanalysis Unit, University College London, and former President of the British Psychoanalytical Society. She is a child, adolescent and adult psychoanalyst, having trained at the Tavistock Clinic and at the British Psychoanalytical Society. She is the former London editor of the *International Journal of Psychoanalysis* and currently sits on the Board of IJP. She has written numerous papers and book chapters and edited *Kleinian Theory, A Contemporary Perspective* and co-edited *The New Klein-Lacan Dialogues, Attacks on Linking Revisited and On Freud's "The Uncanny"*. She works in London in private practice and at the Brent Adolescent Centre.

Sara Flanders, PhD, is a Training and Supervising Analyst of the British Psychoanalytical Society. She has worked many years at the Brent Adolescent Centre, seeing patients and supervising. She edited *The Dream Discourse Today*, published by the New Library of Psychoanalysis, and with Dana Birksted-Breen and Alain Gibault, edited *Reading French Psychoanalysis*. She has written many articles, on adolescence and other subjects, and serves on the Executive of the College of the IJPA. She is co-chair of the Forum on Adolescence of the EPF.

Other contributors

Christine Anzieu-Premmereur is an adult and child psychiatrist and psychoanalyst. Member of the Société Psychanalytique de Paris and of the New York Psychoanalytic Institute, she is faculty of the Columbia University Psychoanalytic Center, where she directs the Parent–Infant Training Programme. She has published "The Process of Representation in Early Childhood", "Attacks on Linking in Parents of Young Disturbed Children", "A Psychoanalytic Exploration of the Body in Today's Psychoanalysis", and in French on play in child psychotherapy and on psychoanalytic interventions with parents and babies.

Leontine Brameijer is a psychotherapist and psychoanalyst seeing adolescents and adults in private practice in The Netherlands. She is a Training Analyst and Supervisor of the Dutch Psychoanalytic Society (NPaV) and teaches on their training course. She has supervision and participates in a clinical seminar with Kleinian analysts in London, and for the past decade has been advocating their approach in The Netherlands, where it is now firmly taking root. She has recently contributed to the first Dutch translation of a work by Melanie Klein, *Our Adult World and its Roots in Infancy*, with an introduction and a short biography of Klein.

Mónica Cardenal is a Training Analyst at the Buenos Aires Psychoanalytic Association; former Scientific Secretary Chair of IPA Committee on Psychoanalytic Assistance in Crises and Emergencies; Consultant of IPA Committee on Child and Adolescent Psychoanalysis; Associate Professor in Clinic Psychology and Infant Psychiatry; Director of Bick's model of Infant Observation and of seminars at the University Institute of the Italian Hospital, Buenos Aires; Supervisor on Early Childhood at the Pediatric Mental Health Service, Italian Hospital, Buenos Aires; Supervisor of Work Discussion groups, Programme for "*homeless children and young refugees*", in Puebla, Mexico, JUCONI Foundation; and author and co-editor of many international publications.

Simon Cregeen is a consultant child and adolescent psychotherapist (Member, Association of Child Psychotherapists) and a couple psychoanalytic psychotherapist (Member, British Psychoanalytic Council). For many years he was Head of Child and Adolescent Psychotherapy in Manchester and Salford NHS CAMHS, where his primary clinical interest was work with "Looked After Children", adoptive families, and associated networks. He now works privately with adolescents, young adults, and couples in Manchester. Simon recently retired as a clinical tutor at the Northern School of Child and Adolescent Psychotherapy (Leeds). He continues to teach and supervise other psychoanalytic clinicians and is a Trustee of Manchester Psychoanalytic Development Trust (mpdt.org.uk). Simon has had papers published in the *Journal of Child Psychotherapy* and elsewhere. He was involved with the IMPACT adolescent depression RCT and is a co-author of *Short-term Psychoanalytic Psychotherapy with Adolescents with Depression: A Treatment Manual* (2016, Karnac).

Joshua Durban is training and supervising child and adult psychoanalyst at the Israeli Psychoanalytic Society and Institute, Jerusalem and Tel-Aviv (IPA), where he also teaches. He is on the faculty of the Sackler School of Medicine, Tel-Aviv University, the Psychotherapy Programme, Post-Graduate Kleinian Studies. He is a member of the IPA inter-committee for the prevention of child abuse. He has a private practice in Tel-Aviv and specialises in the psychoanalysis of autistic spectrum disorders (ASD) and psychotic children, adolescents, and adults. He has written many papers on the psychoanalysis of children and adolescents and on other subjects.

Susan Donner is a child, adolescent and adult psychiatrist and psychoanalyst in private practice in Woodland Hills, CA. She is a Training and Child, Adolescent and Adult Supervising Analyst, Chair of the Child Psychoanalytic Program and Director of the Child and Adolescent Clinic at the New Center for Psychoanalysis in Los Angeles. A graduate of Harvard University and University of California at San Francisco School of Medicine, she is also an Associate Clinical Professor in Psychiatry at UCLA Geffen School of Medicine. She has contributed a number of chapters and articles in the psychoanalytic literature and has presented at conferences of the International and American Psychoanalytic Associations, American Psychiatric Association and American Academy of Child and Adolescent Psychiatry.

Florence Guignard is a Swiss and French psychoanalyst, and honorary training member of the Paris Society. Past Chair and present counsellor of the IPA Committee On Child and Adolescent Psychoanalysis (COCAP); the founder in 1994 of the European Society for Child and Adolescent Psychoanalysis with Annie Anzieu (SEPEA); and past chief editor of L'Année Psychanalytique Internationale (Annual French translation of Selected IJP Papers). She has published: more than 200 papers in French, several of them translated into different languages; four books in French, two of them translated into English: P*sychoanalytic concepts and Technique in Development. Psychoanalysis, Neuroscience and Physics* (The New Library of Psychoanalysis, Routledge, 2020) and *The Infantile in Psychoanalytic Practice Today* (Routledge, IPA Coll., 2021); and two books not yet available: *Conversations psychanalytiques, une autobiograhie* and with Sylvie Reignier *Le psychanalyste dans la cité.*

Angela Joyce is a Fellow, and Training and Supervising Psychoanalyst and Child Psychoanalyst with the British Psychoanalytical Society. She trained as a child analyst at the Anna Freud Centre and worked there for 20 years as well as being a founding member of the pioneering Parent–Infant Project applying psychoanalysis to working with babies and their families, and jointly leading the child psychotherapy service. She now works full-time in private practice in London. She is currently Chair of the Curriculum Committee at the BPAS and a member of its Education Committee; Chair of the Winnicott Trust; a Trustee of the Squiggle Foundation; and has been an Honorary Senior Lecturer at University College London. Amongst her publications, she was a contributing author to the groundbreaking *Psychoanalytic Parent Infant Psychotherapy: Claiming the Baby* (2005 and 2016) and *Relational Trauma in Infancy* (2009); she edited *Reading Winnicott* with Lesley Caldwell (New Library of Psychoanalysis Teaching Series, 2011); Introduction to Volume 6 of *The Collected Works of D. W. Winnicott* (OUP, November, 2016), and *Donald Winnicott and the History of the Present* (Karnac, November 2017).

Mariângela Mendes de Almeida is a psychoanalyst with the Brazilian Association of Psychoanalysis of São Paulo (SBPSP), Brazil, with an MA from the Tavistock

Clinic (Child and Family Department) and University of East London, and PhD from the Federal University of São Paulo. She is head of the Parent–Infant Services, Paediatric Department/Federal University of São Paulo; member of the Parent–Infant Clinical Service of the Prisma Group on Psychoanalysis and Autism (SBPSP), and IPA Research Fellow; co-editor of *Looking and Listening* by Karnac Books and *Infância, vínculos e diversidade profissional* by Blucher; and scientific coordinator of Cippa LA (professionals working with autism in Latin America), member of Alobb (Latin American psychoanalytic observers), Rieppi (international network of psychoanalytic work with infants), and Inspira (interregional group discussing clinical psychoanalytic work with autism).

Kerry Kelly Novick is a child, adolescent and adult psychoanalyst on the faculties of numerous psychoanalytic institutes around the United States. A founder of Allen Creek Preschool, she is past President of the Association for Child Psychoanalysis, a Councillor-at-Large for the American Psychoanalytic Association, and past Chair of the IPA Committee on Child and Adolescent Psychoanalysis. Author of many papers and book chapters, she has also written five books with Jack Novick – the latest is *Freedom To Choose: Two Systems of Self-Regulation*, which have been translated into Italian, German, Spanish, Finnish, Chinese, Turkish, Japanese, and Hungarian. The *Parent Work Casebook*, an edited volume, was published in 2020 and the *Adolescent Casebook* in early 2022.

Maria Rhode is a member of the Association of Child Psychotherapists, a clinical associate of the British Psychoanalytical Society, and Emeritus Professor of Child Psychotherapy at the Tavistock Clinic, where she was a co-convener of the Autism Workshop. Her main interests have been in childhood autism and psychosis, language development, and infant observation; she has written papers and book chapters on these subjects, and is co-editor of three books on autism and psychotic states in children. Her most recent paper concerns an audited case series of toddlers at high risk of autism.

Björn Salomonsson is a medical doctor, psychiatric specialist and an adult, child, and parent–infant psychoanalyst of the Swedish Psychoanalytical Association, Stockholm, working in private practice. He is also a consultant at the Mama Mia Child Health Centre. Associate Professor at the Unit of Reproductive Health, Department of Women's and Children's Health at the Karolinska Institute. His research compares psychoanalytic mother–infant treatments with Swedish routine baby care. Salomonsson has published papers on containment in child psychoanalysis, the analysis of children with ADHD, the aesthetic experience, various subjects on the theory and technique of infant–mother psychotherapy and, with Johan Norman and individually, on analytic case presentation according to the "weaving thoughts" method. His book, "Psychoanalytic Therapy with Infants and Parents: Practice, Theory and Results" was published by Routledge in 2014 and translated and published in Italian, Catalan, and Portuguese. Another book, written with Majlis Winberg Salomonsson, was published by

Routledge in 2016: *Psychoanalytic Dialogues with Children and Adolescents* (In French: *A quoi pensent les enfants*. 2014, Toulouse: Erès). A third book, *Psychodynamic Interventions during Pregnancy and Infancy*, was published by Routledge in April 2018. He is a member of la Société Européenne pour la Psychanalyse de l'Enfant et de l'Adolescent, Paris, an honorary member of the Psychoanalytic Center of California, an Honorary Research Fellow, Anna Freud Centre, London, and a co-founder of the "A Primo Foundation", a knowledge centre in Stockholm for infant and parent psychology.

Carlos Vasquez is a clinical psychologist and child and adolescent psychoanalytic psychotherapist. He studied Clinical Psychology in Perú at the Pontificia Universidad Católica del Perú and Child and Adolescent Psychotherapy at the Tavistock Clinic in the UK. He has worked in clinical institutions both in Perú and in the UK, in services such as the Children, Young Adults and Families Department at the Tavistock Clinic and also the Brent Centre for Young People in London. He has taught at the Tavistock Clinic in London and in Perú. Currently, he works in private practice full-time in Lima, Perú, with children, adolescents, and adults. He teaches in different psychotherapy training institutes in Lima, such as Intercambio and Centro de Psicoterapia Psicoanalítica de Lima.

Gianna Williams is an adult and child analyst in the British Psychoanalytical Society. She is a former consultant child and adolescent psychotherapist at the Tavistock Clinic and has introduced Tavistock Model Child Psychotherapy Courses in five Italian towns. She has developed Infant Observation as a compulsory module for child neuro-psychiatry students at the University of Pisa. Has been Consultant since 1999 to the NGO "Juntos con los niños", organisation for street children in Mexico. She is a visiting lecturer on the Tavistock Clinical Doctorate and teaches at the BPAS analysts and child analysts in training. She has published a large number of articles and book chapters and written or co-edited several books amongst which are *Eating Disorders in Adolescence* and *Internal Landscapes and Foreign Bodies: Eating Disorders and other Pathologies*.

Foreword

The analyst's identity challenged by the reality of today's adolescents: Climate disaster, solitude and lockdown, sex and gender transformations, social and cultural networks

Florence Guignard

Adolescent's experience of external reality today in western Europe

Adolescence is the main crossroad of an individual with his/her actual social environment, where the boundaries of various parts of external and internal reality permeate.

Nowadays, in addition to the normal turmoil of puberty, adolescents have to deal with several aspects of reality that took place recently:

- a new and sudden pandemic with many deaths and repetitive lockdowns;
- a catastrophic degradation of the climate, which is a serious threat for their future;
- and an ever-increasing immigration of people who have lost everything: their country, home, work, and culture.

These new vertices took place in a short space of time, after 50 years of economic expansion and a rather hedonistic mentality in the middle-class population. During this period of time, three generations – at least – enjoyed being their children's mates rather than their stern educators; the classic family structure changed tremendously, and medically assisted procreation gave a new orientation to the desire of two people to form a couple. Most often, children have to live in "recomposed" families and to share the time of their everyday living between separated parents.

Added to these social data, the present events add huge turmoil to the "normal" adolescent disorganisation of the balance established during childhood between the two principles of mental functioning – the pleasure/unpleasure principle <–> reality principle.

Normally, adolescents address their rebellion to the previous generations. But today, parents are embarrassed to face adolescents properly, both because they too were taken fairly unaware by the present situation of emergency, and also because, behind the deafness of their silent denial, they know they are collectively responsible for the calamitous state of today's pandemic and climate situation they are handing to future generations. This reality leaves little opportunity for today's adolescents to work through a post-oedipal, healthy ambivalence together with their external family and their internal parental objects; introjective identifications, supposed to increase during the second part of adolescence, remain fairly problematic.

When the turmoil of puberty makes family life more complicated, adolescents spontaneously turn to more or less structured forms of life in groups. The repeated lockdowns due to the pandemic hit successive blows to that vital vertex of construction of the adolescent Self. To compensate for the loss of real meetings, virtual encounters, starting already from a high rate, increased to an incredible extent. New websites appeared, gathering most parts of the adolescent "chats", whilst they quit earlier ones, used by their parents, thus increasing the gap and the difficulty of communication between generations.

The need to "belong to" brings with it the danger of getting trapped in various conspiracy theories, or situations of harassment or pornography. "Group mentality", as described by Bion, is quickly spreading, with its narrow-minded "basic assumptions": fight/flight, pairing, and dependence.[1]

Intimacy, extimacy.

Body and mind are linked together from *intra-uterine* existence onwards. We know that much drive energy is needed for their association, but we do not yet have enough keys to understand everything about the pre- and perinatal psychosomatic levels of functioning in a human being. Neither are we aware of how many mutual sacrifices body and mind have to accomplish to keep alive a coherent identity feeling through so many experiences in the external and internal world, from birth to death. Still, we know that, to develop properly, body and mind have to interact within a certain degree of *intimacy*, the constitution of which is congruent to the development of the Ego and the Self. The mother's psycho-sensory and motor attitude plays an important role in the early relationship that allows the creation of an internal space of intimacy for the *infans*. At the borders of Self and object, the experience of his/her own body is the first situation of intimacy, not only external, but also internal, in a transitional space (Winnicott).

The word *"extimacy"* was created in 1923 by Albert Thibaudet, a French writer. Rarely used, it was significantly described by Jean Echenoz, to express the demeanour of a character in his first novel *"The Greewich meridian"*.[2] This character, named "Byron" was behaving and relating to other people in an identical way, wherever he was, and whatever the nature of his relation to the person. The author intuitively stresses Byron's *absence of attention for, and of sensitive attachment to* his human environment. Today, the pathology of ADHD confirms the capital role of these two competences at the onset of psychic life.

The concept of "extimacy" was briefly tried by Lacan, who equated it to "the uncanny" and gave it up rapidly.[3] Serge Tisseron[4] uses it, as opposed to "exhibitionism" in his study *Loft Story*. For this author, intimacy and extimacy are the systole and diastole of self-esteem in the constitution of identity.

Biological puberty is an experience of unwilling exposure of one's body to extimacy. It transcends the borders of the private sphere and exposes intimacy to the outside, the public, and the unknown. At a primary, unconscious level of somato-psychic experience, waking up with a broken voice, seeing hairs appearing all over his body and face, having nocturnal pollution, or else seeing her breasts grow and experience her first menstruations, is confronting the teenager to the uncanny experience of becoming alien to himself/herself.

With puberty, the limits of the psychosomatic space of intimacy are deeply disorganised; identity consistency becomes particularly vulnerable, new defences appear, that lead teenagers *now* to hide in a *claustrum*[5] of inhibition and secrecy, and *then* to use provocative exhibitionism, putting to test the new limits of their body and psyche. Tattoos and disguises express something of the uncanny that burst into the teenager's body image.

Chats on the web offer teenagers a *pseudo-intimacy*, in fact, a manic *extimacy* replacing the silent work of mourning the body of childhood, as evidenced by many videos on social networks. But extimacy does not feed much the feeling of identity. To be "popular" is a poor sweetener that does not replace the caloric components of true love, needed for building an adult identity. Psychic transformations necessary to integrate bisexuality require a long-lasting work.

The *sight* of the teenager's pubescent body is also disturbing to his/her environment. Family becomes the place of projection of a past the child has to mourn, including his familiarity and ease with his own body. When parents are consulting for their pubescent child, we are often struck by the gap existing between the real body of their teenager, and the parent's narrative, which seems to deny unconsciously the perception of their child having suddenly become such an uncanny being ...

Together with somatic disorders, a*cting* – in and out – and enactments are the most common defences against intimacy, including psychoanalytic intimacy, that might then regress to a "de-symbolised", eroticised level.

The onset of puberty in today's world

Today, social freedom to talk about sexual orientation, parenthood, sex, and gender identity in society does not erase the complexity of psychic conflicts and object relations. Adolescence is the playground *par excellence* of all kinds of identificatory movements, projective, adhesive, introjective, particularly around the transformation of the Ego Ideal of childhood into an adult Ideal of the Ego.[6] Such a turmoil brings the latest fashion trends in the outside world to meet with the deepest layers of the Superego, made of the parents' internal objects – i.e. the grand-parents' mentality, as Freud stated.

The observation is congruent with the discovery made about ten years ago by searchers in genetics: severe traumas are printed in our epigenesis for at least three generations.[7]

But this also means that we need three generations to accept any consistent discovery, at least at a conscient level, like the facts that the Earth is not the centre of the Universe, that there exists about 96% of black matter, totally unknown yet, and so on. Discoveries about mental functioning, social organisation, and education are

treated in the same way – to say the least, and no to mention the repetitive movements of regression towards long periods of obscurantism.

Adolescent mentality is the only exception to such a repetitive denial of the
quick pace of time and events.

We should be more open to listening to what is expressed nowadays by adolescents, as they are both knowledgeable and primarily concerned by the future of
pandemic and climate. (Some characters are able to keep lifelong such a mentality, like Edgar Morin who, in 2020, a few months before his hundredth anniver-
sary, published a new book with the title: *Let's Change Lanes. The Lessons of
Coronavirus.*)

Whilst the previous generations persist in their ideal of hedonism, ego-centred
preoccupation and old fashion group mentality of "more money, more exploitation
of natural resources, more robotization, more worldwide immediate communication of information – true or fake … and you will obtain total freedom", what
adolescents denounce is "more burn out, more poverty, more violence, and an increasing malaise about gender identity".

Any psychoanalyst who listens today to an adolescent is confronted with a mixture of anxiety, disappointment, even violent bitterness towards this adult who is
pretending to help him/her and who *does not tell the truth* about the actual state of
the world in which adolescents will have to live tomorrow. Confronted with such
a precarious future, today's adolescents address us: "How dare you?!" said Greta
Thunberg in front of the United Nations Organisation.

Because we, psychoanalysts, consider the search for truth as the most important
tool for our therapeutic action, one should not deny our common responsibility
and our concern about the state of the "Blue Planet" we are handing to the next
generation. If we do not do so, how could we help adolescents to pay attention to
their psychic reality and, for instance, interpret their senseless violence as a projective identification of the way their parents and grand-parents totally destroyed
thousands of species of animals, insects, and plants, for the only sake of their own
greediness?

Our analytic competences are seriously put to test, as well as our own identity
balance. Past might not be so much of a treasure anymore, something to explore,
analyse, and overcome, for the sake of a promising future; it might well appear as
an illusionary and poisoned gift hypocritically proposed to new generations. "What
is the use of understanding the past", said a 14-year-old boy, "since we are all going
to die very soon?" Although the situation is not quite new, nevertheless it is the first
time since psychoanalysis exists, that psychoanalysts of the whole world have to
cope with being such transference objects.

Family and sexual orientation of the adolescent.
The question of sex and gender

Traditional family structure has been largely replaced today by new ways of living, with frequent changes of hetero or homo partners in the parental couple of an

adolescent, various step-brothers and sisters growing in his/her environment, when s/he was not brought up by a single parent, most often a mother.

Together with the extension of the "culture on the net", the softening of social rules facilitates the adolescent's questioning and observations at the dawn of his/her own experience of an adult form of sexuality. But this new freedom does not prevent harassment from spoiling his/her relationships with peers. It does not give him/her either a magic pass for acquiring a happy and stable sexual identity. Erasing outside difficulties tends to bring inside ones to the fore. To some adolescents, the more impossible or useless the fight against outside rules, the more urgent it is to find a new target to fight against, in order to keep on splitting and projecting as far as possible the inexorable destiny of puberty: to mourn childhood and its infinite potential, and to become a determined, already partly limited adult.

Some of us had an opportunity to talk with adolescents who declare that they want to change gender and/or sex. A few days ago, I saw a picture of a poster pasted on the streets of Lyon, in France. It shows an androgyne teenager who says: "nobody (is allowed to) define my gender for me". Literature written by people who decided to change gender or sex[8] expresses a tremendous disarray and rancour against a society supposed to have *imposed* on them a body impossible to live in. Paranoid persecution does not succeed in containing melancholy. Such a quest for omnipotence is the most archaic and pathetic defence against infantile helplessness. Concreteness has regressively invaded the whole field of symbolisation and there is not much of a transitional space left for the analyst to work in it.

As an analyst, it is impossible not to listen to what is murmured beyond that concreteness, and to try to make links with such a deep existential pain. Impossible also to find a univocal interpretation that would explain all the cases of this increasing phenomenon. Personally, I can only wonder about the role played by the ideal of narcissistic hedonism claimed by their parents, grand-parents, and grand-grand-parents, in such an unrealistic and contagious claim for deciding of their sex and gender.

During the same recent period, the omnipotence of previous generations has considerably transformed the way people are considering inner psychic life and its suffering. A combination of hatred against the unknown, uncanny, unpredictable unconscious, together with the illusion that the binary system of artificial intelligence will tame once and forever the world of emotions, anguish, and fantasy, invaded the group mentality of adult generations, up to certain parts of scientific methodology. Note that such a tendency to mix up technological sophistication with authentic scientific research enhances the denial opposed to adolescent anxieties about their identity, proposing to them a few external, supposed, solutions to their internal disease. The mere idea of having recourse to a psychotherapy to help any situation has become despised. However, in the same way several writers during the last five years accused their parents of not having transmitted anything to them; some of the people who got a medical and surgical treatment to get the appearance of a sex different from their biological one, sued their parents several years later, for having accepted their desire as a child or adolescent, and ordered and paid for such a concrete solution to their existential malaise.

To conclude: "making the best of a bad job" (Bion)

Violence was always one of the hazards of the adolescent process. The considerable push of the drives, together with the body modifications out of their control, always brought adolescents to burst out, whenever a situation is overwhelming their capacities of mastering it. Uncertainty about finding oneself within so many new parameters is the core of their violence. Emotional conflicts do not reach an internal, intra-psychic status. Psychoanalytic work is difficult to establish because psychic envelopes[9] are as defective as social ones. The uncanny part of any new psychoanalytic encounter often contains too little good and too much bad, too little familiar and too much unknown of the object.

Such a challenge has always urged the psychoanalyst's creativity to find a minimum of interests that they share with an adolescent who is consulting, often reluctantly. Today, we are in a new situation, with many more adolescents who need help because of their legitimate anxiety about the state of the world, but many fewer adults who trust psychoanalysis and look for us to help them and their family. This is also true of the medical environment.

This might be a good opportunity for us to have a serious look at the important changes that occurred in the society and family structure, and to test our basic identity feeling as analysts, shaken by the necessity to modify our usual rules of setting in our psychoanalytic practice. It might well be that our adolescent patients bring us new paths to discover where to go, keeping the essence of our practice, even when external components of the *setting* are not any more available. I do not think only of the sessions on the web, but also of the frequency of sessions accepted by the adolescent and his/her family.

Of course, nobody will deny how fruitful a sufficient number of sessions is, to establish an analytical process. Nowadays, we have to do hard work to convince people that psychic life exists, living at its own pace and needing intimacy to develop and be explored, and that we are experts in the matter of caring for it. Treating adolescents puts us in the best place: they will oblige us to consider the changes that occurred in the society and family in which they grew up, and to examine them at the rate of our analytic assumptions. Today, we have to mourn the old sayings that pretend we are the only ones to *know*. We do not know much, neither about the future, nor about the psychic resources that will be at hand tomorrow.

In spite of the sociological break-down of a consistent Oedipus complex, we still have real and precious assets to accompany those adolescents who would be interested to work with us: we know the richness of the unconscious mind and the creativity of dreams; we know how important it is to establish or repair a consistent container/contained relationship in order for an individual to trust himself in life; we know that relation between body and mind is capital and everlasting; we know that identity feeling is constantly in movement and so quick to feel threatened by new persons, events, emotions; we know also how our own "Infantile" – the most vivid unconscious/preconscious part of our Self – is in condition to help our patient whenever we are ready to observe and analyse a "blind spot" occurring in the analytic field.[10] In other words, we know some capital things about human relations and identifications, how to listen to suffering, and how to try and make them useful, with the help of the patient.

What we do not know is how long we will be able to use these assets, because of the state of illness in our world.

In these conditions, we should do our best to use all the means available *today* – tomorrow might be too late. And here, we should be very grateful towards the binary system used by artificial intelligence, which allows two or more human beings to obtain an immediate and prolonged communication on the web, whatever the geographic distance between them. We should use such a means as much and as long as it is needed and desired by our patients, and know that they also will come – or come back – to a closer contact with us – if and when it will be possible again – which means to examine many outside, but also inside reasons to be frightened by it.

We should also acknowledge in front of our adolescent patients that we are part of the generations who destroyed the world they are going to inherit from us. (Of course, many previous generations should have done that as well – we still discover non-exploded bombs of the Second World War.) This might help *them* to listen to us as to human beings rather than to oracles. This might help *us* to observe the consistency and the changes that occurred over a hundred years, since the birth of psychoanalysis, in the realm of Western society and family, so that we would not interpret wrongly our patient's fantasies, dreams, and beliefs. For instance, the actual role of the father has changed considerably over the past 50 years. Simultaneously, the women's place in the world of work, the tolerance to homosexuality, to families "other", to medically assisted procreation, and so on … all this has to be confronted in the personal primal scene of an adolescent of 2021, and also to our own beliefs.

Because we had the privilege of accomplishing many years of personal psychoanalytic treatment several times a week, we know how the delicate balance of any identity feeling is easily disturbed, and because we trained our projective identification to become a constant capacity of reverie, we are able to *feel* distressed under violence, despair under manic defences, and trust under arrogance.

Let's do everything in our power to keep contact with adolescents, relentlessly, even when they want to escape from the dialogue with us. Any other so-called *rule of setting* resembles a denial of reality: the world has changed more quickly and deeply than it had during the past five, ten, or twenty centuries, maybe more – this is the work of historians to be more precise.

Mine is to acknowledge reality and to try going on doing my impossible job: being an analyst. I guess you are in the same situation …

Note

1 Bion W. R. 1948 *Experiences in Groups*, London, Tavistock, 1961.
2 Echenoz J. 1979 *Le Méridien de Greenwich*, Paris, Éd. de Minuit Il fait de Byron, son héros, un personnage : « sans attache sensible, sans ancrage particulier. Ne s'attardant

ni aux objets ni aux décors, il traversait l'espace avec une inattention sincère. Jamais il n'avait pu acquérir la notion de domiciliation, se mouler à l'impératif civique du lieu privé, intime, adhésif. [...] Ainsi, à Paris, son bureau du boulevard Haussmann et son appartement de la rue Pétrarque, pôles rigoureux d'une quotidienneté binaire, lui étaient également familiers et étrangers, intimes autant qu'extimes, semblables en cela, par exemple, à une cabine d'ascenseur, à la salle d'attente d'un dentiste, ou à la terrasse d'un tabac du quai Voltaire ».

3 Lacan, J. 1969 *Seminar XVI, The Other Side of Psychoanalysis*. New York: W. W. Norton & Company, p. 249.
4 Tisseron S. 2001 *L'intimité surexposée*, Paris, Ramsay.
5 Meltzer D. 1992 *The Claustrum. An Investigation of Claustrophobic Phenomena*. With an essay by Meg Harris Williams: "Macbeth's Equivocation, Shakespeare's Ambiguity" Strathtay (Scotland): Clunie Press.
6 I am referring here to a difference made in French, thanks to Cathy Bronstein for making it clear for English readers!
7 Cf. Giacobino A. 2013 *Rev. Med, Suisse*, 9(396): 1600.
8 For instance, Paul B. Preciado 2019 *Un appartement sur Uranus*, Paris, Grasset
9 Anzieu D. 1985 *Le Moi-peau* Paris Dunod.
10 Guignard F. 2021 The Infantile in Psychoanalytic Practice Today. IPA podcast, https://link.chtbl.com/p-eqlPO-

Introduction

Catalina Bronstein

In July 2019 the British Psychoanalytical Society (BPAS) organised a conference on Child and Adolescent Psychoanalysis.[1] This conference was the result of the awareness by the BPAS and by several organisations from different parts of the world of the need to address and think together about the challenges we are facing regarding child and adolescent mental health. Beyond the familiar internal and external issues affecting children and adolescents which influence their mental health, we must also consider societal changes that impact them. These include the challenges brought about by changing sexualities and family structures, by new technologies such as the internet and world wide web, by societal and political conflicts, and by the extension of knowledge in the areas of diagnosis and treatment.

The editors of this book felt that there was an urgent need to increase awareness of the extent of emotional and mental suffering in many vulnerable children and adolescents and of the widespread deficiency in health systems to recognise this and to provide proper psychotherapeutic help to those in need of it. Without timely support, children and young people's problems tend to worsen increasing the risk of creating chronic mental disturbances that will affect them for the rest of their lives.

This book is the result of this conference. It contains the main papers that were presented then as well as other papers that we felt would enrich our thinking on child and adolescent mental health in a changing world. Since the conference, we have been deeply affected by several other traumatic issues that crucially impacted on children and adolescents. The increased awareness of the disastrous effects of climate change together with the COVID-19 pandemic brought a sense of helplessness and a higher level of anxiety across different age groups about the precariousness of life. The pandemic with its prolonged periods of lockdown greatly impacted on children's and adolescents' usual ways of socialising and increased the potential for conflictive relationships with their families.

All chapters are clinically based and have been written from a psychoanalytical perspective. Whether we think of psychoanalysis as a particular tool to help psychological disorders in an individual way – and/or as a theory of mind that informs many other approaches such as those involving family work, group work, and parental help amongst others, psychoanalysis continues to provide the most in-depth understanding of the mind and of how to help those in need.

One of the main aspects in the development of child and adolescent psychoanalysis was the realisation of the specificity of this field. Whilst the general psychoanalytic understanding that arises from treating adults and the theory behind it informs its findings, there was a need to find specific theoretical and clinical pathways to understand children and adolescents and establish a meaningful contact with them. Since the beginning of psychoanalysis, the pioneers in child analysis have strived to find these ways. The technique of free association used in our work with adults had to be modified into a particular technique suitable for accessing the children's minds. Klein's discovery of the psychoanalytic play technique was fundamental to this development. The development of the child play technique which Klein thought to be the equivalent of free association paved the way to the profound understanding of the child's inner world (Bronstein, 2001). Explorations by child analysts such as Melanie Klein, Anna Freud, and Winnicott gave place to a very rich field of thought and research where individual cases treated in an intensive way gave rise to many exciting discoveries about the child's unconscious thoughts and phantasies, anxieties, and defences. Understanding the role of developmental phases as propitiated by Anna Freud and of the impact of the relationship to the mother as proposed by Winnicott and later Bion, enriched this field and created many further developments in child analysis across the world. Similarly, as with the child, adolescent problems with their own specific sets of anxieties and defences that needed specialised attention brought questions on how we could address the complexities that characterised understanding and helping this age group. We are convinced that psychoanalysts and child and adolescent psychotherapists must work together to further our understanding of this field that is constantly impacted upon by new challenges, as society, family attitudes, technical advances, and many other stimuli, both positive and negative, impact on the mental health of children and adolescents.

The early work of different psychoanalytic pioneers is reflected on the diverse theoretical approaches that stem from them and that different schools of thought have further developed. Some authors pinpoint the need to understand the early anxieties and defences that are seen to arise from an early sense of self, an ego that can experience anxiety from the very beginning of life. Other authors see the early relationship between infant and mother as one that is initially symbiotic and look at the difficulties in the process of individuation and separation. We can also see an emphasis on issues surrounding the different phases of development. However, despite the different theoretical and clinical approaches, there is still much common ground. The role of primitive anxieties and agonies, the impact of the early relationship with the mother, the role of oedipal conflict and of the Superego, the relevance of phantasy, both conscious and unconscious, the different ways in which children suffer from fears and phobias, from obsessional thinking and states of panic, the impact of early trauma, the relevance of suicidal impulses in adolescence and the beneficial role of psychoanalytical and psychotherapeutic treatment to help both children and adolescents are accepted by all. We can add to this the recognition of the importance of providing psychoanalytical psychotherapy to help parents as well as families of children and adolescents.

Even though human beings struggle with impulses, anxieties, and defences that stem from very early on in our lives each age group requires specific attention concerning the needs and abilities to process emotions and thoughts. The needs of a one-year-old infant are different from the adolescent's needs when struggling with issues related to his/her gender identity. Child and adolescent psychotherapists are very attuned to these differences and to the various skills, they must employ to understand and reach their patients, to be in touch with their emotional and specific maturational development. These factors, plus the intense emotional experience of working with desperately troubled children and adolescents explain in part why child and adolescent's psychoanalytic psychotherapy can be very demanding and challenging whilst being at the same time creative and rewarding.

For reasons of clarity, we have divided the book into three sections that place an emphasis on some particular problems and ways of approaching them though we are fully aware that any "cataloguing" of difficulties cannot be absolute. The human condition inherently presents us with a changing kaleidoscope. However, we also need some order from where we can think about these issues more clearly. Each section has an introduction that we hope will help the reader navigate the different chapters.

The first part, on "New frontiers, diagnostic, theoretical and technical challenges" has been helpfully introduced by Mónica Cardenal. How can we sustain a capacity to think and to help when we are met with suffering babies and toddlers whose parents feel submerged in a difficult relationship with their baby? As Mónica Cardenal highlights, psychoanalysis has benefited from psychoanalytical infant observation (Bick, 1964, 1968). Infant observation, which is now part of the requirement at many child psychotherapy and psychoanalytic trainings has in itself furthered the understanding of the early relationship between mother and baby. Not only this, but it has also greatly helped many aspiring professionals learn how to find the right distance from where we can both get emotionally involved with the observed baby/primary object and at the same time keep an internal space where we can think about the emotional experience elicited by them. This learning experience will prove extremely helpful in the future psychotherapeutic work, a first step towards bearing the complexities that we will have to deal with when meeting the intense transference and countertransference elicited by our young patients.

In 1930, in a pioneer analytic work where she showed how anxiety affects the development of symbol formation, Melanie Klein wrote a paper on the analysis of a child who suffered from what we would now describe as autism, though at that time this would have still been seen as a psychosis (Klein, 1930). The understanding of autism has developed significantly since 1943 when Leo Kanner wrote the first systematic description of early autism (Kanner, 1943). At times it is not very easy to work out the clinical differences between psychotic states and autistic states of mind as they can sometimes overlap whilst autistic and psychotic anxieties can be seen in various forms of cognitive impairment, so it seems of fundamental importance to continue to explore and write about these pathologies (Rhode, 1997). Following Kanner's work, there were many important psychoanalytical contributions such as those from Tustin (1972, 1983, 1992), Meltzer et al. (1975), Alvarez (1977, 1996), Haag (1997), Houzel (2004), among many others. Progress in the understanding of autism was challenged by the arrival of a more organicist way of thinking that aimed at trying to cancel the knowledge provided by psychoanalysis rather than explore the possible complementarity between physical and psychological explanations. Both Maria Rhode's and Joshua Durban's chapters give a clear account and further develop the exploration of autistic mechanisms, of autistic spectrum disorders (ASD) and of the possibility of helping these children and adolescents.

Staying with the complexities underlying early emotional disturbances and the intricate quality of difficulties in connection to the relationship between mother and baby, both Christine Anzieu-Premmereur and Björn Salomonsson write on the work they do with babies and parents. We can see the impact of this interaction in the here and now of the sessions. We can also see the relevance of how the baby was conceived and cared for, the role of the embodied relationship with the mother as well as the development of a sense of identity (Stern, 1998). One of the issues we are now confronting is the assisted reproductive technology which has introduced many complex changes in family dynamics and in the children who have been conceived following them (Haynes & Miller, 2004; Ehrensaft, 2008). The relevance of studying and developing possible ways of helping mothers and babies is quite crucial and Salomonsson gives us a rich account of this possibility through PIP (Parent–Infant Psychotherapy)

The second part on "Children on the edge" addresses *domestic and social violence, abuse, and deprivation*. Of course, these are not new issues in the history of humanity. But, as Kerry Kelly Novick states in her introduction to this section, we can now see far clearer than before the amount of children who are suffering from living in conflict zones, from wars, having refugee status, suffering from neglect, domestic abuse, social discrimination. The treatment of deeply traumatised children and adolescents needs special psychotherapeutic skills. It also brings an enormous emotional challenge to child psychotherapists as they must withstand intense projections plus the despair, hopelessness, sadness, and unbearable feelings that are often elicited in the countertransference. The three children written about by Cregeen, Joyce, and Mendes de Almeida had a profound impact on their therapists who, as Flanders states in the introduction, need to be sustained by the belief "*that there is meaning in the most confusing and distressing, even repellent symptoms presented by young people*". There is a distinction between reproducing the trauma in the therapeutic situation by means of action and the possibility of symbolising it, being able to think about it with the help of the therapist. Cregeen mentions both Boston and Rustin's ideas on the therapist's need to be able to survive, to be able to wait and to be willing to take risks (Boston and Szur 1983; Rustin, 2001).

The complexities brought by intergenerational trauma, that as Joyce, following Anna Freud, sees as connected to "underlying primary deficiencies" that bring developmental delays and states of "proto-meaning" can be helped by careful psychotherapeutic intervention which in this case included non-interpretative techniques

and interventions. In the case of Lisa, described by Mendes de Almeida, the therapeutic space helped the development and expansion of internal representations. In
all these cases the development of a capacity for symbol formation helped towards
the substitution of the repetitive patterns caused by trauma with a more thought-
enabling capacity.

The title of the third part is "New realities, new challenges". One of the current
changes we must engage with and understand is the one happening in connection
to states of "gender dysphoria". The search for sexual and gender identity which is
one of the paramount tasks in adolescence offers now different possibilities for resolution. The clearer binary gendered way with which we used to navigate has been
replaced by several possibilities that can offer both solace and/or anxiety, clarity,
and/or confusion to many children and adolescents. Issues related to gender, sexuality, and the impact of the internet are clearly presented by both Flanders and
Donner. To try to understand how we construct our world-model (Money-Kyrle,
1961), especially in adolescence, I think is worth thinking about how we react to
the reality of a changing sexuality, a changing body that imposes itself on us. Curiosity about the world becomes heightened in adolescence. Adolescence is a fertile
ground from where we can start to explore in greater depth what is going on in the
world, what lies beyond ourselves, close friends, and family, in politics, history,
literature, and science, to look at those questions that haven't yet got answers and
to formulate new ones. The internet with the world wide web offers an immense
opportunity for exploration and it is of great attraction to this age group. But for
that to develop freely, adolescents should have had the experience of carrying the
germ that will enable them to explore themselves and others without undue stress,
anxiety, shame, and guilt. These are all developmental steps that must be met but
that need the solid ground on which the adolescent's acceptance of reality and a
feeling of being in peace with it has been developed from birth onwards.

We can see the impact of the internet and of cyberspace in connection to both
positive developments as well as to the place it occupies in disturbed adolescents.
The internet played also a very important role during the Covid pandemic, enabling
the continuity of psychotherapeutic treatment, as Vásquez describes in his work
with his patients.

Allowing for movement between what we know and the unknown is central
to psychoanalysis. We continually transit in between these two states, holding on
to the certainty of what we know as a base from where we can also approach the
unknown and often unknowable. The psychoanalytic setting helps us with this, offering stability, a sense of continuity and a "Third" that enables space for thinking
when thinking is being attacked, a setting that tends to be maintained as invariable
(Bleger, 1967) In child and adolescent psychoanalysis and psychotherapy analysis,
the consulting room, the box of toys, the sense of a containing physical environment, and the consistency of frequent weekly sessions provide a safe setting that
therapists rely on when they are usually exposed to a level of action and sometimes
physical aggression that is part and parcel of children's way of communicating
their difficulties. The safe setting that was created by the analyst had to be changed

during the Covid pandemic and catapulted therapists into an unknown space, wondering about how to continue with the work when we could no longer rely on the usual frame. Different ways of approaching children and adolescents had to be developed and quickly put into practice. Innovative ways proved to be helpful and necessary, whilst it is also important to acknowledge the loss of the more personal one-to-one encounter. For therapists, the loss of the actual "feel", the loss of the possibility to have the child and adolescent in the room involved several adaptations that included having to use the type of media – even the virtual space that children and adolescents spend many hours immersed in. I personally think that we are not yet able to assess the impact that this change in the setting will have on the future of the profession.

But the internet is more than just a tool. It can have a large impact on how we see ourselves (Antinucci, 2013; Marzi, 2013; Turkle, 1997). This is particularly relevant in connection to issues related to identity, including sexual and gender issues. We could say that the contemporary ways by which adolescents approach their gender and their sexuality are greatly influenced and connected to the internet and the exchanges that happen through it. Physical catastrophes such as the changing world due to climate change are something that is new and they can be seen as clear evidence of the damage humans produced sometimes unwillingly but other times knowingly. The fear of a potentially irreparable lethal situation is having an impact on both children and adolescents. The pandemic has confirmed these anxieties too though in a different way. The Covid pandemic added much complexity to disturbed children and adolescents who were already struggling with persecutory fears and anxieties. This, such as in the chapter by Williams and Brameijer, could be understood in connection to some adolescents' huge fears of intrusion into their bodies, the "no entry patients" as has been described by Williams (1997).

We can now say that the field of child and adolescent psychoanalysis has grown and expanded and enjoys the expertise of many professionals who continue to research, treat patients of all ages and provide new ideas that fertilise the discipline.

Time does not stay still. Whilst human suffering and human predicament contain something universal and, in many ways recurrent independently from the times we are living, we could say that human society is always changing and presenting us with new elements that we need to deal with. As psychoanalysts and child psychotherapists, we shouldn't stay still and ignore the changes that are affecting children and adolescents both physically and emotionally. All these changes must be seen in conjunction with considerations about the unconscious inner world of impulses, phantasies, anxieties, and internalised objects, when both objective reality and subjective experience come alive within the transferential process of the analytic relationship. It is impossible to isolate the exact factor that causes pathological responses in a child or an adolescent, but the psychoanalytic exploration of the young person's internal world opens the door to the possibility of understanding and changing the rigid defensive organisations which children and adolescents create in order to survive.

Note

1 This conference was organised under the auspices of the British Psychoanalytical
Society (BPAS) in collaboration with the International Psychoanalytical Association
Committee on Child and Adolescent Psychoanalysis (COCAP), the British Association of Child Psychotherapists (ACP), the Boston Psychoanalytic Society and the Israel Psychoanalytic Society

References

Antinucci, G. (2013) Identity work in the time of cyberspace. In Marzi, A. (Ed), *Psychoa-
nalysis, Identity and the Internet*. London Karnac, pp. 77–109.
Alvarez, A. (1977) Problems of dependence and development in an excessively passive
autistic boy. *Journal of Child Psychotherapy*, 4C(3): 25–46
Alvarez, A. (1996) Developmental psychotherapy for autism. *Clinical Child Psychology
and Psychiatry*, 1(4).
Bick, E. (1964) Notes on infant observation in psychoanalytic training. *Int. J. Psycho-Anal.*, 45.
Bick, E. (1968) The experience of the skin in early object-relations, *Int. J. Psycho-Anal.*,
49: 484.
Bleger, J. (1967) Simbiosis y ambigüedad. Estudio psicoanalitico. Buenos Aires: Paidos.
Also republished in 2013 as *Symbiosis and Ambiguity*. London: Routledge.
Boston, M. & Szur, R. (Eds) (1983) *Psychotherapy With Severely Deprived Children*. Lon-
don: Routledge and Kegan Paul.
Bronstein, C. (2001) Melanie Klein: beginnings. In Bronstein C. (Ed), *Kleinian Theory. A
Contemporary Perspective*. London: Whurr, pp. 1–16.
Ehrensaft, D. (2008) When baby makes three or four or more: Attachment, individuation,
and identity in assisted-conception families. *Psychoanalytic Study of the Child*, 63: 3–23.
Haag, G. (1997) Psychosis and autism. Schizophrenic, Perverse and manic-depressive states
during psychotherpay, pp. 189–211. In Rustin, M., Rhode, M., Dubinsky, A., Dubinsky,
H. (Eds), *Psychotic States in Children*. London Duckworth.
Haynes, J. & Miller, J. (Eds) (2004) *Inconceivable Conceptions: Psychoanalytic Aspects of
Infertility and Reproductive Technology*. Hove: Brunner-Routledge.
Houzel, D. (2004). The psychoanalysis of infantile autism. *Journal of Child Psychotherapy*,
30(2): 225–237.
Kanner, L. (1943). Autistic disturbances of affective contact. *Nervous Child*, 2: 217–250.
Klein, M. (1930) The importance of symbol-formation in the development of the ego. *Inter-
national Journal of Psychoanalysis*, 11: 24–39.
Marzi, A. (2013) *Psychoanalysis, Identity and the Internet*. London: Karnac.
Meltzer, D., Bremner, J., Hoxter, S. Weddell, D., & Wittenberg, I. (1975) *Explorations in
Autism*. Strath Tay: Clunie Press.
Money-Kyrle, R. E. (1961) *Man's Picture of His World: A Psychoanalytic Study*. London:
Karnac, 2014.
Rhode, M. (1997) Discussion. In Rustin, M., Rhode, M., Dubinsky, A., and Dubinsky, H. (Eds),
Psychotic States in Children. Tavistock Clinic Series. London: Duckworth, pp. 173–186.
Rustin, M. (2001). The therapist with her back against the wall. *Journal of Child Psycho-
therapy*, 27(3), 273–284.
Stern, D. (1998) The *Motherhood Constellation. A Unified View of Parent-Infant Psycho-
therapy*. London: Karnac.

Turkle, S. (1997) *Life on the screen: Identity in the Age of the Internet*. New York: Touchstone.

Tustin, F. (1972) *Autism and Childhood Psychosis*. London: The Hogarth Press.

Tustin, F. (1983) Thoughts on autism with special reference to a paper by Melanie Klein. *Journal of Child Psychotherapy*, 9(2): 119–131.

Tustin, F. (1992) *Autistic States in Children*. London & New York: Routledge (revised edition).

Williams, G. (1997) *Internal Landscapes and Foreign Bodies*. London: Duckworth.

Part I

New frontiers, diagnostic, theoretical, and technical challenges

Mónica Cardenal

Introduction

I am grateful for the opportunity offered by the editors to comment on the chapters in this section of the book which encompasses "New frontiers, diagnostic, theoretical and technical challenges" in child and adolescent psychoanalysis. I consider that it is through this area that extraordinary contributions to the development of psychoanalysis, its theory and technique, have been made in recent times. As well as its vitality, I would add.

We are facing critical changes in today's world, and I believe that we child analysts are willing to address them for the benefit of our young patients and their families. The four chapters presented here are a testimony of that. In this part we find ourselves before analysts who work very closely with their young patients, inviting us to reconsider the quality of our relationship with them.

The human cub is the most vulnerable of all the species, it does not talk, it cannot flee from what frightens it, and is dependent for its survival. It is our speciality as analysts to get close, to "observe" what the baby is communicating, and help the parents to understand something about this. I get the impression that Björn Salomonsson's work is centred on this delicate and very committed task. I believe that for this reason the author proposes a permanent test of transference and countertransference as a means of researching the work carried out in Parent–Infant Psychotherapy, in my view, the best way to research in psychoanalysis, different from other possible ones.

Salomonsson introduces us to the PIP technique, presenting his theoretical principles as well as the debates and controversies that this psychoanalytic approach technique for babies and parents generates. In this form of intervention, the analyst addresses the babies and talks to them about what he detects that is happening to them in the bond with those significant objects of love. In this way, he puts the babies' phantasies, anxieties, and defences into words and communicates them in an easy and sincere way which is close to their parents. It is evident – as explained by the child psychoanalytic clinic as well as infant observation – that young children

DOI: 10.4324/9781003216360-1

feel relieved when adults communicate the fact that they are trying to understand what is happening to them, even without knowing the full content of their anxiety. As the author mentions, babies perceive an emotional atmosphere of dedication towards them and their parents. In my experience, babies pay a lot of attention to adult language and body rhythms and tones of voice. There is a sensorial plane of the language that babies recognise from the uterus, it is part of their innate knowledge at birth. I agree with Salomonsson that babies receive the mental dedication of an adult who is not their mother or father, and who is close to them trying to contain their anxieties, from the most painful to the most persecutory, some even downright terrifying.

I would highlight the value and the bravery of the analyst in talking to the babies with sincerity about what they are feeling in the bond; their pain, their fear, their anger, and their love.

Christine Anzieu-Premmereur leads us through her chapter to new problems of our times linked to the astonishing technological advance and its consequences on mental health, which encompass the individual subjectivity, the family group and the social fabric. It is a reality that in our times children are gestated and born in different ways. The phantasies about one's own origin in the face of the new techniques for assisted reproduction are particularly relevant. In this way, the author invites us to think about the anxieties that can be awakened in young children when the gestation does not derive from sexual intercourse between the parents, and the family secrets that can surround that gestation. Filiation has always been an interesting issue for psychoanalysis, and the author wonders how parenting occurs in a family who seeks to have a baby outside it. Aggression, guilt, narcissistic aspects, depression, feeling of strangeness, inadequateness, are all signs of the parents' emotional drama in this type of experience. The second skin phenomenon (Bick, 1968) and an attack on loving dependence are some of the defences that the author detects in children who have gone through an atypical gestation. These interesting ideas will be developed through the presentation of three clinical cases. In this way, the analyst contacts us with the baby's emotional world, while she makes a thorough study of the anxieties and fears of the parents. What type of pain does resorting to assisted fertilisation involve? The chapter makes us think about the place of the body and emotional life in modernity. As analysts, we are inevitably led to opening paths towards the comprehension of certain medical interventions, their conscious and unconscious effects, in the present and the subjective future of the child and the parents. Unconscious infantile sexuality and the development of family bonds will be key issues to investigate in the new generations and their evolution in the world. The author alerts us about this through precious clinical materials.

In her chapter, María Rhode proposes a debate on the early interventions in babies at risk of autism and the challenge the new theorisations imply for psychoanalysis – among them the organicist ones and those of psychiatry – and the possible agreements, divergences and complementarity.

Given the author's significant experience in this field, I would like to highlight the interventions based on the psychoanalytic observation of the Esther Bick method, acknowledged to be therapeutic observation, in which the inclusion of the parents is fundamental when dealing with babies or young children. We know that for the baby's "world" is the mother's body, for this reason some of the intervention models are carried out in the family home. Clinical observation helps the parents understand what is happening to the young child whose conduct or way of bonding is so hard to understand and contain, and opens a perspective which I consider to be central since it redeems what they have to offer to their child which is very valuable, as well as the possibility of detecting, together with the observing therapist and in identification with him, the most positive signs, which otherwise could go unnoticed by the parents. Rhode points out that the behaviour of these children always communicates their experience of the world, obviously loaded with sensoriality. The author illustrates her presentation through her own work in collaboration with a group of colleagues, on interventions with children at high risk of autism who were observed weekly for a year together with the fortnightly work with parents as part of a pilot programme (Rhode, 2007).

Rhode introduces us to a baby who begins treatment at 16 months, with therapeutic informed observations, until 3 years of age. At this moment, due to the evolution the treatment veers towards an individual therapy. In this way, she invites us to inhabit his inner landscape. It is always a pleasure to read about María Rhode's clinic, she is a "diver" expert in those landscapes. Her work will help us understand that to these children words may sound in the mouth like babies making noises, in a mother's house – body. Intense anxieties and worries can originate about whether the analyst has a skin, and this will be touchingly displayed in the transference. She shows us how the body must organise itself at a mental level for the language to occur, how dreams can appear, even nightmares, instead of a terrifying nothingness, as well as how the behaviour of these children frequently shows an identification with "siblings" in the mind of the mother, alive, dead, or vengeful (Rhode, 2005). I would state that a geographic perspective of the mind (Meltzer, 1967, 1992) is present in the form of comprehension of the author. Rhode therefore makes us face the determining issue regarding the way to help these children to "be born in their personality", to help them, I would say, to feel lodged, received in the interior of the object, in order to be able to develop their own mental capacity to lodge and introject, the only alternative of the mind to grow and live.

Durban begins his chapter by focusing on the anxieties in their different dimensions described by Melanie Klein, on the one hand, as the motor for mental functioning and the bonds, and as they become excessive, hindering the integration of the Self and the contact with the object, even to the point of paralysing the psychic functioning. Referring to Tustin and Suzanne Maiello, Durban mentions those "anxieties-of-being" as the most primitive in which the Self inhabits a uni- or bidimensional world, with no interiority within itself or within the object. The sensations of free-falling, disintegration, breaking into pieces, freezing, among others, are the ones that define this desperate way of being in the world. How to exist in a world plagued with these sensations? The author mentions the complex defensive organisations that the autistic patient can set in motion, surprising us in the treatment. Moving between adhesive and obsessive mechanisms, where they can confuse us in terms of what they are communicating. I am very interested in the idea that some defences are built against others, setting the very oscillating course in the treatment. He thus propounds the idea that very primitive anxieties are still unchartered territory. Extreme fears appear when the autistic defences are broken in analysis, and the world is there to be apprehended. How to prepare the patient for this new perception of himself and the world? In a personal communication at home in Amersham in 1990, and supervising the material of a young autistic patient, Frances Tustin told me that the most critical moments in the treatment might be when the autistic defences fall, since despair can give signs which are completely unknown to the analyst. Emerging from autistic isolation can be traumatic for the patient and for the analyst, Durban declares. Sensorial forms of relating, even perverse, can prevail in that period of the treatment in contrast with the creativity linked to the introjective processes. Projective identification is in its splendour due to the self's despair which already recognises the object in the external world, and desperately needs to control it. We face important theoretical and technical challenges, he states, and tells us about his experience accompanying his autistic child patient move towards the world of adulthood. The difficulties in emerging from the autistic world to the one of relations will have enormous effects on the transference. The words of the young patient moved me: "*I wish you would have left me as I was. It was good to be autistic. Who gave you the right to cure me!*" The confession of the analyst's hopelessness before the omnipotent and perverse defences of the patient also moved me, as well as the effort of his comprehension. I wonder what challenges and pains we analysts are exposed to when our autistic child patients grow up, on the road of adult sexuality, and are more vitally faced with their vulnerability? An experience which is not frequently found in psychoanalytic literature.

Child psychoanalysis has the possibility to investigate the early mental states that are key for the personality and for its development towards maturity. This type of contribution, which would undoubtedly benefit the future of our societies, can only be offered by psychoanalysis, complementing other branches of knowledge.

1

Early intervention for toddlers at risk of autism

Theorisation, controversies, convergences

Maria Rhode

In this chapter, I discuss a number of recent developments in early intervention for children at risk of autism. Autism has long been an exceptionally contentious area. Psychoanalytic discoveries arising out of work with autistic phenomena include technical and theoretical innovations that are fundamental to the understanding of the beginnings of mind and of primitive emotional states in adults as well as in children. But the biologically based position of many psychiatrists and psychologists remains that autism is a life-long neuro-developmental disorder, and that emotional interventions are therefore irrelevant if not dangerously misleading, even though authors such as Anne Alvarez (1992) and William Singletary (2015) have worked to integrate biological and cognitivist perspectives with psychoanalytic findings. We have needed to keep reminding ourselves of Bjørn Salomonsson's (2004) point that psychoanalysis and neuropsychology address different realms – emotion and aetiology respectively – so that it is not meaningful to speak of a conflict between them.

But the last few years have seen the publication of a number of revolutionary research papers by psychiatrists and psychologists. First, there is Fein's (Fein et al. 2013) description of so-called 'optimal responders': children with an unimpeachable diagnosis of autism who mysteriously become indistinguishable from controls. Then there are two studies – one a longitudinal investigation (Wan et al. 2013), one a randomised controlled trial (Green et al. 2017) – documenting the overriding importance of the interactional style between infants and toddlers at risk of autism and their parents. One offshoot of this has been a new emphasis on early, parent-mediated intervention – which is precisely what some psychoanalytic clinicians have been providing, though workers on the ground are often not aware of this convergence, or indeed of the implications of the research papers.

I will describe one such psychoanalytically informed intervention: a modification of the therapeutic variant of infant observation that the psychoanalyst Didier Houzel had introduced into child psychiatry provision in Brittany and Normandy (Houzel 1999). Like Wan et al. (2013) and Green et al. (2017), Houzel stressed the importance of adult receptivity. The present modification overlaps in important ways with the video interaction guidance described in Green's RCT, but is flexible enough to move into more conventional psychoanalytic child psychotherapy

DOI: 10.4324/9781003216360-2

if that seems indicated. In fact, Wan's longitudinal study shows that those children at risk who benefit from helpful interactions with their parents and do not receive a diagnosis still have important residual difficulties, and I would argue that the possibility of addressing these difficulties is a major strength of the psychoanalytically informed observational intervention.

I will begin by summarising the two research studies and describing the principles of Houzel's therapeutic observation. I will then discuss an audited case series of toddlers at risk of autism who were treated by the modified version of this, and consider convergences with the psychiatric findings as well as differences. Finally, I will give a case example of a little boy who received this intervention and suggest how the process might be theorised. I hope this will illustrate how psychoanalytically informed early intervention sheds light on very primitive mental states – and thus helps us to understand such states in adults – while also promoting healthy development and alleviating the suffering of both children and parents.

Psychiatric research approaches

In a particularly interesting paper, Wan and colleagues (2013) investigated the relative importance of autistic features and parent–infant interaction in predicting an autism diagnosis at the age of 3. Like many researchers, these worked with younger siblings of children with an autism diagnosis, who are much more likely than normal to get a diagnosis themselves. They found that the autistic features of 1-year-old at-risk siblings did not predict a diagnosis; what did predict it was the parents' interactional style. Siblings with high scores for autistic features and whose parents scored low for sensitivity and high for directiveness tended to receive a diagnosis: siblings with high scores whose parents showed high sensitivity and low directiveness did not. They did, however, have numerous residual difficulties: The authors called them the 'other concerns' group. This has also been my experience with the toddlers in the present case series, and, as I have said, I think that the scope for psychoanalytic workers to address these 'other concerns' is a particular strength of our approach.

Until very recently, only the Early Start Denver Model (Dawson 2008; Dawson et al. 2012) led to significant improvement (including brain changes) in randomised controlled trials of two years of highly intensive behavioural and parent-mediated work. Then, in 2017, Jonathan Green and colleagues reported an RCT on the effects of 6–11 sessions of modified video interaction guidance (VIPP-auti) provided to at-risk siblings between 9 and 14 months of age. VIPP-auti is aimed at helping parents to be more sensitive to the meaning of their infants' behaviour as well as to the timing of their own response. Green found a considerable decrease in autistic features, as well as an increase in parental non-directiveness and in children's attentiveness to the parent and initiation of interactions. These changes became significant on follow-up a year later, which suggests that parents and infants had internalised the intervention though the improvement in the parents fell off at 27 months. However, no effect was seen on the incidence of an autism diagnosis.[1]

The observationally based intervention

A number of psychoanalytic clinicians (including Acquarone & Jimenez Acquarone 2016; Anzieu-Premmereur 2018; Laznik 2007; Lechevalier 2004) have treated very young children with autism together with their parents. Another approach is therapeutic, or participant, psychoanalytically informed infant observation, which has been used for a wide variety of problems in very young children whose parents might have difficulty attending clinic appointments (e.g. Cardenal 1998; Delion 2000; Gretton 2006; Houzel 1999; Lechevalier et al. 2000; Wakelyn 2011; Wedeles et al. 2002; Williams et al. 2002). Observers are offered ample seminar time to help them to understand what they are witnessing and to process their countertransference. Houzel (1999), who has reported gratifying improvements in very young children with autistic features, emphasises the importance of the observer's receptivity. He distinguishes three levels: perceptual, emotional, and unconscious, of which the unconscious level, which does not obey an effort of will, is the most important. He stresses just how incompetent the mothers of these children have often come to feel, and how easily invalidated by 'expert' professional input coming on top of the invalidation their children subject them to. An observational stance, he thinks, goes a long way towards countering this and reminding the parents that they have something important to offer; and after a time of being respectfully listened to themselves, they begin to identify with the observer's receptive capacities. This converges with the emphasis on parental sensitivity in the research studies I have mentioned, though these do not consider unconscious elements.

Participant observers vary in the degree to which they make comments. Working observationally in a clinic setting, I have tended to draw the parents' attention to what their children were doing, sometimes directly, sometimes by means of a descriptive comment to the child. My aim is to see whether I can observe anything in the child that might open up the possibility of making contact – often by imitating them, a strategy that many interventions for autism make use of. Besides listening to the parents' concerns and trying to attend to them as well as to the child, I hope to be able to 'introduce' their child to them, and particularly to point out things he or she might be doing that the long discouragement they have suffered might make them unlikely to notice. My hope is that, in this way, a benign cycle may be set in motion and that the parents begin to value their own capacity to pay attention. This does indeed often happen, though sometimes not without a lengthy initial period in which the parents either say that I must be mad to think their child is capable of meaningful behaviour; or else themselves interact so sensitively with the child as to make me feel I have nothing to add.

The parents' ability to notice positive signs is fundamentally important on many levels. We know that being seen and having one's feelings recognised and witnessed has existential importance (Winnicott 1967); on a more behavioural level, what isn't noticed can't get built on. In the arising vicious circle of discouragement, the parents' lack of expectation prevents them from recognising and responding to the child's often atypical attempts to engage, and the child withdraws even further (see, for example, Rhode 2007, pp. 202–4, 2019). Pointing out what the child is doing therefore overlaps with video interaction guidance, though it happens in real time.

Obviously, this is not child psychotherapy or parent–infant psychotherapy: it does not focus on the child's inner world or on the parents' representations. The parents' point of departure is that autism is a life-long neurological condition: they do not want to be 'therapised'. What they do want is to discuss their experience of their child in the present, what they might hope and fear for the future, what they should make of all the assessments and interventions being offered. On the other hand, if parents do bring up issues of their own, the framework is flexible enough so that the worker can respond. As Bick (1964) said of classical infant observation, we take our lead from what suits the parents.

As long ago as 1966, Mattie Harris, in describing brief therapeutic consultations, wrote:

> the containing role of the therapist is similar in some ways to that of the observer in baby observation, yet may be effective in a few brief sessions. A genuine interest, conveyed without any claim to 'magical expertise', can aid in restoring the parents' own creativity, putting them back in touch with their own 'unique knowledge of themselves and their child'.

After Harris's first consultation with a hyperactive toddler, the mother said she felt she had got through to him for the first time: Harris saw this as reflecting the mother's experience of getting through to her during the session. In other words, the behaviour of an unresponsive child can link in the parents' mind with the experience of unresponsive internal figures, and, in favourable circumstances, respectful attention to the parents can trigger a cascade of positive developments.

In attempting to theorise this way of working I have drawn on a paper by Salo Tischler (1979) called 'Being with a psychotic child'. Tischler explicitly links the traumatically painful experience of having an unresponsive child who behaves in incomprehensible ways with the pain that accompanies our relationship to the 'bad' facets of our internal figures. An unresponsive baby reinforces these 'bad' aspects of a mother's internal mother; it becomes harder to access and identify with the 'good, forgiving, blessing [internal] mother' who supports a good relationship between mother and baby. A vicious circle may be inaugurated or reinforced. On the other hand, if and when the child improves, the bad internal voice becomes less strident and the parents are freed to persist with new approaches. Viewed in this way, the intervention is in fact addressing the parents' representations, but on the more concrete level of helping the child (and so counteracting the undermining voice) rather than through insight-based interpretations.

The audited case series

Nearly 20 years ago, I joined with Judith Trowell, David Simpson, Elizabeth Nevrkla, and Martin Bellman to look for toddlers at high risk of autism who would have a year of weekly observation and fortnightly parent work as part of a pilot study (Rhode 2007). The observers were trainee child psychotherapists, supervised by Margaret Rustin (2014).[2] The pilot soon proved to be impractical because of the geographical difficulty of matching observers to families. Since then, I have seen toddlers myself in a clinic setting; in the absence of NHS pathways for children of this age, it has taken some 15 years to put together a case series of eight children, including two from the pilot. Throughout, we used the Checklist for Autism in Toddlers (CHAT) as a baseline screen.

The CHAT (Baron-Cohen et al. 1996) is a very simple, well-standardised screen, valid between 18 and 24 months, that targets pretend play and joint attention. Children who do not perform any of the tasks have an 83% chance of a diagnosis at 3½ (High Risk); in the Medium Risk category, the risk of autism is 50%. Results on the CHAT cannot rule out a later diagnosis (its sensitivity is only 25%); but if a child is seen to be at High Risk, that is very unlikely to be wrong. This meant that a small number of High-Risk toddlers who did well with an intervention would support a prima facie case for a 'proper' study.

In the end, 50% of the toddlers received an autism diagnosis as against the 83% predicted by the CHAT. A statistician specialising in small samples (Rhode & Grayson 2021) found this to be significant at the level of p = 0.03 (Fisher's Exact Test). Obviously, then, this intervention is not a panacea, but it does seem worth pursuing.

Clinical illustration

I will now attempt to illustrate how the modified observational intervention can work in practice by discussing the case of Jacky, who came to treatment at 16 months. Jacky was not part of the case series as he fell in the Medium Risk category of the CHAT, with a 50% risk of a diagnosis, rather than the High-Risk Category; but the very fact that his condition was less serious makes it easier to trace continuities between his early behaviour and themes that came up in individual therapy after 18 months of parent–toddler work. In that sense, he is an example of Wan's 'other concerns' group, and shows how some of these residual concerns may be addressed.

Jacky was the youngest in a large family. They had been shocked by two traumatic events some years before he was born: his mother had suffered a late miscarriage after an uneventful pregnancy, and Jonathan, one of the older children, had been diagnosed with autism at the age of 2½, having previously given his parents no cause for concern. Jonathan was to become increasingly violent. Understandably in view of the unexpected miscarriage, all of mother's subsequent pregnancies had been overshadowed by anxiety, though the babies had fortunately been born safely. Jacky was born three weeks early, but could soon be discharged from intensive care. His mother told my colleague and me that breastfeeding had gone very well, but that Jacky, like many children with autistic features, took badly to the introduction of solids at 6 months, and had serious problems with feeding by the time he was 11 months old. When he came to treatment, he was refusing anything but purées. At nearly 1½, he was not yet babbling or walking: he shuffled on his knees instead, and often obtained sensory stimulation by bouncing on them. He was frightened of falling asleep. He was affectionate, but his mother described him as withdrawn and 'sensory seeking'. People said that he was improving, she told me, but then Jonathan hadn't been diagnosed until he was considerably older. I said that seemed to mean that she couldn't trust any progress – again, this is often the case for parents of such children – and she agreed: 'No, I don't trust it at all'.

First session

In fact, when she brought Jacky the following week, I was surprised by how good his eye contact could be. He was an endearing little boy with dark curls and a cheeky face, except for the many times when he went blank, with vacant eyes, and clutched his tummy button while sucking his fingers. He was not yet babbling, but was capable of pretend play, and provided us with numerous cups of 'tea', then took back the cup and pretended to drink himself. Sometimes he refused to let go of the cup, as though possessing it were vital. Similarly, he repeatedly took the lid off the teapot and clamped his mouth onto the exposed rim. He put the lid's knob in his mouth, then turned the lid over so that it covered his mouth and chin. He persisted with determination at fitting it back onto the teapot, as though this were really important. I wondered whether he felt that he might damage the pot if he took over the lid. Anxieties concerning a damaged mouth are of course often encountered in children on the spectrum (Tustin 1972), and a fear of damaging others was to be a feature of Jacky's treatment as it is for many of these children (e.g. Klein 1930; Meltzer 1975, p. 10).

This first session introduced themes that were to prove central: Jacky's obvious interest in making contact and exploring, alongside his worry about inflicting damage when he asserted himself and the way he frequently turned to sensory means of reassurance (Tustin 1981a), for example, by clutching his tummy button and sucking his fingers. His mother related warmly to him, but this was often overshadowed by her fears about his fragile development and a feeling that death was always around the corner. Throughout the first three terms, it was rare for Jacky to come two weeks running, generally because of one of his many siblings was ill; I often heard about journeys to A&E in the middle of the night. In spite of this, he clearly retained the memory of previous sessions, and linked back to them in his play.

When Father came some weeks later, he mentioned additional worries. Jacky was frightened of falling, and he habitually stiffened his fingers and made a tight fist, though he did not carry hard objects around with him (as many children on the spectrum do). Through their experience with Jonathan, the parents knew that these were autistic features: Father said explicitly that he saw Jacky in terms of Jonathan. I said that I could well understand how that could be so, but reminded the parents of hopeful signs we had witnessed that day: many instances of social referencing;

pretend play with pouring and offering tea; increased pointing to indicate interest. His mother agreed, and added that, at home, Jacky had begun to look at an object if someone pointed at it. Throughout this first term, she told us about progress in a number of areas, but without quite being able to believe in it: for example, Jacky had fed himself lots of new solids in a café, but then this new behaviour disappeared. That, she said, was part of a pattern with him, and it felt utterly disheartening. The issue of precious things getting lost was to come up in Jacky's own material two years later. This illustrates how important – and difficult – it is not to forget that these children's behaviour is not just a function of their limitations, but can communicate their experience: a perspective that can easily get lost when one is faced with the feelings of hopelessness about damage and permanent incapacity that they can so readily evoke.

Early themes: 'dark' and 'broken'

Throughout the first terms of treatment, Jacky made steady progress in developing a play vocabulary for representing his experience, and also in his capacity for spoken language. An enduring worry seemed to be that having something for himself (like the teapot lid in the vignette above) meant damaging something or someone (the teapot). The state of the teapot continued as a major theme; he clearly equated it with his mother's state of mind (like many children with autistic traits, he was acutely sensitive to what others were feeling). For example:

> In his third term, after a few weeks' absence, Jacky was delighted when he could make the computer screen light up (when it was off, he would say 'dark' with distress, and was obviously worried it might be broken). I said how pleased he was that it was working, not broken. His mother meanwhile described how dreadful it had been during the break when the children ran around uncontrollably during an outing: she had burst into tears when she felt unable to keep them safe. Jacky, listening to her, shrieked, arched his back, and tried to put the lid back on the teapot but wasn't able to. His mother tried to cuddle him, but he shrieked again and arched away. I said that mummy had been talking about being upset, and he got worried about things being broken: that she was going to try to sort things out, and that it wasn't because of him that she was sad. He calmed down, listened, and very seriously managed to put the lid back on the teapot. As she went on talking, he cried and arched away and again the lid came off, but when I described this he calmed down again and they both enjoyed a very loving cuddle.

Falling, other children, and words

The following week, he returned enthusiastically, made urgent noises indicating that I should turn the computer screen on and was delighted when it lit up. While waiting for this to happen, he clutched at his tummy button and sucked the fingers

of his other hand. He then tipped out all the little wooden people from their individual holes in a wooden block, looking at mother and me to make sure that we had
noticed. He replaced them in their holes, tipped them out again, and repeated this
a number of times.

At first, I simply described this, then began to speak for the little people ('oh,
please don't tip me out, it's horrible falling, oh thank goodness I'm back in my
place, oh dear, I'm falling out again') and so on, finally saying he couldn't believe
that we didn't want him to feel like that. He proceeded to put the teacups (decorated
with little bears) inside the dolls' house, rang the bell and looked through the window trying to find them. I described seeing them inside, and he continued moving
them around and locating them behind different windows, moving his tongue in
his mouth as he did so, as though there was a parallel between 'bear-children' in
the house and the tongue in his own mouth.[3] This period of treatment was in fact
marked by masses of new words tumbling out, though his pronunciation could still
be inaccurate and he did not develop full sentence structure until he had been able
to strengthen his sense of agency and to feel that the consequences of his aggressive impulses could be repaired. Language development is of course underpinned
by symbolic capacity, which requires the child to feel that his love as a separate
person will be stronger than his hate (Segal 1957). But it also depends on feeling that his body coheres as part of a coherent, orderly world, in which sensory-
perceptual integration has won out over primitive bodily anxieties, and that the
bodily apparatus (including particularly the organs of the mouth) is his to use in the
service of articulate communication.

Bodily scattering and sensory reassurance

That was not something Jacky could take for granted, and he often needed to turn to sensory reassurance. Throughout the first term, he repeatedly scattered pencils all over the room and then clutched his tummy button and sucked his fingers while I gathered them up. After we had come back from the first holiday, he began to be able to pick up the pencils himself, and then rapidly moved to scattering them with intent and showing that he could retrieve them. The colleague with whom I had worked from the beginning unfortunately had to leave after a few months. Jacky obviously missed her, and spent a number of sessions on a cotton-reel game (Freud 1920), throwing objects away and showing that he could recover them: this was immediately followed by his beginning to walk, as though his ability to process my colleague's departure had allowed him to integrate his feet more fully into his body image and use them to support himself. (Indeed, Haag (1991) has proposed that, in normal development, the child's ownership of his limbs depends on his internalisation of the link to his caregiver on both sensory and emotional levels). His mother, too, became more able to help him when he withdrew. For example, when he clutched his tummy button while looking blankly at the leafless trees that he could see through the window, she asked him, 'Are you looking at the dancing branches?' and they danced together delightedly.

Communication through projection

In the second term, Jacky began to play a game with the telephone in which he pretended to ring me, and then rang off as soon as I said 'Hello'. I said how disappointing and upsetting this was: I'd thought he was there, and then he wasn't, or he was and disappeared straight away. This game sent him into fits of laughter, and he modified it continually as his confidence grew that important people came back. In the beginning, if I asked whether Jacky was there, he would answer 'No' or simply remain silent, whereas after two years, he would say 'I'm here!' and 'yes, I'm coming back'.

Some 18 months into treatment, he could play with different sounds on the telephone, and when a mechanical, ghost-like sound came on, he explained, 'It's Nothing' (and 'Nothing' was clearly an active presence). He also became more able to own frightening impulses: he indicated the little wooden people inside the brass Tibetan musical bowl and said: 'I want to eat them', and his eating improved after that. Such frightening impulses are of course a part of normal development, during which caregivers help the child to overcome fears of retaliation and to feel that the world is reasonably benign.

Phobia and nightmares

It was after his fifth break, a summer one when he was nearly 3, that his mother told me Jacky had had what sounded like a panic attack at a children's zoo. Previously he had enjoyed stroking baby animals, but this time he happened to be watching at

the precise moment when a baby chick came out of its shell. Jacky shrieked, began to shake, and nothing his mother could say or do had comforted him though she had held him for 20 minutes. Since then he'd kept saying that the chick was on his skin; he had been unable to sleep unless he was in bed with one of his brothers, and even then woke with bad dreams. His mother agreed with me that he might benefit from some individual work, and since then we have moved to more conventional once-weekly child psychotherapy, with his mother joining us once a month.

Internal speaking presences or empty darkness

In an early individual session, Jacky touched the cuddly peacock's beak and said it couldn't talk.

He rang the doorbell of the little dolls' house, and after a minute, when no one seemed to respond, he opened the door and said, 'It's dark'. I said he was telling me that the house was dark and empty, with no people in it. At first he enjoyed my pretending to speak for people in the house ('Hello, Jacky'). After a while, I

moved on to saying that there needed to be people inside the house who could talk, who could answer, so the mummy-me-house wasn't dark and silent, and he agreed emphatically, 'Yes'. He poked out his tongue and grinned, as though linking back to his earlier equation of his tongue with people in the house, and I poked mine out, too.

The following week, he turned on the computer, rang the doorbell of the house and said it was so dark there. He put a full cup in the garage as though to enliven it (later he was to call this 'warming up' the house, the expression mother used when the computer was slow to boot up). He then 'wrote' his name, which was pretend but with the proper movements, and said at once that he needed to replace the pencils in their pot. I said he couldn't believe it was okay for him to take them and use them, to drink and grow, and it wouldn't leave me dark and empty. He asked whether it was time to tidy up, but then banged as hard as he could with the beater on the Tibetan bowl, with great enjoyment, and repeated this with the little wooden people inside it. Again, as with the dolls' house, it seemed to be the children inside an object that were responsible for the sound it made.

Hostile presences

Some weeks later, Jacky stared blankly out of the window. I asked whether he liked the leaves he could see on the trees or was frightened. He said 'frightened', and when I asked of what, he said of the owl. I said that was a night-time bird. He sucked his fingers while clutching his tummy button, and I said he needed to feel safe. He answered, 'Mummy picks me up'. I said perhaps he didn't really believe it was all right to be Jacky, to eat and grow and learn, and that the owl with its hooting and big eyes wouldn't want to hurt him. He leant against my knee, and I put my hands on his back and tummy while I talked, saying that perhaps he got cross when he thought of me with other children, like the little wooden people he'd been putting inside the house, and he agreed enthusiastically: 'YES!' He noticed that I had a plaster on my arm, and wanted to look underneath it: 'Does it hurt?' I said he didn't believe that I had skin that could heal, as he did. He took the toy peacock apart, then put it back together correctly, and said that he would fix mother and me. I said that was Daddy's job, but when he got cross with me, he wanted my Daddy-man to beat me instead, the way he himself did with the bowl and the beater, and to get rid of the other children that way. Again he said 'YES'. I said that perhaps when it was dark, either that was frightening because no one was there, or else someone nasty was there like the owl or the chick. Again he said 'YES', emphatically, cleared up cheerfully and waved goodbye.

Over the next few weeks, he reprised this material: the house was dark and empty ('that's a bad dream'), or else he went blank, and talked about a bad dream where a scary owl with claws wanted to get into his hair. His mother told me that he was no longer waking up at night, though he was still in an older brother's bed. A month later, he talked about the moon not being there, then said that he had 'roared' at a bad dream. The critical issue now seemed to be the presence or absence of a protective moon, rather than the alternatives of frightening nothingness or a frightening presence (Bion 1962; O'Shaughnessy 1964).

This was something of a turning point, as Jacky's material now came to be much more focused on whether he could hold on to good internal presences in spite of absences and holiday breaks. The emphasis was on his acknowledged wish to be with his mother and me at night-time, linked to anxieties about being able to break the door of the dolls' house. The focus of the most recent term has been on hostility and reparation, with the increasing ability to own and even enjoy his anger, as when he throws the dolls' house emphatically onto the floor. In parallel, he increasingly shows his pride at being stronger and able to do new things: he says with delight, 'I did it', which in turn delights his mother. His increasing confidence allowed him to articulate, before a recent break, 'I lost my calendar!' and ask me to make him a replacement, reminding me of his mother's early description of how his new achievements often seemed to get lost.

Discussion

Jacky undoubtedly had some characteristic autistic behaviours and anxieties: his fear of falling; his sometimes vacant glance; his experience of a scattered body;

his need for something separate (like the teapot lid) to be part of his own mouth. Turning to self-generated sensations for reassurance is also typical (Tustin 1980): he still did so even after two years, clutching his tummy button, sucking his fingers and looking blank if he was worried about loss. In his early sessions, such behaviour merely looked like a typically autistic pattern: with the progressive elaboration of phantasy over the course of treatment, it became increasingly meaningful in the context of anxieties concerning damage, siblings, and oedipal exclusion. This is perhaps the most obvious example of the continuity between Jacky's later difficulties (what Wan et al. (2013) called 'other concerns') and his early autistic features. The dreams appear to mark a decisive moment in his capacity to represent his conflicts and to be increasingly able to engage in the family and at school, and it is striking that he has always come back from separations having made a step forward.

The dual constellation of dark nothingness and frightening presences illustrates the fears Jacky has had to deal with in coming alive. It links with Tustin's (1978) account of the autistic anxieties concerning sibling-like entities that can often underlie phobias, and calls to mind Durban's (2019) recent description of the relationship between autistic and psychotic features on what he describes as the autistic–psychotic spectrum. One could see Jacky's anxieties as partly reflecting reality, with the dark house as a representation of his parents' traumatised state of mind after the miscarriage and the terrifying chick as an amalgam of a returning unborn child and Jonathan's violence. In my experience, the behaviour of children on the spectrum often reveals an identification with sibling figures in the mother's mind, whether these are thought to be dead or alive and vengeful (Rhode 2005; see also Barrows 1999 on an adult patient). Jacky's dreams show him taking the important step of being able instead to represent the state of these internal figures.

While Jacky's teachers and other professionals say that they now have no concerns about him, he had in fact begun to imitate some of Jonathan's behaviour. One could imagine how he could increasingly have come to be seen as being 'like Jonathan' and to attract an autism diagnosis, particularly as this is behaviourally based and his extreme anxiety would have made it difficult for him to engage properly with a diagnostic assessment. It is the clinician's task to resonate with intimations of a child's potential, so that these can be incubated in what Tustin (1981b) called a 'mental uterus' and be born into his personality.

In describing Jacky's treatment, I have attempted to illustrate the convergence of the parent–toddler phase of this observationally based approach with video interaction guidance and to show how Jacky's situation after 18 months of work together with his mother corresponded to Wan's 'other concerns' group. I have suggested that this particular way of working highlights the continuity between autistic behaviour and 'other concerns', and can help to address these. It is my hope that this may contribute towards the recognition of convergences between organicist and psychoanalytic findings, and to a lessening of the polarisation between these approaches.

Notes

1 Since this chapter was written, Whitehouse et al. (2021) have reported significant differences in the rate of later diagnosis between very young at-risk siblings who received ten sessions of iVIPPauti plus usual care, and those who received usual care only.
2 Of these, Agathe Gretton (2006) has published an account of her observation of a toddler at risk of autism, while Jenifer Wakelyn (2011, 2019a, 2019b) has extended the method to infants in foster care with emphasis on the theorisation of attention. Instruments were administered by Becky Hall.
3 Children can sometimes be seen to equate the words in their own mouth with babies inside a house representing the mother (Rhode 2015).

References

Acquarone, S. & Jimenez Acquarone, I. (2016). *Changing Destinies: The Re-Start Infant Family Programme for Early Autistic Behaviours*. London: Karnac.
Alvarez, A. (1992). *Live Company: Psychoanalytic Psychotherapy with Autistic, Borderline, Deprived and Abused Children*. London & New York: Routledge.
Anzieu-Premmereur, C. (2018). 'Bodily experiences and the developing capacity for representation – psychoanalytic psychotherapy with an autistic toddler and her depressed mother'. Paper presented to the English-Speaking Weekend Conference of the BPAS, 29 September 2018.
Baron-Cohen, S., Cox, A., Baird, G., Swettenham, J., Nightingale, N., Morgan, K., & Charman, T. (1996). 'Psychological markers in the detection of autism in infancy in a large population'. *British Journal of Psychiatry* 168: 158–63.
Barrows, K. (1999). 'Ghosts in the swamp: Some aspects of splitting and their relationship to parental losses'. *International Journal of Psycho-Analysis* 80: 549–61.
Bick, E. (1964). 'Notes on infant observation in psycho-analytic training'. *International Journal of Psycho-Analysis* 45: 558–66.
Bion, W. R. (1962). *Learning from Experience*. London: Heinemann Medical.
Cardenal, M. (1998). 'A psychoanalytically informed approach to clinically ill babies'. *International Journal of Infant Observation* 2: 90–100.
Dawson, G. (2008). 'Early behavioural intervention, brain plasticity, and the prevention of autism spectrum disorder'. *Development and Psychopathology* 20: 775–803.
Dawson, G., Jones, E. J., Merkle, K., Venema, K., Lowy, R., Faja, S., & Webb, S. J. (2012). 'Early behavioural intervention is associated with normalised brain activity in young children with autism'. *Journal of the American Academy of Child and Adolescent Psychiatry* 51: 1150–9.
Delion, P. (2000). 'The application of Esther Bick's method to the observation of babies at risk of autism'. *International Journal of Infant Observation* 3: 84–90.
Durban, J. (2019). 'Making a person: Clinical considerations regarding the interpretation of anxieties in the analyses of children on the autisto-psychotic spectrum'. *International Journal of Psycho-Analysis* 100: 921–39.
Fein, D., Barton, M., Eigsti, I., Kelley, E., Naigles, L., Schultz, R. T., &Tyson, K. (2013). 'Optimal outcome in individuals with a history of autism'. *Journal of Child Psychology and Psychiatry* 54: 195–205.
Freud, S. (1920). *Beyond the Pleasure Principle. SE* 18. London: Hogarth.
Green, J., Pickles, A., Pasco, G., Bedford, R., Man, M. W., Elsabbagh, M., & the BASIS Team (2017). 'Randomised trial of a parent-mediated intervention for infants at high risk

for autism: Longitudinal outcomes to age 3 years'. *Journal of Child Psychology and Psychiatry.* DOI: 10.1111/jcpp.12728

Gretton, A. (2006). 'An account of a year's work with a mother and her 18-month-old son at risk of autism'. *Journal of Infant Observation* 9: 21–34.

Haag, G. (1991). 'Nature de quelques identifications dans l'image du corps (hypothèses)'. *Journal de la Psychanalyse de l'Enfant* 4: 73–92.

Harris, M. (with Carr, H.) (1966). 'Therapeutic consultations'. *Journal of Child Psychotherapy* 1: 13–9.

Houzel, D. (1999). 'A therapeutic application of infant observation in child psychiatry'. *Journal of Infant Observation* 2: 42–53.

Klein, M. (1930). 'The importance of symbol-formation in the development of the ego'. In *Love, Guilt and Reparation: The Writings of Melanie Klein, Vol. 1*. London: Hogarth Press, 1975, pp. 219–32.

Laznik, M.-C. (2007). 'Joint mother-baby treatment in a baby of 3 ½ months who shows early warning signs of autism'. In Acquarone, S. (Ed.) *Signs of Autism in Infants: Recognition and Early Intervention*. London: Karnac.

Lechevalier, B. (2004). *Traitement Psychanalytique Mère-Enfant: Une Approche au Long Cours des Psychoses de l'Enfant*. Paris: In Press.

Lechevalier, B., Fellouse, J.-C., & Bonnesoeur, S. (2000). West's Syndrome and infantile autism: The effect of a psychotherapeutic approach in certain cases. *International Journal of Infant Observation* 3: 23–38.

Meltzer, D. (1975). 'The psychology of autistic states and of post-autistic mentality'. In Meltzer, D., Bremner, J., Hoxter, S., Wedell, D. & Wittenberg, I. (Eds) *Explorations in Autism*. Strath Tay: Clunie Press.

O'Shaughnessy, E. (1964). 'The absent object'. *Journal of Child Psychotherapy* 1: 34–43.

Rhode, M. (2005). 'Mirroring, imitation, identification: The sense of self in relation to the mother's internal world'. *Journal of Child Psychotherapy* 31: 52–71.

Rhode, M. (2007). 'Helping toddlers to communicate: Infant observation as an early intervention'. In Acquarone, S. (Ed.) *Signs of Autism in Infants: Recognition and Early Intervention*. London: Karnac.

Rhode, M. (2015). 'Autistic children: Bodily factors in the use of language'. *Psychoanalytic Study of the Child* 69: 275–90.

Rhode, M. (2019). 'Finding one's feet: Body, affect and identification in a pre-autistic toddler learning to walk'. *Bulletin of the British Psychoanalytical Society*, April 2019.

Rhode, M. & Grayson, K. (2021). 'An observationally and psychoanalytically informed parent-toddler intervention for young children at risk of ASD: An audited case series and convergences with organicist approaches'. In Fitzgerald, M. (Ed.) *Autism Spectrum Disorder: Profile, Heterogeneity, Neurobiology and Intervention*. DOI: 10.5772/intechopen.95628

Rustin, M. (2014). 'The relevance of infant observation for early intervention: Containment in theory and practice'. *Journal of Infant Observation* 17: 97–114.

Salomonsson, B. (2004). 'Some psychoanalytic viewpoints on neuropsychiatric disorders in children'. *International Journal of Psycho-Analysis* 85: 117–35.

Ségal, H. (1957). 'Notes on symbol formation'. *International Journal of Psycho-Analysis* 38: 391–7.

Singletary, W. M. (2015). 'An integrative model of autism spectrum disorder: ASD as a neurobiological disorder of experienced environmental deprivation, early life stress and allostatic overload'. *Neuropsychoanalysis* 17: 81–119.

Tischler, S. (1979). 'Being with a psychotic child: A psycho-analytical approach to the problems of parents of psychotic children'. *International Journal of Psycho-Analysis* 60: 29–38.

Tustin, F. (1972). 'Psychotic depression'. In *Autism and Childhood Psychosis*. London: Hogarth.

Tustin, F. (1978). 'Psychotic elements in the neurotic disorders of children'. *Journal of Child Psychotherapy* 4: 5–17.

Tustin, F. (1980). 'Autistic objects'. In *Autistic States in Children*. London: Routledge. Second revised edition, 1992.

Tustin, F. (1981a). *Autistic States in Children*. London: Routledge. Second revised edition, 1992.

Tustin, F. (1981b). 'Psychological birth and psychological catastrophe'. In *Autistic States in Children*. London: Routledge. Second revised edition, 1992.

Wakelyn, J. (2011). 'Therapeutic observation of an infant in foster care'. *Journal of Child Psychotherapy* 37: 280–310.

Wakelyn, J. (2019a). 'Clinical research and practice with babies and young children in care'. In Rustin, M. E. & Rustin, M. J. (Eds), *New Discoveries in Child Psychotherapy: Findings from Qualitative Research*. London: Routledge.

Wakelyn, J. (2019b). *Therapeutic Approaches with Babies and Young Children in Care: Observation and Attention*. London: Routledge.

Wan, M. W., Green, J., Elsabbagh, M., Johnson, M., Charman, T., Plummer, F., & the BASIS Team. (2013). 'Quality of interaction between at-risk infants and caregiver at 12–15 months is associated with 3-year autism outcome'. *Journal of Child Psychology & Psychiatry* 54: 763–71.

Wedeles, E., Grimandi, S., & Cioeta, M. (2002). 'From traditional observation to participant observation in the case of an infant who was failing to thrive'. Paper presented at the Third International Conference for Teachers of Infant Observation, Tavistock Clinic, London (March).

Whitehouse, A. J. O, Varcin, K. J., Pillar, S., Green, J., & Hudry, K. (2021). 'Effect of preemptive intervention on developmental outcomes among infants showing early signs of autism: A randomized clinical trial of outcomes to diagnosis'. *JAMA Pediatr.* 175(11): e213298. doi:10.1001/jamapediatrics.2021.3298

Williams, G., Grimandi, S., & Cioeta, M. (2002). 'From traditional observation to participant observation in the case of an infant who was failing to thrive'. Paper presented at the Bick Centenary Conference on Infant Observation, Krakow (August).

Winnicott, D. W. (1967). 'Mirror role of mother and family in child development'. In *Playing and Reality*. London: Tavistock Publications, 1971, pp. 111–8.

2

The role of early anxieties when emerging from autistic pathological organisations

The dilemma of cure

Joshua Durban

Introduction

Kleinian psychoanalytic theory and practice has always given a central role to un-conscious anxiety and its psychic content, in both normal development as well as in the formation of early developmental pathologies. Anxiety has been understood as a double-edged sword. On the one hand, unconscious anxieties push the infant to develop, to seek the object and gravitate towards its bisexual, integrative contain-ing and holding functions, and through that to gradually connect with reality so as to escape from the horrors of an anxiety-flooded internal situation. A healthy infant, according to Klein, can draw comfort from reality. On the other hand, when anxie-ties are excessive, and when the infant's innate capacity for processing stimuli and anxieties is impaired, object-seeking might be jeopardised. In extreme cases, such an anxiety state might bring about withdrawal and paralyse psychic development.

Melanie Klein's groundbreaking discovery of the paranoid-schizoid and depres-sive anxieties, their concomitant defence mechanisms and the constant kaleido-scopic, non-linear interplay between them (in what she called positions) paved the way for a more profound and deeper understanding of psychic reality. While the paranoid-schizoid and depressive anxieties are located in and directed towards an object or a part-object and therefore necessitate a rudimentary sense of self, or part-self, our accumulated experience with severely autistic, autisto-psychotic, and schizophrenic infants has revealed that there are even more primitive, archaic lay-ers of unconscious anxieties in which the perception and experience of both self and object often fail to develop. Frances Tustin (1981, 1987, 1990) was the first to realise that infants who are constitutionally hyper-sensitive, hyper-permeable and hyper-vulnerable often fail to establish a sense of a coherent, integrated, solid, con-tinuous, well-defined, bounded, and three-dimensional entity that exists in time and space. As Suzanne Maeillo beautifully demonstrated (2021), these infants do not feel that they have a body, or some-body, therefore being nobody, not having any-body (object), and being nowhere. This sense of "Nowhere-ness" (Durban, 2017a) is strongly affected by an influx of what might be called "anxieties-of-being": fall-ing forever, falling into bits, burning, freezing, liquefying, dissolving, having no skin or a skin full of holes, having no sense of time or space, and existing in a

DOI: 10.4324/9781003216360-3

unidimensional or bidimensional world. These anxieties are experienced in a very concrete, bodily fashion and, as a consequence, any interaction with the internal or external world, mediated by an object, is extremely traumatic.

An even more primitive layer of unconscious anxieties fails to be located in the fragmented body. These osmotic/diffuse anxieties (Durban, 2021), first described by Rosenfeld (1987) as an intra-uterine "osmotic pressure" exerted by the maternal unconscious toxic material, which infiltrates the defenceless foetus, are experienced as being everywhere yet nowhere. They are undetectable in neither object nor self.

To complicate things further, it is often the case that an individual patient might move along a whole spectrum of anxieties ranging from the better-developed and differentiated depressive and paranoid-schizoid anxieties, to autistic anxieties-of-being and even to osmotic anxieties. In a previous paper (2019) I have shown how, in the course of an analysis, a patient might fluctuate between psychotic and autistic anxieties in often confusing ways. This poses great theoretical and technical challenges for the analyst. Anne Alvarez, in her pioneering work (1992, 2012), has shown how important it is to use several levels of interpretation in accordance with the child's level of self–object differentiation and level of symbolic meaning.

A staple of classic Kleinian technique, which I still find true and relevant, is to try and detect the deepest, most primitive anxiety at each moment in the session, and interpret it in its own language, at its point of maximal urgency. However, due to the perplexing, concrete, and often pre-symbolic nature of these early anxieties, and to the rapid movement between various anxiety levels which characterise autistic patients or those with autistic pockets, the analyst's task becomes very difficult indeed.

In addition, the patient might resort to various defensive organisations or concrete "mantles" whose main function is to alleviate these anxieties by creating physio-mental "covers". This mantling process (Durban, 2017b) involves covering up with various artificial defences, which are at first very bodily and concrete, as in the case of autistic objects and autistic sensation shapes. As the analysis progresses, these mantles are composed of bits and pieces which are annexed (Rhode, 2012) from the external layers of the analyst or caretaker and whose function is to ward off any real contact with the object. What at first seems to be communication is, in fact, pseudo-communication, or what may be described as an autistic false self. These annexed mantles are adhesive, imitative, and obsessive in nature and therefore cannot be described as proper containers and are neither internalised nor identified with. These autistic defensive organisations often alternate with better-developed psychotic organisations or psychic retreats, described by Steiner (1993, 2011), and the patient might constantly oscillate between these defensive organisations, with each defensive structure serving as a defence against the other. These archaic anxieties undergo considerable modification in the course of the psychoanalyses of autistic or autisto-psychotic patients. However, it is still rather unchartered territory and therefore a challenge for further exploration and understanding.

The hazards of autistic evolution in the course of psychoanalysis

It is not often that we have the possibility of accompanying children on the autistic spectrum into their adulthood within an ongoing intensive psychoanalytic process. When we do, we can witness, time and again, how the process of change, difficult as it is for everyone, is especially so for the autistic or autisto-psychotic child (Durban, 2017b, 2019). Noam, the young adult patient whom I shall describe, has asked me a few times over the last year, "Who asked you to cure me? I didn't want it! Nobody asked me. I was much better off being autistic than this ongoing, horrid pain of living to which I'm now subjected". I have heard similar complaints from other patients whom I have analysed for many years from a young age.

Picasso said that every act of creation is first an act of destruction. Change is the creation of new internally related forms, and for the ASD child this is concretely experienced as destruction of the autistic, encapsulated pathological defensive organisation with no hope in sight. The child therefore destroys the possibility of change so as not to be destroyed by it. This raises an interesting question concerning the role of the death drive in autistic phenomena and the danger of the de-fusion of drives involved in such patients' unique process of change. When they emerge from their autistic shelters the death drive poses a seduction of "mental suicide". That is, it offers a regressive withdrawal into mindlessness and disconnectedness from the precariously established internal objects as well as from the emotions associated with forming stable relationships with them.

The autistic "creation" in the process of emerging, therefore, is mainly composed of defences against changing and against being in touch with both the internal world and with that of the analyst as an other. Our patients very often prefer the monochromatic, unidimensional or bidimensional safety of their own self-generated retreats over the colourful complexity and real creativity of various affective, object-related states. I think this "affective-blindness" often reflects, and is reflected in, the sensorial difficulties and fragmentation which we encounter in such patients (Durban, 2019). A little ASD girl once said to me, "I don't want to live in the world of colours. I want only white-on-white or black-on-black". When she dared to emerge into the "land of colours" she became more integrated into her sensorimotor abilities and exhibited a development in her emotional and attachment capacities as well. She became obsessed with the paintings of Caravaggio and, like them and through them, was able to experience and express the colours of love, fear, jealousy, and longing against the background darkness of separation and loss. It is interesting, however, to note that throughout her development in analysis a number of factors remained constant: her preference for the concrete and sensory modes over the psychic ones; her omnipotence; her heavy use of obsessive-compulsive mechanisms (which, with her omnipotence, formed part of her manic defence); and finally, a fascination with perverse modes of object relations. I shall return to these factors when discussing the case of Noam, demonstrating that even with some limited modifications, these dynamics stubbornly persist.

Change for the ASD child entails leaving the safety – pathological and delusional as it might be – of the autistic encapsulation and organisation and having to endure an intense flooding of anxieties-of-being and osmotic/diffuse anxieties. In the initial phase of emerging from the primary autistic retreat, we mainly encounter those anxieties relating to losing the skin, becoming shapeless, liquefying, burning, freezing, fragmenting into bits, losing orientation, having no connection to the body, and falling forever. However, when a measure of self–object differentiation is achieved, the child experiences a mixture of archaic anxieties together with more developed psychotic ones such as invading the object and being invaded by it, devouring and being devoured, mutilating, robbing, possessing, poisoning and being poisoned. In other words, the child experiences all the anxieties typical of the paranoid-schizoid position described by Melanie Klein, which intermingle with the more autistic primitive ones.

As a result, it is very difficult for the analyst to anticipate – and very often deal with – the variety of defensive pathological structures which the patient "creates". There is a back-and-forth movement between different anxiety levels and different levels of identifications and organisations: autistic ones based on adhesive or osmotic identification; projective identification and, occasionally, even full internalisation. It is a never-ending task to recognise which kind of anxiety is being experienced at each given moment and to try and interpret it in its own language.

Another worldwide problem is that not many children are able to maintain their analyses into adolescence and early adulthood. We therefore have much to explore regarding their development as they grow up. For example, what kind of balance could they achieve between healthy developmental traits and pathological consolidations? What would be the nature of their internal objects and of the accompanying unconscious phantasies?

In Israel, we are fortunate to have conducted quite a few long-term analyses of autistic patients. We are therefore trying to accumulate more information regarding the salient themes, dynamics, and problems involved in such endeavours. The case I shall present demonstrates many of these points. Although my patient Noam has a remarkably high level of intelligence and verbal ability, the themes and dynamics found in his case are also often present in lower-functioning ASD adults, as well as in adults with a propensity for autistic pockets and enclaves.

In this chapter, I shall describe the progress of the five-sessions-per-week analysis of 21-year-old Noam which began 13 years ago when he was 8 and is still in progress. Since he is a high-functioning ASD patient, albeit with quite distinct autistic mechanisms and features, he can provide us with some insights regarding the difficulties, satisfactions, and horrors of emerging from an autistic universe into the world of communication and relationships, with which he is still courageously struggling.

The patient's journey passed through three main stages: autistic encapsulation; autistic-psychotic defensive organisation, and, finally, autistic-manic-perverse pathological organisation, with severe obsessive-compulsive defences that help him ward off the pains and anxieties of otherness and dependence.

Central to this patient's journey is what Irma Brenman-Pick (personal communication, 2020) has called "the dilemma of cure", namely, accepting the analyst's offered cure over his own autistic self-generated, omnipotent one. I think this dilemma can often deteriorate to a standstill that might even result in a negative therapeutic reaction. However, if we have the patient's deep anxieties concerning change in sight while, at the same time, we relate to his aggression, destructivity, and omnipotent-perverse need for a new protective structure, some further, benign object-related changes might emerge. This calls for the analyst's open acknowledgement of his or her responsibility for the inevitable anguish and pain he is causing the patient with his analytic "cure".

I am reminded of Bion (1976) who said, "It took me a very long time to realise that the actual experience of being psychoanalysed was a traumatic one, and it takes a long while before one recovers from it". In fact, the process of emerging from isolation to loneliness and gaining some awareness of the basic pathological situation can prove to be quite traumatic for both patient and analyst.

Noam

Noam, now 21 years of age, had been given the diagnosis of high-functioning autistic spectrum disorder (ASD) when he was 8 years old. The reason for that rather late diagnosis was that both parents were convinced that Noam was a genius and thus, "justifiably" they said, a bit peculiar. Although they deeply cared for their children, both parents managed to ignore the fact that Noam was an extremely withdrawn child who did not speak until he was 4. He avoided eye-contact and any other human contact. When he did initiate interaction, it was in an adhesive and obsessive way. He needed to touch, hug, and rub everything with his saliva as if to glue himself to the object. This was accompanied by obsessive masturbation, hand flapping, and by the use of a variety of autistic objects and sensation shapes. Noam's coordination was poor, with a floppy upper body and a noticeable confusion between front and back, left and right. He demonstrated hypersensitivity to the auditory, visual, tactile, and olfactory modes.

When Noam began to speak at the age of 4 it was in a bizarre way. He seemed to master Hebrew at an uncanny level, using outdated and special Biblical terms combined with words he invented. He would talk incessantly in endless sentences which closer listening revealed to be nonsense. It seemed he was not using language in a communicative way but rather as an autistic sensation shape or mantle. At that time, he talked in different voices and intonations, all imitated, annexed, and mixed up. Noam spoke with a strange diction, an outcome of the peculiar use of his tongue. He later told me he tried to speak without his tongue touching his palate. It was as if he were refusing to acknowledge the penetration into or the protrusion of his tongue from his oral cavity and not allowing for a union between soft and hard, mother and father, inside and outside. He was thus both replicating yet avoiding what Didier Houzel (2019) describes as a failure in establishing a bisexual psychic container. Later in his adolescence, this omnipotent, terrified denial took the form of undifferentiated sexual activities even though he said he was not quite sure he really liked sex at all. During his childhood, Noam used to calm himself by covering up in his mother's dresses while rejecting her live presence. It is interesting and worrying to see that many such patients exhibit what might be mistaken for gender dysphoria or fluid sexuality in their adolescence, with often tragic and irreversible results as a consequence of sex-change surgery. Their basic inability to create a mental body, and their avoidance of the bisexual container is often a manifestation of their inability to integrate between the track of drive development and that of object relations. There is often the underlying phantasy of being re-born in a better way in a new body-mantle.

Noam is now working and studying successfully. He has been in a steady relationship with a young woman for over a year. His previous obsessive thoughts have been replaced by new ones. He constantly checks the location of his penis, keys, iPhone, and wallet. Because of Covid, I have only seen Noam online and this is our first session in person.

Monday

Upon arrival Noam, without looking at me or saying hello, walks straight into my waiting room, takes a glass and pours himself some water. He then steps into the consulting room with the glass in his hand and lies down on the couch.

I'm feeling quite annoyed by this familiar mixture of Noam ignoring my presence yet being all-over-the-place. Is it because I was unconsciously hoping to see he was improving, being in better contact (thus making me the good, helpful, analyst)? Or is it because I felt some provocation there and held myself back from engaging in one of his sadistic modes of communicating? At the same time, I was also thinking that since it was an incredibly hot summer in Tel Aviv it was only natural for him to need some water. But I immediately felt this was not real concern but rather a rationalisation.

J: No Joshua, just Joshua's water, now Noam-water. (I used to interpret like that when he was still manifestly autistic.)

N: (Checks anxiously his keys and his iPhone and then breathless and without any pauses starts talking) I had a dream yesterday with a monster, an octopus or a monster squid, it was on the beach and sent its giant tentacles towards anything that was on a beach, destroying part after part of the beach and then it reached the part where we were and my brother and I ran downstairs in our old school. And then we were with some other people and there was a giant wave, it arrived, passed above us, and then another one came and again crashed above us onto the shore. It was clear that the next wave will drown us. There was a woman who escaped but I did not follow her. We had to climb on the rocks in order to survive and escape from the wave, but I did not succeed and then I saw everyone but I was already dead.

Noam immediately goes on "to associate", as he calls it, in a very robotic, detached way and, in fact, shuts me out. He becomes his own analyst.

N: I've got an ear infection and I fear it will never go away, it stands for my problems from which I'll never be able to escape, that I'm cursed, nothing works and nothing will work, and I left my antibiotics out in the sun and it spoiled but it was by mistake, for a few hours. I was afraid all the time, I have this very strong anxiety. Like when I was a child. I'm afraid now that it will never disappear, never get solved easily, nothing gets solved easily with me. The bottle touched my infected ear and it will contaminate the antibiotics and then will get back into my ear. (He's silent for a moment and then says) I'm afraid of everything.

J: It seems to me you're afraid of me today, perhaps after not seeing me in person after such a long time. You needed something vital from me, the water, but that was too frightening so you ignored me, like you were giving the water to yourself. You then felt guilty for taking things from me and I became this scary, deadly monster-wave which would kill you.

N: Covers his ear and says it's infected. (The infected ear is the one facing me on the couch.)

J: Listening to me feels like getting infected.

N: I don't think you're infecting my life. Everything is infected inside and out. I wish I could detect the source of infection.

J: (Thinking we moved from the initial autistic anxieties into the paranoid level and now the osmotic/diffuse one) The infection is everywhere yet nowhere. Perhaps it's all confused – am I the infection or the helpful antibiotics?

N: (Silent)

At that point, I'm thinking that in fact N feared that he had contaminated the antibiotics/me. I am thinking how, in his dream, it is unclear why his brother managed to escape the wave and he did not. Then, to my surprise, N says:

N: In my dream, I was trying to hide and did not succeed. I didn't follow the right path. I had to follow the woman who was there because she managed to escape, but I chose not to.

He then begins to talk about his fear of the wave and of drowning but "It would be nice to be like water – having no shape, no thoughts, no emotions, just flowing and flowing".

I suggested to Noam then that his hostility towards the woman in his dream and the envious realisation that she was real and that he needed to rely on her, follow her, and thus be saved, led him to choose the opposite. I said: "You'd rather become water, shapeless, inanimate and even turn into a living-dead than acknowledge the fact that you need me/mother in order to survive". I added, "You're afraid that this will never change and that I'm a mother who is impervious to your fears and suffering".

N stays silent, a rare thing for him and then suddenly says he fears our relationship is damaged, ruined. "Please don't leave me".

I feel rather detached and cold when he cries and ashamed of these feelings. Has he managed to turn me into his cold internal mother and his judgemental father? Or is there something in his crying that feels inauthentic?

Although I fear falling into one of Noam's sado-masochistic traps I say:

J: I'm thinking about these waves and your choice to let them get you, and then these explanations that it's ok … or your attempts today through tears and some more water, to make me say that's it's ok, whereas in fact I'll be ignoring that part of you that's drowning, that wants to live, to get nourished by me and get in touch with me in a loving, grateful way.

        He is silent and then says:

        You've always been here for me and yet I hate you (bursts out crying).

This time I feel touched.

It's like I'm expecting you to always be here for me and I can go on and do whatever I want. It's the same with H (his girlfriend). I know I need structure, a link, something to hold me together but I always find fault with everything and attack it.

J: Like attacking me and your analysis. Is it just another attack or could it be an attempt to get through to me?
N: (Shouting) What do you expect me to feel – all this anger, and fear, and loneliness, pain and sadness? It's all over me.
J: It's the octopus's tentacles.

We reach the end of the session.

N: (Gets up and looks at me, his eyes full of tears) I don't know how I'm going to survive. He obsessively starts checking and re-checking his keys, iPhone, and looks intently at his penis.

Tuesday

On the Tuesday session, N walked in robotically saying that the room smells nice. He said he read poems which are obsessed with death. He then speaks about his girlfriend being jealous and envious of him.

J: After yesterday's session you felt more alive. Yet the octopus, this death obsession, is still there and holds great charm for you. I think you might have experienced me yesterday as arrogant, jealous, and envious towards you and were relieved to deposit it in H, your girlfriend.

N:	(Silent) I watched a lot of porn. I was happy before that and then I was plunged into this dark, black hole. I can neither enjoy sex nor masturbate like these men can.
J:	How terrifying it must be to feel that instead of a penis there's this black hole into which you fall endlessly.
N:	(Becomes very anxious) He goes on to talk about penises and how Judaism regards the foreskin as a useless piece of flesh.
J:	I feel you're cutting me off and turning me into a foreskin – a useless piece of flesh detached from a person. I'm wondering whether this is how you are feeling right now, after what I said which made you very anxious.
N:	(Silent) I'd like to write a short story about a man who is a mental illness salesman. He convinces people that mental illness has a lot of beneficial things and he then implants it within them. For instance, my obsessions. They turn everything into clear-cut, simple things. There's no complexity or confusion. Just instructions and manuals – check this or that. It's like Hitler and the Jews; he provided a simple, easy solution. A final solution.
J:	I think you're really seeking some final solution for all this madness and murderousness inside of you, that threaten to kill you from within. One such solution would be to drive me mad and annihilate me, covering it all up with a nice smell. Yet, there's another part of you that feels like a threatened Jew and wants to live, to take pleasure in life and not in death.
N:	I get what you mean. It is too much for me, too complex to live, so I turn everything into one confused mess. But then I lose you. It's like this poem where a ship stuck in the stillness of the water "perched on emptiness". This emptiness is my death-sentence.

As Noam speaks, I am thinking that much of his talking is composed of "death sentences" in the sense that it does not promote real thinking and creativity but rather an emptiness and a denuding of meaning.

J:	So, it's either this deadly stillness or the pain and confusion of life, with all the envy and jealousy it arouses in you …
N:	(Interrupting my words) I'm afraid of my analysis. But you know me best. I told H that I was literally born here, with you. I wish you would have left me as I was. It was good to be autistic. Who gave you the right to cure me! (weeps silently)
J:	Would you wish to go back to this death-sentence rather than this life-sentence, as painful and complicated as it might be?

Noam is silent for a minute and then tells me that he bought himself a necklace, a good-luck charm, like the one Harry Potter had. He said he was hoping it would protect him from his obsessive thoughts and compulsive actions but the necklace broke and now he feels exposed, helpless and hopeless.

He starts a long monologue about Harry's magical powers, his ability to overcome the worst troubles by himself, without any help. He cannot trust anyone.

I suggest to Noam that he really and very concretely believes that he can overcome everything by himself, with his omnipotent, magical powers – his rituals, autistic objects, and sensation shapes as well as his omnipotent phantasies of creating a pathology of his own choice. He thus turns me and the things I say into a useless, broken necklace. He once admitted that many times, as I was speaking, he was breaking my sentences into words and syllables so that the words do not connect: "like a broken chain". When he refuses to take my protection and care he is, in fact, turning me into the demented, indifferent mother who does not respond. He thus becomes an empty and isolated child in the world, without any colours and emotions. Furthermore, he is beginning to realise that staying in this omnipotent, magical world of objects, rituals and delusions is not a real cure and might even end up in death, like in the novel he was writing.

Noam did not respond. I felt a great fatigue descending upon me. It was like all our many years of work have resulted in this impasse. I felt helpless and inefficient in the face of his omnipotent, manic, and perverse autistic defences.

After a while he said, "I'll always be so ill, won't I? But now I'm ill and I know it. I see this sick and twisted thing and I can't change it".

I suddenly remembered the way he described the breaking of the Harry Potter necklace and how vulnerable, exposed, and helpless he felt. It further occurred to me that Harry was orphaned from both parents and brought up by people who betrayed him. They offered him care which turned up to be abuse. When, eventually, Harry discovered his unique nature as a magician, it only confronted him with many mortal dangers. So, emotional contact with the truth and the relief it carried were dangerous.

I then said, "I know that what I'm offering you is difficult, confusing, and painful. I'm sorry for that and for how vulnerable, helpless, and hopeless it makes you feel. But as long as we're trying, there's life and hope".

Noam turned his head to look at me. He was clearly relieved and somehow looked more integrated and present. The session ended. Noam walked out, stopped at the door and said, "Thank you". I felt he meant it.

Some concluding thoughts

A central question in the psychoanalyses of autistic states is if, how, and to what extent will the patient be able to achieve better connection and integration in his body-mind experience and to internalise a good reliable object. What is the nature of the anxieties and internal objects of such patients, and how do they deal with reality?

In Noam's case, as in many patients who emerge from the primary autistic organisation, we can witness increasingly sophisticated uses of self-generated or annexed mantles or covers. These covers mask a deep confusion between bodily parts, self and object, unconscious phantasy and reality. Noam's early use as a child of adhesion to autistic objects and to people-as-concrete-objects or covers, soon gave way to using speech and intellect as autistic sensation shapes and a form of masturbatory self-excitation. Furthermore, Noam uses the analyst and the analysis as one such cover. Later on, he relies mainly on grandiose, omnipotent, and manic mechanisms and on a perverse sexualised use of objects.

Underlying these defensive organisations, we can find a confused and confusing array of osmotic/diffuse anxieties, anxieties-of-being, and psychotic anxieties. I think one of the common solutions to this confusion in our emerging patients is to retreat into a grandiose omnipotent phantasy of having the cure for their sufferings. They maintain the delusion, often very concrete and bodily of being the breast, the sucking mouth, and the penis, all in one. This phantasy replaces the more primitive modes of autistic encapsulation, self-excitation, and retreat. This "cure phantasy" is strengthened by paranoid anxieties of contaminating and being contaminated by the analyst and by the cure he or she offers. It is a more developed way of avoiding the pains of separation, dependency, rivalry and envy. Very often we find a perverse identification with a sadistic, destructive and deadly "octopus" object. This death object (Durban, 2017c) is the sum total of the autistic child's near-death experiences or "death equivalents", which from very early on are personified and with whom various unconscious pacts and agreements are formed.

Upon re-reading the clinical material, the first thing that strikes me is how really confused (and confusing) Noam is about who is who, and who does what to whom and why. This confusion is immediately reflected in my own countertransference. Am I the unhelpful parent or may I be Noam the infant, who may want to be recognised and is in the presence of an arrogant or indifferent figure?

But Noam, or at least some part of him, is *really* in a state of mind where he is the one who has it all. He is, at one and the same time, the sucking mouth, the penis, and the breast. He becomes, and acts, like a bizarre combined object.

I wish to underline how *concrete* these feelings are; how for the first two years of the analysis I was really so sleepy, confused, and detached. This is a distinctive feature of such patients. Their seemingly symbolic thinking is very often a thin façade over both symbolic equations as well as concrete and adhesive projections which are aimed at sedating the analyst so that the patient can mantle himself with his external properties. Noam does not know whether his lips are there to suck/take in from the object or to suck-up to/make the object feel better about himself. We need to remind ourselves that Noam's precarious internal object is narcissistic – wanting to be made to feel good about himself and thus hanging on to the "genius" child.

Thus, when I interpret that Noam is making my water his own, I think I do not take into full account that there is a danger of speaking to him as though he is saner than he is – that perhaps I am not quite understanding how Noam knows or is convinced that it *is* his – he is the breast, the army commander, the analyst, and the one who has the cure.

Noam responds to the interpretation by telling me of his dream about a monster octopus. Again, I would suggest that this is Noam's response to the interpretation; that he does not quite know if it is a dream. Is he asleep or awake? That is, in his mind it becomes a reality that I come in like a monster (baby) wanting to destroy Noam's view of himself. Does this dangerous wave go over Noam's head (shall he ignore what I am saying)? Or, if he hears it, will it kill him? And indeed, he becomes dead and robotic.

We can see how Noam is unable to secure an internal good object and how, instead of internalisation, there is an intensified cycle of projection and re-projection/introjection happening very *concretely* and very fast.

So, the alternative to being all-powerful is to be done away with. I think that with such patients we need to keep in mind that the alternative to being this all-powerful person, is to be an absolutely helpless, fragmented infant at the mercy of such a confusingly cruel and sadistic object.

Noam continues that he has an ear infection that will never go away. Something is getting into his ear which upsets him and that is followed by the account of the antibiotics which have been left out in the sun.

I think if he lets my interpretations in, it will mess up his "cure", namely, to be the all-powerful one who has it all. However, Noam does not know whether his cure was the mistake, or would the mistake be to let my words come in. Because if he does let them come in, then he is faced with his need for and dependency on me and therefore he is in danger of feeling left out (in the sun) when I am not there. The bottle, the breast, my words touched his infected ear and contaminated his "cure".

Do I represent the wave trying to drown him or should he rather withdraw autistically to *be* the water that just flows and flows, and will drown my words? I think that there is a sane part of him that does really connect with me. However, there is also a sadistic and terrified part of Noam that flirts with my interpretations, partly out of cruelty but also because he feels it is too dangerous to really *engage* with them.

Noam believes that either I am a cut-off impervious mother or that I am the octopus's tentacles. I just cruelly want to have total power over him and make him suffer.

When I tell him that he is talking about something being wrong in the relationship he is suddenly frightened. "Don't leave me". I am then the mother knowing there is something wrong with the relationship, and Noam fears I will choose to leave him. "In the end, it will catch up with him", the seduction back into autistic isolation and mindlessness.

The session ends with:

N: (Shouting) What do you expect me to feel – all this anger, and fear, and loneliness, pain and sadness? It's all over me. (gets up, looks at me, his eyes full of tears) I don't know how I am going to survive.

And indeed, can he cope with this anger with me for ending the session, for bluntly confronting him with my separateness, with the fear that I will leave him forever and with the pain of guilt and sadness? It is a deep question for him and for me, when Noam feels so moved by me, can he survive the pain of separation and rivalry (he has to be the famous poet/analyst), and the pain of guilt?

On the one hand, Noam fears that he has contaminated me. It would be a terrible thing if he has contaminated me with his disease. But it is also a terrible thing if he hasn't, because that would mean that I am yet another impenetrable, impervious object. It would be a terrible thing if I were just like his parents, but it is also a terrible thing that I am not. If I have been able to survive his attacks and not retaliate and go on thinking I am provoking, besides dependency, rivalry and guilt also his envy.

I am often moved to think what a long way Noam has come; how he has to keep hidden both his destructiveness and his neediness, and now his guilt.

Now, as he gradually becomes better located in his body and in his mind, he feels so vulnerable and so exposed. Can he survive that?

I feel that besides the close interpretation of the different and often changing levels of anxieties, unconscious phantasies, and self–object differentiation in the patient, we must also take some responsibility for the fact that for our emerging patients the very process of being analysed could be traumatic. When we recognise that and perhaps allow ourselves to feel this too, with the patient, a depressive connection can be established and with it some hope for further change and integration.

References

Alvarez, A. (1992). *Live Company. Psychoanalytic Psychotherapy with Autistic, Borderline, Deprived and Abused Children.* London: Routledge.
Alvarez, A. (2012). *The Thinking Heart.* London: Routledge.
Bion, W. R. (1976). *The Tavistock Seminars.* London: Karnac, 2005.
Brenman Pick, I. (2020). Personal communication.
Durban, J. (2017a). "Home, Homelessness and 'Nowhere-Ness' in Early Infancy". *Journal of Child Psychotherapy*, 43: 175–191.
Durban, J. (2017b) "'The Very Same is Lost': In Pursuit of Mental Coverage When Emerging From Autistic States". In: *Engaging Primitive Anxieties of the Emerging Self: The Legacy of Frances Tustin*, edited by H. B. Levine, and D. G. Power, 129–150. London: Karnac.
Durban, J. (2017c). Facing the Death-Object: Unconscious Phantasies of Relationships with Death In: Erlich-Ganor, M. (Ed) *Not Knowing, Knowing, Not Knowing: Festschrift Celebrating the Life and Work of Shmuel Erlich.* New York: International Psychoanalytic Books, 85–115.
Durban, J. (2019). "Making a Person": Clinical considerations regarding the interpretation of anxieties in the analyses of children on the Autisto-Psychotic Spectrum. *The International Journal of Psychoanalysis*, 100: 5, pp. 921–939.
Durban, J. (2021). Where does the Covid live? Osmotic/diffuse Anxieties, isolation, and containment in times of the plague. In: Howard B. Levine & Ana de Staal (Eds) *Psychoanalysis and Covidian Life: Common Distress, Individual Experience.* London: Phoenix Books.
Houzel, D. (2019). *Splitting of the maternal container, psychic bisexuality and autistic sensation shapes.* Paper presented at the IPA international congress, London, 27 July 2019.

Maeillo, S. (2021). *On the absence of bodily awareness in autistic children*. The Frances Tustin Lectures, Tel Aviv University

Rhode, M. (2012). Whose memories are they and where do they go? Problems surrounding internalization in children on the autistic spectrum. *Int. J. PsychoAnal*. 93: 356–376.

Rosenfeld, H. (1987). *Impasse and Interpretation*, London: Routledge.

Steiner, J. (1993). *Psychic Retreats*. The New Library of Psychoanalysis. Hove and New York: Brunner: Routledge.

Steiner, J. (2011). *Seeing and Being Seen*. London and New York: Routledge.

Tustin, F. (1981). *Autistic States in Children*. London and Boston: Routledge.

Tustin, F. (1987). *Autistic Barriers in Neurotic Patients*. London: Karnac.

Tustin, F. (1990). *The Protective Shell in Children and Adults*. London: Karnac.

3

Questions of origins and identity in today's children

Christine Anzieu-Premmereur

In recent decades, we have observed the emergence of specific issues in child and family dynamics related to developments in reproductive technologies that have enabled new medical and legal options for becoming a parent. These technologies are also part of larger trends, from social media to migration, affecting the social fabric, individual psychological development, and family dynamics

Global health and mental health data are disturbing—even from before the COVID-19 pandemic, which has taken a significant toll on mental health across the globe.

Depression has been named the number-one illness in the world by the World Health Organization (WHO 2018). After serious concerns about increases in addictions, to video games, pornography and to drugs, reports of self-harming have tripled among adolescents worldwide.

Group psychology is very important in children's lives, since they place a high value on peer relations and being abreast of social trends. Much of their lives take place online and many feel most comfortable expressing themselves and interacting through social media. However, unconstrained online communication of extremist views has too often fueled violence.

As Sherry Turkle (2015) wrote a few years ago, "reclaiming conversation" has been a priority for adults, who themselves are isolated, reinventing transitional objects to soothe themselves without taking care of others. Worried about global instability, and needing to keep time for themselves, young adults are having fewer children. Babies and toddlers now face screens more than anything alive. But at the same time, the development of new technology and artificial intelligence is booming, with young adults revealing a huge creativity. Artists are showing us the role of sensitivity and bodily experiences to stay alive.

This is a world of both excess and scarcity. Excess of stimulation and novelties, lack of relatedness and attention. That's why we should apply the psychoanalytic theory with its economic view of the psyche as the mean for regulation and discharge of quantities of affects.

DOI: 10.4324/9781003216360-4

Infants and their distressed mother

Depending on the parents' circumstances, needs, and choices, babies can be born in several different ways. The development of medical techniques and surrogate pregnancy arrangements have opened multiple routes to parenthood. What do the parents have in mind when they consider the origins of their new baby, how do they think about their child's identity, and importantly which fantasies are involved in the cathexis of a child with origins outside the family who will raise him/her? Internal conflicts, feelings of guilt, and/or omnipotence can create a narcissistic component in the parents' investment in and love for the baby (Nayar-Akhtar 2014).

What is the child talked about its origins? Is the parents' conflictual position toward reproduction a source of curiosity and questioning for the child or, on the other side, a source of cognitive inhibition? I have seen babies and toddlers whose mothers were overwhelmed by anxiety at not being able to identify with the "foreign" child and felt depressive feelings at not being able to love the new baby.

The complexity in filiation is not new, and post-partum issues are not specific to assisted reproduction. Pregnancy after sexual intercourse and adoption can also be accompanied by internal conflicts in parents and many families benefit from the multiple routes to parenthood and enjoy raising their children without significant psychic conflict. The discussion below is not meant to imply that assisted reproduction is inherently associated with psychic distress or conflict. Rather we are focusing on cases where specific anxieties around the medical and social arrangements resulting in the child's presence in the family affect the family dynamics and eventually play a role in the child's ability to figure out its origins.

In some cases, the atypical origins of the child—and/or the secrecy surrounding them—can reactivate primitive anxieties in the parents, oedipal conflict with the fantasy of an incestuous child, or narcissistic anxieties at not being able to identify with the new baby.

Some mothers may not experience libidinal sensuality with their newborn, waiting for the baby to recognize them as the legitimate mother. Gay male parents may struggle with the wish to give their baby a maternal figure. The grandmother can play that role, making some feel deprived of full "ownership" of their child.

We observe how becoming a parent signifies confronting a "developmental process of mourning" for the new parent (Palacio Espasa 2004) who must now cede the role he had previously occupied as the child of his parents. The presence of the infant requires the couple to assume the parental role, in an interactive dynamic between identification with the child and libidinal and aggressive drives. Many couples who have consulted with me after egg donor pregnancy have developed a "masochistic" relationship with the baby.

Guilt feelings vis-a-vis the donor often results in submission to the child's demands without any limit, as well as a need for expiation, while projecting onto the infant a grandiosity associated with all the narcissistic wishes that often accompany this difficult pregnancy. The mother feels inadequate; any symptom in the baby, including feeding, sleeping, and anal issues, may reactivate infantile sexuality fantasy and conflicts, and be interpreted as an accusation (Winnicott 1947). Aggression is projected onto the baby, as most baby girls are said to be mean. Those difficult emotions and projections leave the mother in a manic state of non-contained agitation. The sadomasochistic quality in the dyad, with the strong superegoic source of intense guilt, plays later on a role in the child's low self-esteem and depressive reactions (Anzieu-Premmereur 2011).

A disorganized 2-year-old

Anna, a 2-and-a-half-year-old toddler, had been conceived with the father's sperm and an egg donor and surrogate mother.

The parents think that their child is already disturbed because of the surrogate mother's own psychological issues, and they feel disappointed to have a child with "defects," as they had wanted a smart girl. Their little girl was so agitated that she couldn't sit to take a test for entering preschool.

On the family's first visit with me, she ran around my office without ever stopping to rest, opening the Russian nesting dolls, and looking at me intently. I told her that the doll's babies were inside their mommy's belly. She looked at her mother who told me she didn't know what to say; she already thought it had been a mistake to engage a surrogate with borderline features.

I told the mother that she had time to think of what to say to her child when she is old enough to understand reproduction, but as a toddler she needed a secure representation of her link to her mother. I understood the girl's hyperactivity as the result of her anxiety at feeling the parents' detachment from her. So I said that all babies emerge from their mommy's mind, body, and belly, and that Anna was in her mom's and dad's heads for a very long time before being born. A strong emotion overwhelmed the mother who took her child on her lap, confirming in her own way that the child had been a precious gift (Winnicott, D. W. (1956).

An intense oedipal rivalry between the mother and her own mother had made her, since adolescence, "envious" of the fertile uterus that she fantasized her mother owned. Her infertility became to proof of this representation. Having a baby girl coming from a surrogate was confusing for her (Guignard 2002).

It took only a few sessions to improve the mother–child relationship and Anna's anxious behavioral symptoms. But both parents needed more time to elaborate on the pain associated with infertility and their narcissistic cathexis on an imaginary child, which was interfering with their capacity to enjoy and interact with Anna.

An untouchable 5-month-old boy

A dyadic twice-a-week therapy helped to contain a tyrannical disorganized 5-month-old infant. Persecutory representations invaded the analytic room. The mother experienced herself as a failure confronted with an omnipotent mother figure and an intense guilt regarding her disorganized sexual life at a time when she would have been more likely to get pregnant. She had to buy another woman's eggs through the internet and go through a painful process of IVF, because of being too old to develop a pregnancy. Exploring those issues when the baby finally fell asleep in her arms led to the awareness of the lack of pleasure she experienced with the baby's body. She realized she never felt any pleasure at looking at the frightening infant, neither at touching his skin or hair, nor at feeling the warmth of his body when giving the breast. She had dissociated herself from any feeling and sensation, functioning in a concrete mechanical way, like in the "blank depression" behavior described by Andre Green (1993). By talking directly to the baby about his need to trust his mother, and about the maternal ambivalence toward this difficult infant, I enabled the mother to find ways to contain the helpless child.

I named some feelings of sadness and anger, of distress at not loving a helpless infant. She cried while talking about conflicted emotions, and feeling connected to the baby's sadness. The mother and child were then able to find ways to experience pleasurable moments together and soothing capacities.

However, the mother then developed a paranoid anxiety toward her babysitters, while also experiencing a reactive negative transference toward me: She experienced that I had been emotionally close to the infant before she was able to have any feelings for him. And she had fears that the babysitter could steal the child, like in horror stories. When we were able to connect these fears with her feelings about the egg donor and the fantasy that that she had stolen the eggs, the mother could associate with her shame: For years she had opposed the idea of buying eggs from another woman, and had many rounds of IVF with her own eggs, each one followed by miscarriage.

Her mourning for her own imaginary children was then associated with the crying baby and the fear that he could die from infection. She reported how she insisted that the baby not to be touched by anybody, even the father; contamination was her fear, which we were able to associate with the fecundation of the foreign egg. When this symptom disappeared and she could enjoy touching the baby—who reacted positively, she then developed a denial of the baby's genitals, as if the boy has been of a "neutral" gender. Remembering her own issues with anal pleasure and control since toddlerhood, we were able to talk about the oedipal issues toward the baby boy who was very attached to his father (Freud 1905).

Whatever their biological origins, children develop interesting theories of the primal scene, but those who are forbidden or inhibited to figure out their own origins also have to deal with symbolic and cognitive issues. This is a source of insecurity regarding one's own identity (Faimberg 2005).

A 14-month-old toddler with hair-pulling symptom

Discontinuity in an early relationship and experiences of neglect and absence during infancy can lead to deficiencies in psychic functioning that evolves into unbearable internal conflicts. In psychoanalytic theory, the forgotten economic view underscores the importance of the quantity of emotions and affects. When experiencing excess and lack from the maternal object is part of the daily life of a baby, there are often psychosomatic consequences. We also see in adult patients how excess and deficiency play a role in regulating their internal life, when they complain about the lack of intimacy with their mother or partner, but cannot stand too close to a rapprochement.

Nelly was a 14-month-old girl whose mother had to "be submitted to," as she said, an IVF procedure to become pregnant, after her infertility had made her very depressed. When they came to see me, Nelly moved slowly on her tiny legs, proud to be able to walk, even unbalanced. Her parents didn't reach out a hand to help her enter my room, as if they didn't see the same baby I saw. Their expressions and behavior conveyed the sense that they saw her as an independent and difficult character, with whom they felt little connection. They didn't reveal any empathy toward her—the father laughed each time his daughter teetered while trying to reach a toy; the mother was anxious but powerless, puzzled by her daughter who was for her like a stranger. I was not sure if the father's reaction was embarrassment and shame in front of a non-harmonious baby, or a narcissistic aggressive reaction like an older brother disparaging a younger sibling.

Nelly didn't smile, her face was stern and unemotional. Her hair was very sparse, which gave her a strange look. She had started pulling her hair dramatically 4 months earlier when the family moved to a new apartment and she was placed in daycare, her first separation experience. The parents reported that she pulled her hair compulsively each time she had to deal with frustration.

I wondered if this sad fragile baby was confused, anxious, or disorganized. But when I engaged her in doll play with me, she seemed to be reorganized though she mostly avoided looking at me. She was more interested in the mechanics of toys than in their symbolic meaning. When playing with the Russian dolls she was amazingly capable of putting the pieces back together. I understood that she was having a reaction of stranger anxiety to me, and already had the cognitive capacity and skills to focus her mind inward and on manipulating the objects around her, withdrawing from the human beings who were making her anxious. This enabled her to feel separated and strong in the face of that anxiety.

Since the mother was smiling, pleased, and surprised that I was able to engage her baby in play, I thought I would try to reconnect the two of them, enabling them to experience tenderness and mutual enjoyment together. So I offered Nelly the opportunity to play with a bag of stuffed animals, hoping to explore her attachment issues, regression tendencies, and the ability for transitional functioning. But she was not interested in touching the furs and the soft fabrics of the toys. She chose some round-shaped animals and we played at rolling them between us.

I also thought that this baby was dealing with feelings of aggression that she couldn't discharge in a harmonious way. Her parents were so afraid of any sign of aggression, that it was immediately repressed. They frequently interrupted our play to instruct her to thank or reply to me as if she were guilty of wrongdoing: "Say Sorry to the doctor, say thank you!" each time she picked up a toy.

I felt they were uneasy and anxious, feeling judged by me, without any concern for Nelly's experience. At the same time, they reported that they often screamed at their child out of irritation: the mother was experiencing a huge distress at night when alone with her daughter after picking her up at the daycare. She didn't to work but wanted to have time for herself, and I thought she couldn't deal with the regression stimulated by being with a young child. This was the mother who complained about her life being difficult and tiring. This young woman was frustrated and irritated without any awareness of the depressive component of her distress, and she presented an obsessive defense that made her unavailable to satisfy her daughter's needs. She forbade the child to touch anything in the kitchen while she was cooking and violently interfered with the girl's exploring the concrete world. Nelly was under her strict control at home and "abandoned" during the day. Her mother appeared unaware of her emotional separation and physical rejection of her child, who was already presenting an attachment disorder. The lack of physical and mental holding was serious and the mother's vulnerability was obvious. She didn't report anything about her own family for a while, but later I would learn about the maternal grandmother's inability to care for her daughter who felt rejected and abandoned.

The father was so irritated by his daughter pulling her hair every night when he came home, that he couldn't repress screaming and threatening her. He knew how inappropriate this was, but he couldn't contain his anxiety and anger, and, I will add, his feeling of powerlessness. He said he didn't know which emotions he was feeling; he was just repeating his own father's behavior.

I jumped on the opportunity to play at being upset when a toy fell on the floor. I said, "Bad toy," and looked at it as if I were punishing it, and I threw it on the floor. Nelly was immediately interested, she asked me with her eyes to repeat the game, and then she did it by herself, taking a big breath in an active discharge of her stress. It was a less pleasurable play than an acting at mastering intense emotions.

The parents were shocked—both that I offered the girl this type of play and how interested she was in it. We repeated this pattern many times during the hour, up to a point when she was showing pleasure at doing it. She left the room after keeping a small stuffed animal to take home, and saying goodbye with a good look into my eyes. She had never smiled during the session. The parents reported afterwards that it was very important to her to repeat that game at home.

I saw Nelly three times with both parents, and then twice a week with her mother. During this time, the child improved, and the mother changed her way of interacting with her daughter. The parents were reluctant to have more sessions, which I interpreted as reflecting their fear of facing their own issues with abandonment and aggression. The father complained about wasting time for sessions where he didn't understand anything, and the mother was very defended against not being in total control of her life, as if coming to see me on a regular basis would place her in a maternal transference frightening and symbiotic, in which she would lose her autonomy.

The mother had a positive transference toward me, even with a lot of anxiety, and since she lacked empathy toward her child and had allowed her daughter to be detached from her, I worked in a guidance style, instead of delving into the mother's issues with her own mother (though we talked about them). I thought the baby didn't have to time to wait for a major change in the mother's emotional reactions to her own childhood.

So I told the mother that I was concerned that Nelly was too independent, and treated by her parents as a provocative teenager, when I saw a vulnerable, sad child confused about her own feelings. The mother immediately picked up on this understanding and started to give milk bottles to Nelly, which she had stopped abruptly recently, and to put her daughter on her lap when feeding her or reading a book. She also created a nightly ritual to help with transitions, as I suggested to her, explaining that even if she seemed very independent, Nelly was suffering a lot during separation and transitions. Nelly used to appear detached when she was left at the daycare, or indifferent to having her mother back at night. Then the mother observed that Nelly started to have emotional reactions when her mother left her and she asked the daycare for a transition with music and songs.

Each session showed me how Nelly was happy to come back, her eyes were more excited, and she started to babble. She wanted to repeat the same type of playing, the same pattern of throwing "bad" toys on the floor; she was less and less interested in aggressive play and more in symbolic ones. She started drawing with a lot of focus on making round figures. Interacting easily with me, she finally smiled twice during the third session. Playing was interpreted by Freud (1920) as an activity that maintains a psychic balance in order to deal with anxieties for object loss and depressive feelings. This toddler's playing shows how she was dealing with the mother's absence by mastering a toy's disappearance, playing at being active instead of passive, and expressing her feelings of abandonment and anger (Anzieu-Premmereur 2013).

As I was facing an ambivalent transference from the mother and a resistant anxious, almost negative transference from the father due to his narcissistic vulnerability, I felt relieved to interact with Nelly exhibiting a positive transference. This young toddler was adept at using my attention and our playing together as a strong support for her sense of self. She regularly remembered every detail of each session, and enjoyed having a kind of control over me as well as over the objects in the room. I felt that her transference and cathexis was, as always with young kids, a maternal transference and a cathexis toward a new real object, not only toward me but in a more global sense toward the setting and the content of the room.

The role of play

In Donald Winnicott's theory of play, the ability to play is an achievement of emotional development. In playing, the infant, like the adult, bridges the inner world with the outer one within and through the transitional space. In the analytic relationship, playing is an achievement of psychotherapy because through playing can the self be discovered and strengthened. Winnicott was more concerned with the playing child than with the content of the play, emphasizing the way the individual uses play to process experience, and at the same time, to communicate. The quality of play is a signifier by itself, showing the capacity for integrating emotions, anxieties and aggression. Play is best understood in relation to the developmental process, from the absolute dependence of the baby, to the toddler's ability to trust in his environment, and later, to the child's capacity for symbolic activity.

> Playing is immensely exciting ... The thing about playing is always the precariousness of the interplay of personal psychic reality and the experience of control of actual objects. This is the precariousness of magic itself, magic that arises in intimacy, in a relationship that is being found to be reliable. To be reliable the relationship is necessarily motivated by the mother's love, or love-hate, or her object-relating, not by reaction-formations.
>
> (Winnicott 1971)

The magic is inspired by the infant's experience of his mother's empathy through communication and mutuality.

The child is active in the playing, but needs the mother's support and sharing. The psychoanalyst's role is mostly to provide them with a safe, contained space that will allow them to develop this quality in their relationship.

For young infants, bodily sensations and experiences are the primary way of interacting with the world. The integration of sensations, of the arousals is a work of linking that is provided through the daily contact with the mother: by the imitation interplay, the sound of the voice, the subtle adjustment of their rhythm. When this adjustment fails because of a pathological interaction due to the baby's temperament or problems, or to parental pathology or other problems, the child's establishment of a stable identity is at risk. The therapist can help by offering the child some attention to his troubles and needs, and by providing an opportunity to interact with an understanding, responsive partner. At the same time, the therapist can provide the parents with a space to voice their concerns and anxieties about their child and to recover from their depression and conflicts.

Another important benefit of therapeutic play activity with babies is that it enables the young child to have a real experience in the analytic office. Winnicott pointed out that psychoanalysts can give an "object lesson" to a child by providing an environment that facilitates the opening of a transitional space; and playing that allows the child to have a complete experience with an object. That object can be the analyst as the one who offers the representation of the internal object: the control or mastery over the object, the playing in front of the parents who react to it, is by itself a therapeutic experience. In Winnicott's view:

> What there is of therapeutics in this work lies, I think, in the fact that the Full course of an Experience is allowed. From this one can draw some conclusions about one of the things that go to make a good environment for the infant. In the intuitive management of an infant, a mother naturally allows the full course of the various experiences, keeping this up until the infant is old enough to

understand her point of view. She hates to break into such experience which is of particular to him as an Object-lesson.

(Winnicott 1941)

The object lesson here implies increasing the infant's capacity to use and control objects.

Parental distress and narcissistic negative projections

Nellie's mother reported that her daughter was becoming increasingly able to connect with her, was more "soft and tender," sleeping better, and was less focused on being in control. Instead, she was more interested in interacting with others. But during one session with Nelly and her mother, I observed the girl actively detached from her mother and aggressively moving to sit away from her. I touched her body at that moment, because she was about to fall from a chair, and the level of muscular tension in her tiny body surprised me (Bick 1968).

Nelly's two young parents were both dealing with sadness and anger toward their own parents who didn't come to see the new baby or offer any help. They had to move to new apartments three times after the birth, as a result of bad experiences with cold and noisy apartments that overwhelmed the mother with non-pleasurable sensations. They were loving parents, lost in parenting, eager for help and advice, repeating patterns of neglect and authoritarian behavior from their own upbringing.

The mother's unconscious hatred toward her own neglectful mother and toward her baby as the source of the painful and shameful medical interventions she had undergone, contributed to her own depressed detachment from her child and negative projections into her.

The father was very critical of his wife and child for coming for treatment, and I asked him why he was so opposed to my helping them. He said his daughter was born a difficult child and that's it, you cannot change the genes. I wondered aloud whose genes it could be that made Nelly so unbearable and he immediately associated with his younger brother who always was spoiled by his parents and whom he hated when he was a child. I said that this association helped me a lot to understand his despair at seeing his own child being "unlovable."

I said that it seemed that he felt as if there was no hope for change and that this was a kind of punitive repetition of his past bad sibling situation. Could he be feeling any guilt from his childhood? He denied that but said that association with his brother made him very angry at his daughter. I told the parents that Nelly needed an intervention now since her psychological development was at risk, and that her symptoms were manifestations of suffering that would interfere with her ability to develop a positive sense of herself.

At the same time, Nelly who was putting toys in a container with my help, turned her head toward her father, babbling "Dadada," and giving him a toy. I said that Nelly was telling him how much she loved him and needed him as a father. He was very moved by this insight and started to cry.

Offering parenting guidance was a way to expedite change since the mother was leaning on the maternal transference to me. After those first three sessions, interacting with Nelly was more pleasurable for the mother. Her aggression was still low, and only manifested in occasional hair-pulling.

I never observed the symptom during our sessions but I was very concerned by the damage to her skin and the intensity of her need for self-containment. I asked the mother to put a soft cap on Nelly's head to protect her hair and skin, by making it difficult for her to reach the hair, and to take Nellie in her arms when she was trying to pull her hair, in order to offer the calming she needed so much. Winnicott introduced holding as the main maternal position, with the idea that the infant integrates this pattern of containment. An infant, under its mother's care, receives both stimulation and interaction, and thus the establishment of the skin-ego responds to the need for a narcissistic envelope and creates the assurance of a constant, basic well-being (Anzieu 1985).

I knew I was asking the mother to repress her own anger, but I hoped that she could derive pleasure from holding her baby, and find fulfillment in the experience of being able to mother her child. In "Project for a scientific psychology" (1966), Freud explained that the mother acts as a protective shield against stimuli, and her role is as essential in maintaining the internal balance in the child's developing psychic functioning as it is in stimulating pleasure and desire.

The mother's conscious and unconscious interactions with her baby are essential to the development of the child's primary narcissism, psychosomatic balance, libido, and identifications and attachment, including the capacity to develop an oedipal conflict. The maternal function in calming and containing the child's emotions is fundamental at the economic level associated with Freud's constancy principle. At the libidinal level associated with the pleasure principle, the mother's role in offering satisfaction and the capacity to develop the hallucination process and object relations is fundamental to the ability for representation and symbolization.

After the sessions, Nelly had stopped most of the time this self-injury symptom, and began sucking her thumb, a sign that a libidinal exchange with the mother had been internalized. But when angry or frustrated at night, or left alone in the back seat of the car or on the couch at home, she continued to pull her hair. So the parents became creative when I told them Nelly needed to explore new soft and calming sensations. They found a doll with long hair, they offered soft fabrics to touch, they discovered songs and music with rhythms Nelly loved; and the family was finally able to find pleasure in playing together.

The lack of autoerotic capacity

We can understand Nelly's symptom as an aggressive reaction connected with grief and rage in a young girl with a series of affective frustrations in her early development.

Trichotillomania is not only aggression against self but can also reflects feeling deserted and unloved. In an attempt to hold onto the self when others fail to provide emotional support, the child learned to "lean on itself" or feel herself through self-injurious hair-pulling. In this way, she satisfied a need for tenderness and contact, albeit in a primitive way. In sum, disturbed bodily feelings, detachment from the mother, and suppressed impulses had led to the development of trichotillomania.

Esther Bick (1968) in her comments on infant observation has associated babies' hair-pulling with the experience of the loss of the nipple at weaning time. Renata Gaddinni has described pre-transitional activities with the mother's hair as linked with autoerotic pleasure and the fantasy of a common skin with the mother. In contrast, Nelly's hair-pulling was a type of "second skin" formation. With her non-harmonious body feeling 'like a bag of potatoes', she failed at finding autoeroticism and couldn't displace into a play activity her despair at being detached from the mother's body. The self-soothing repetitive symptom was calming an internal tension by creating a motor excitement, which became a compulsion without any fantasmatic representations that could allow for real autonomy (Gaddini 1978).

The mother couldn't develop a healthy symbiosis with her first baby because of her own unresolved emotional conflicts and intense, unsatisfied dependency needs. The term "healthy symbiosis" is used to emphasize the mutual dependency between mother and child that occurs in normal development. The deep failure of representation in both of these depressed parents led to the absence of a libidinal quality in their relationship with their baby. It left Nelly without an object or channel for her emotions and excitements other than to be discharged onto her own body.

The introjection of the negative cathexis of the mother who couldn't touch her infant made the baby precociously independent but lacking pleasurable associations with the presence of the object. The destructiveness integrated from the mother's own detachment is reflected in the violence of the compulsive activity.

However, it seems that the father's attitudes and behaviors were at least an equally important determinant. His passivity seemed to prevent him from pulling the child out of the symbiotic relationship with the mother, in contrast to the course of normal development, where the child is attracted to the father as the "first stranger," actually the first "non-mother," as part of the process of separation–individuation. He didn't support the mother–child dyad in their need for a calm symbiotic time, because of his own anxiety regarding his professional life and his infantile need to be supported by his wife. But when Nelly developed this precocious, almost "False Self" independence, he didn't help her to be an autonomous proud girl. Instead, he reacted to her initiatives with anger and frightening screaming. I tried only one time to interpret the father's behavior to him, in order to help stop his abuse. After he had reported about his siblings, and while he was laughing arrogantly at Nelly's unbalanced way of walking, I told him: "I heard a teenage boy laughing at the helplessness of his little sister, as if he were jealous of the new baby in the family." He was shocked and angry, and then interested, asking me if parents sometimes feel like being children again.

Kernberg (2008) emphasizes that ego weakness is linked to the child's problems in establishing object constancy. The child who has not achieved object constancy cannot evoke the image of the mother consistently, and therefore remains reliant upon physically sensing and/or being near her. Such a child develops little tolerance for temporary separation from loved objects, and reacts calamitously to the loss of an object. Most significantly, the child does not relate to objects as whole entities but, instead, largely in terms of part-objects, like one feature of a person—for example, the mother's breast. Nelly had to deal with an early separation from the breast and from the mother's body while drinking her milk from a bottle alone on a chair, and then from any nipple when the parents decided to stop the bottles.

The perception of proprioceptive, interoceptive, kinesthetic, and labyrinthic experiences stirs up awareness of the presence of the body. At every stage of development, there is a perception of the body. The ego is in a constant relation with the body and with the external world. It is through narcissistic identification that the child integrates a sense of her own body. This means that it is mostly through the mirroring function that the body acquires knowledge of itself. Seeing, hearing, smelling, tasting, and touching, give the infant a first perception, a knowledge and the illusion of a control of the mother, enabling a capacity for anticipation, and eventually for representation during the absence of the maternal object.

The self is a "body-in-relation" self. The importance of libidinization of the baby's body by the earliest contact with and tactile ministrations of the mother has been emphasized by Hoffer (1949). The sensori-perceptive interchange not only facilitates differentiation, and thus eventually separation–individuation, but seems to be a *sine qua non* of the earliest sense of the body-self as an entity. This in fact seems to be the condition on which the feeling of "being alive" rests. When there is neglect or deficiency in the mother's libidinal contact with the child, boundary sensations and the sense of "being alive" appear to be missing.

In order to "feel alive" Nelly compensated with aggressive overstimulation of her skin and body. These manifestations were the result of a disintegration of instinctual drives and failure of integration. Her vehement self-injury behavior revealed a psyche at risk of disorganization. Nelly was looking for a painful sensation and this self-aggression could be interpreted as masochistic. But sometimes it serves more as a discharge of distress reflecting an urge to feel something intense. When the compulsion can be linked with a libidinal interest, due to an investment in the object, then masochism is associated with her compulsion that made it less repetitive and offered some transition to a more playful activity.

The parents finally agreed to more sessions. The first time the family returned, Nelly ran into the room eagerly, and put her head into the big bag full of stuffed animals, choosing the softest ones, screaming for joy and excitement as if recovering a lost object and the good memories of a maternal transference. The mother said how happy she was to see her daughter being joyful for the first time, even smiling at home. She reported that her baby used to cry a lot each time she woke up in the morning and after the nap, and that had changed recently. This made her wonder whether Nelly had suffered from depressive feelings. She expressed some empathy toward her child, and I sensed a closeness between them even if the ambivalence was still there. She was able to report for the first time her disappointment at having had to wean Nelly early because breast-feeding had been too painful for her.

At this point, the mother agreed to come for a few sessions by herself. She talked about her narcissistic withdrawn father, her absent indifferent mother, and a very disturbed younger sister who could have been the source of the projection of negative attributions onto Nelly. She reported having been a sad child who sucked her thumb until the age of 7, feeling loneliness and resentment at the same time. She also remembered moving to the US after Nelly's birth, the cold dark apartment and the need for a mother who could support her while her husband was traveling a lot. She felt her life was chaotic and recalled the urge to get rid of her daughter when she could not stand her crying at night any longer.

I observed that Nelly was more solid on her legs, less unbalanced and fragile, more harmonious in her bodily movements, and, most of the time, her muscles were less tense. She was able to relax on the couch, though at times she would still push her mother away. She had a hyperactive quality, and often demonstrated a need for control, which I explained to the mother was normal in toddlerhood.

I had to deal repeatedly with the parents' decision to stop the treatment, which I interpreted as a kind of acting out, reflecting both phobic reactions to confronting their own psychic baggage related to their experiences with their own parents, and their need to retain full control over their family life, without making any change. When I suggested shortening Nelly's stay at the daycare to make her day less demanding and tiring, the mother objected, arguing that her child needed to keep the same schedule to feel secure.

She had been an inhibited austere mother with limited emotional engagement, leaving Nelly to interact primarily with inanimate objects, and she became a more communicative attentive mother, giving more physical stimulation. She always was an efficient mother, but her affective withdrawal and aggressive reaction to the baby's needs had the same value as neglect for the young child. She was concerned in very specific ways about good infant education and social development. The physical and affective withdrawal from the child was indeed associated with Nelly's obsessive hair-pulling at an earlier age. She was certain that Nelly entertained herself perfectly well alone, and without playthings, for long periods, and should not be allowed to interfere with any of the family's routines; and she did decide to leave Nelly with English-speaking strangers before she had any idea of how Nelly would take to them.

This chronic hair-pulling symptom may have signified a severe anxiety reaction, and formed a base for later on narcissistic issues. Nelly persisted in her hair-pulling when her mother, the main love object, was present. Unable to reach her, Nelly supplied her own bodily gratification-arousal, with the specific aim of re-establishing bodily contact with the mother.

The body remembers early experiences and especially, traumatic ones. Suffering, illness and loss of the bodily connection to the love object interfere with the building of the ego. Pleasurable sensations can also be overwhelming; too much stimulation or intruding interactive patterns can be traumatic events. Like pain, intense sensations leave a scar on the ego. For us as therapists, it is important to remember the strong association between bodily sensation, body image and mental life. Particularly when treating patients who are considering or have experienced bodily modifications such as tattoos, piercings, plastic surgery, gender transformation, and medical technologies for restoring damaged body parts, it is essential to focus on the narcissistic and libidinal qualities of the body as the essential sources of mental life.

To conclude

Patients who choose medically assisted reproduction may feel a sense of loss at giving up some aspect of their transgenerational history, and it is important that they can express this suffering and have others acknowledge and validates the rupture that sperm or egg donation, freezing embryos and surrogate pregnancy may signify in their biography. In short, they need understanding companionship in order to get through this mourning process by accepting and integrating a host of ambivalent emotions.

Assisted reproductive technology brings us face to face with new forms of family structuring which oblige us to rethink the unconscious meaning of origins, sexuality, procreation, and the filiation of family mythology, as well as its entire symbolic system which may be profoundly disrupted by this origin story. Some children integrate well an understanding of their origins, perhaps learning from it that technology can help overcome a lack or fulfill a need; and feel securely attached to their parents. Yet others develop a compromised sense of identity and social belongingness. Future generations of children will need to come to terms with this new world where medical reproduction is a shared reality. What about their superego modifications, identity formations during adolescence, group tensions, gender and sexuality issues and capacity for partnership and relationships? Further case analyses and research are needed to understand the psychic ramifications for the development of their own capability and cathexis for both sexuality and parenting of the next generation.

References

Anzieu D. (1985). *The Skin Ego*. London: Karnac, 2016.
Anzieu-Premmereur C. (2011). Fondements maternels de la vie psychique. In *Revue Française de Psychanalyse*, Le Maternel, 71ème congrès des psychanalystes de langue Française, Paris, LXXV, 5, Decembre 2011, pp. 1449–1488.
Anzieu-Premmereur C. (2013). The process of representation in early childhood. In *The Work of Figurability. From Unrepresented to Represented Mental States*, Howard Levine, Gail Reed, Dominique Scarfone, eds. London: Routledge, pp. 240–254.
Bick E. (1968). The experience of the Skin in Early Objects Relations. *Int. J. Psy*, 49: 484–486.
Faimberg H. (2005). *The Telescoping of Generations, Listening to the Narcissistic Links between Generations*, New Library of Psychoanalysis. London: Routledge.
Freud, S. (1966). Project for a scientific psychology (1950 [1895]). In *The Standard Edition of the Complete Psychological Works of Sigmund Freud, Volume I (1886–1899):*

Pre-Psycho-Analytic Publications and Unpublished Drafts (pp. 281–391). London: Hogarth.

Freud, S. (1905). Three essays on the theory of sexuality. In *The Standard Edition of the Complete Psychological Works of Sigmund Freud, Volume 7* London: Hogarth Press

Freud, S. (1920). Beyond the pleasure principle. In *The Standard Edition of the Complete Psychological Works of Sigmund Freud*, Volume *18* (pp. 7–66). London: Hogarth.

Gaddini, R. 1978 Transitional object origins and the psychosomatic symptom. In *Between reality and fantasy: Transitional Objects and Phenomena*. Lanham: Jason Aronson, pp. 112–131.

Green, A. (1993). The dead mother. *Psyche, 47*(3): 205–240.

Guignard F. (2002). *Mère et fille. Entre partage et clivage*. Paris : InPress, 2002, sous la direction de Thierry Bokanowski et Florence Guignard, Coll. de la SEPEA.

Hoffer, W. (1949). Mouth, hand and ego-integration. *Psychoanalytic Study of the Child*, 3(4): 49–56.

Kernberg, O. (2008). Pathological narcissism and narcissistic personality disorder. In *Aggressivity, Narcissism, and Self-Destructiveness in the Psychotherapeutic Relationship*. New Haven: Yale University Press, pp. 45–59.

Nayar-Akhtar M. (2014). Infertility, trauma, and assisted reproductive technology: psychoanalytic perspectives, in *Psychoanalytic Aspects of Assisted Reproductive Technology*, edited by M. Mann, London: Karnac, pp. 77–98.

Palacio Espasa, Francisco (2004). Parent-Infant psychotherapy, the transition to parenthood and parental narcissism: Implications for Treatment, *Journal Child Psychotherapy*, 30 (2): 155–171.

Turkle S. (2015). *Reclaiming Conversation: The Power of Talk in a Digital Age*. London: Penguin.

WHO – Disease and Injury Incidence and Prevalence Collaborators (2018). Global, regional, and national incidence, prevalence, and years lived with disability for 354 diseases and injuries for 195 countries and territories, 1990–2017: A systematic analysis for the Global Burden of Disease Study 2017. *The Lancet*. DOI: 10.1016/S0140–6736(18)32279-7

Winnicott, D. W. (1941). The observation of infants in a set situation. *International Journal of Psycho-Analysis, 22*: 229–249.

Winnicott, D. W. (1956). Primary maternal preoccupation. In *Through Paediatrics to Psycho-Analysis*. New York: Basic Books, 1975, pp. 300–305.

Winnicott D. W. (1947). Hate in counter-transference. In *Through Paediatrics to Psycho-Analysis*. London: Hogarth Press–Institute of Psychoanalysis, 1982.

Winnicott, D. W. (1971). Playing: A theoretical statement. In *Playing and Reality*. London: Tavistock/Routledge, pp. 38–52.

4

Patient(s) in parent–infant psychotherapy

Björn Salomonsson

Recently, I presented parent–infant psychotherapy (PIP) to a group of students. They had no psychotherapeutic training, so I preferred to describe the method without any professional terms. The theme was if the patient in PIP could be defined as the mother, the baby – or both. First, I stated the evident: a mother or father in therapy is a patient. But then I asked if *the baby* is also a patient and suggested the participants to imagine the following clinical situation.

> A mother arrives with her baby, 5 months old, to my office. She seems unhappy, a bit sad, maybe tense as well. She confides that her feelings about motherhood did not develop as expected. "I don't know if I love my baby". Her confession is accompanied by visible tension and shame. Simultaneously, I notice that the baby is flailing, grunting sometimes, and there is a frown on his forehead. Sometimes, he avoids looking into his mother's eyes.

We agreed that the vignette contained two suffering human beings. But could we speak of two *patients*? One student said, "A therapy patient *speaks* with a therapist in a dialogue. Babies can't speak. The mother may've come to you because she's unhappy about, or with, her baby. But that doesn't make the baby a patient!" I agreed that in ordinary psychotherapy, the terms "patient" and "dialogue" are closely related. The speaker got surprised when I added, "Actually, this is what I do in PIP therapies. I turn to mother *and* baby, because I do not want to talk with the mother *about* the baby". The speaker retorted, "That is not the same as claiming that you *talk to* the baby".

I replied: "If the mother tells me she doubts that she loves her baby son, I will pay attention to her pain and shame. But I will also turn to the boy and address him in plain and simple words, for example: 'Peter, your Mum is not sure if she loves you as much as she'd hoped. That's painful to her. She doesn't want you to notice that she's in pain, but perhaps you note anyway that something changes in her when she thinks about her trouble. Maybe there are two tense people here, you and Mum. I'm interested in helping us find out why Mum, maybe you too, are not as happy as anyone of you wishes'. After a while, the boy's flailing movements may abate, and for a second or two he is looking steadily into the mother's eyes".

DOI: 10.4324/9781003216360-5

At this point, I lost the students' attention. A woman said, "The mother is depressed and needs help. But addressing the baby seems farfetched and even cruel. How do you know Peter discerns her depression? Not to mention that he would understand your speculative and advanced interpretation! And how do you handle the mother's reactions when she hears you talking to the boy about connections between his and her distress?"

The group's critique needed careful consideration. It covered the major questions about the character, aims, techniques, and results of the PIP method. I will approach them in this chapter and make room for speculations about why PIP evokes fascination, resistance, and dispute. Some of the critique could be countered by scientific studies confirming that infants of depressed mothers can react aversively to the mother's emotional state (Blandon et al., 2008; Feldman et al., 2009; Field, 2010; Tronick, 2007). In experiments where mother was instructed to keep her face still, thus mimicking a brief instance of depression, most babies reacted with immediate distress (Adamson & Frick, 2003; DiCorcia et al., 2016; Conradt & Ablow, 2010; Mesman, van IJzendoorn, & Bakermans-Kranenburg, 2009; Tronick et al., 1978). They either became visibly worried and motorically active or turned flat, passive, and dejected. Thus, babies are sensitive to their mothers' emotional state, whether it is happy, anxious, angry, or depressed.

In contrast, the other questions were more intricate: Was my address to Peter farfetched and was there any substance to it? Was it frank or even cruel? Did he understand anything and was it helpful? And how did I handle the mother's reactions when addressing the boy about his distress and how it linked with Mum's sadness and shame? These questions concern clinical method and cannot be answered by experimental lab studies. They require a discussion of clinical material with details about verbal interchanges. We must also submit what was expressed through other communicative modes like body movements, eye contact, tone of voice, cries, bodily tension, sweat, etc. Finally, the therapist would need to consider his or her countertransference reactions, which are often intense and oscillating. A therapist who recognizes and reflects on them will discover a major source for understanding the emotional dilemmas and padlocks that mother and baby are involved in.

What is a patient?

For a psychotherapist working with adults or with children who speak, a patient is someone who wants to talk about his/her suffering. Some languages have a special term, such as the German *Gesprächstherapie* or "conversation therapy". Fair enough, but how should we denote what occurred between me and young Peter? One could claim that I was the only one doing *Gespräch*, thus it was a mere monologue. However, when the students protested that my addressing Peter did not qualify him for the title "patient", they overlooked one detail: The vignette also contained how he reacted after my address; he calmed down and his distressed movements decreased. I wondered why the students paid attention to *Gespräch* between mother and me but showed little interest in his shifting behaviour. I wondered if a further factor was hidden in their refutation, maybe a resistance when hearing me talk about – and with – Peter.

These common reactions have made me speculate that the subject "babies in distress" evoke our anxieties and helplessness. When we are discussing distressed babies and how to help them, privately or professionally, many avoid focusing on the baby's varying reactions and concentrate on the parents. If this reflects a general defence, PIP therapists face heavy challenges. We need to convince parents to take perinatal emotional distress seriously and include the baby in treatment. Second, we need to inspire psychotherapists to consider PIP promptly in cases of early distress, rather than to wait until the baby has become a child, teenager, or adult responsive to traditional psychotherapy. Third, we must persuade psychiatrists and politicians that these treatments are important, and that resources need to be allocated.

The shibboleth of whether the baby is a patient or not depends on if we regard him as in any way taking an active part in the session – or not. Many psychotherapists have published clinical experiences of their emotional contact with a troubled baby. They have described such interchange in detail (Anzieu-Premmereur, 2017; Baradon et al., 2016; Emanuel, 2011; Fraiberg, 1980; Keren, 2011; Lieberman & Van Horn, 2008; Norman, 2001; Paul & Thomson Salo, 2014; Salomonsson, 2014, 2018; Tuters, Doulis, & Yabsley, 2011) and some have even claimed that this recruitment of the baby as patient was essential to therapeutic progress.

A brief canon of the underlying theory and psychotherapeutic technique in PIP could be formulated as follows. PIP therapists observe and communicate with both mother and child. They acknowledge that the baby does not understand the lexical levels of language – and they also take into account his ability to pick up and react to emotional communications within the relationships that the session exposes. They wish to capitalize on such capacities by addressing the baby about his or her dilemmas, feelings, behaviours, etc. In doing this, therapists transmit to baby and mother a readiness to contain their distress. They presuppose that the baby pays attention because he or she senses their willingness to be a *Nebenmensch* or "a fellow human being" (Freud, 1895/1950, p. 331). Up until now the environment, not the least the parents, have met such distress by diverting the baby's attention, comforting him, or feeding him. Now the baby meets with a person interested in understanding the anxieties roaming about in the dyad.

One example is when I said, "I'm interested in helping us find out why Mum, maybe you too, are not as happy as any one of you wishes". As this quote indicates, there are two persons in need of a *Nebenmensch*: the baby and the mother. As for the mother, we need to listen carefully to her reports and feelings about the baby. Her comments will soon intertwine with present and past facts and feelings about herself. Any communication expressed will obviously be picked up by the others. When I speak to Peter about his distress, the mother hears and reacts. When I speak to her, Peter may listen, drop off, cry, become attentive, etc. When he flails and whines, mother and I register it, and we react emotionally. My training gives me an advantage of being able to bear these emotions, submit them to my reverie, and translate them into words often accompanied by some inadvertent gesture or facial expression.

All in all, PIP aims to liberate affects and behavioural patterns in both parties, that is, phenomena that have been forestalling positive development in mother and baby.

To sum up the canon, Peter is a patient in PIP with his mother. He participates in a "trialogue" where he pays attention to mother and therapist. Sometimes, he responds to what was said or not said, or to a change of atmosphere, body language, tone of voice. He may do so by smiling, tension, crying, falling asleep, etc. His attention to the therapist and to the parent often differ. He registers that the therapist is not inclined to play or cuddle but to pay close attention to him. He may also notice that the therapist speaks differently with him than other adults do; simply, plainly, and with a neutral or sometimes sombre tone of voice. If the baby becomes distressed, the parents primarily use diversion of attention as a way of calming him, whereas the therapist facilitates for the baby to stay with the distress so that it could be understood and talked about. This presupposes tact, empathy, warmth, and an astute containing function in the therapist.

A 3-month-old girl and her mother in parent–infant psychotherapy

The presentation to the students needed to be brief, whereas this chapter allows me to go deeper. I will submit a case treated at the Child Health Centre where I work as a psychiatric and psychotherapeutic consultant. I am asked to see Nathalie, a mother of three children. Her 3-month-old daughter is screaming terribly. An even greater challenge for Nathalie is that she cannot decide on the girl's name. Tottering on this issue torments her constantly. During our interviews, I learn about Nathalie's background: her mother's self-preoccupation, her father's demanding character, and her severe anorexia at the time of her parents' divorce when she was 17. After some interviews, we start PIP twice weekly. I will provide material from two early sessions, parts of which were published elsewhere (Salomonsson, 2014). The sessions were video-recorded upon the parents' consent, and the text below has been slightly edited. The paragraphs in italics present my ideas post hoc of how to interpret, from a psychoanalytic vertex, what was taking place between the three of us: Tina, Nathalie, and myself.

During the fifth session, the girl arrives asleep in the baby carriage. Nathalie tells me the family had a christening last Saturday. She managed to overcome her ruminations about names: "Finally, she got her name, Christina Jennifer Martine! Actually, I wanted her to have a name containing 'na', like in my own name. I even fantasized she'd carry my name, but that would be weird! Christina is good, it carries some of my own letters". Yet, Christina is not perfect either because it feels too elegant, says Nathalie. At home, the girl is called Tina. She is already screaming less now compared with when therapy started. Nathalie cannot connect anything inside herself with Tina's screaming attacks.

While listening to the mother, I recognize from previous sessions her ongoing internal conflict between two strands or tendencies; one appreciates everyday kindness and warmth, the other demands perfect elegance. Perhaps the mother's wish that the girl's name should contain letters of her own name can be interpreted as a wish that the girl should function as the mother's mirror object.

The girl wakes up and Nathalie picks her up with a smile and puts her on her lap. Tina and I have eye contact for a minute. She is sleepy and smiles briefly. After two minutes she starts yelling. It is a terrible sound and feels as if it were piercing my very marrow. I have a feeling of someone drilling my head and of my brain swishing about in my skull. Nathalie is visibly tense.

My almost concrete suffering of being pierced by Tina's yell helps me to empathize both with her and mother's agony. It can also be interpreted as an index in Peirce's sense (Kloesel & Houser, 1998), *an exhortation: "Do something, help me, I can't bear this alone!"*

Analyst (to Tina):   "You are screaming terribly, and we don't know why. This must be very hard on you … How are things for Mum?"

One taxing countertransference feeling in PIP is of utter helplessness and a total lack of comprehension paired with an eagerness to help. When I say, "… and we don't know why" it expresses such feelings plus the desire to reach deeper and grasp the emotional situation beneath Tina's yelling.

Mother: "I feel so sorry for her. I don't understand why she's screaming. In these situations, only the breast will do. But it can't be right to breast-feed her every time!"

A: "Tina, I also note that you don't look Mum in the eyes. You were looking at a painting on the wall, but when your eyes returned to Mum's face you closed them. Well, sometimes you do peer at Mum. I wonder why you don't look Mum straight in the eyes".

Infant gaze avoidance is a common but much-neglected sign of distress in the baby and in the dyadic relationship. It often indicates the baby's effort to transmute an internal threat (of an incomprehensible internal object) to an external menace to be avoided (the mother's eyes). It is often very saddening and humiliating to the mother.

M: "Yeah, that's right. I wonder …"

A (to the still screaming Tina):   "Maybe you've got two Mums, Tina? One appears when you smile happily at Mum and look into her eyes. The other one you don't dare looking at. You seem scared of her".

M: "When you mention two Mums, I think of Christina and Tina. The names are so different. Tina sounds nice and cosy, while Christina is old-fashioned and stern. But it also contains 'Stina', which has a gentle ring to it. I have made her confused by

switching between calling her Christina and Tina. I've been jok-
ing that she'll become schizophrenic one day".

By now, the mother connects Tina's two varieties of behaviour (yelling or smiling)
with two varieties of her own self-representations (kind and warm, or elegant and
perfect).
   The girl yells and yells, and Mum offers the breast. She takes it promptly and
calms down.

A: "Perhaps there's a third Mum? I got this idea now that you, Tina, are
        looking drowsy. Maybe 'Drowsy-Mum' would be the third Mum".
M: "It's all my fault! After birth, she always looked into my eyes when she
        was breastfeeding. Meanwhile, I was checking my cell-phone for text
        messages and e-mails! I feel guilty because I turned away from her and
        that's why she doesn't look into my eyes!"

The mother's checking of e-mails cannot be dismissed as mere self-preoccupation.
It also reflects a flight from an unbearable ambivalence, not only towards her
breastfeeding baby but also towards herself. Yet, this flight makes matters worse in
that she feels guilty of neglecting the girl.

The next session

The session the next day starts on a calmer note. Its beginning develops into a sum-
mary of our ideas from yesterday. Mum is relaxed and Tina looks at me with big
and calm eyes.

Analyst: "Tina, you've got big, fine eyes, you're looking at me and smiling. I
           never saw you like that before! Yesterday, one minute of smiling and
           then total screaming. Now, you're fingering on Mum, and you seem
           to like it. You're working with your tongue as well, as if practising
           speaking".

Mum is relaxed and reports that on her way to the session that Tina was screaming.

Mother: "She was distressed, but she didn't have that piercing shriek from yes-
           terday. I thought she was just hungry".

Tina looks briefly into Nathalie's eyes, and I ask Mum what she feels about it.

M (in a brief, dispassionate   "Good – when she's happy. On the other hand,
tone of voice):   I never look at her when she's angry".

Not looking at her angry baby signifies Nathalie's rejection of her non-perfect and non-elegant baby. Perhaps Tina's yelling is a cry of protest about this kind of object relation.

A (to Tina): "We noticed yesterday that you, Tina, sometimes peered at Mum while you were screaming. That gave me the idea about your two Mums, and that one of them is scary to you and that's why you peer at her. Like children watching horror movies".

Mum looks at me with interest, the girl is still calm.

M: "I don't grasp why I'd be scary to her!"
A: "You suggested yesterday it had something to do with Tina and Christina".

Nathalie and I speculate that when she enters a state of mind resembling how she feels about the name Christina, her daughter gets scared and starts screaming. The link is thus being forged between states of mind in mother and baby, respectively. Not in an identical sense, for example, that both mother and daughter would have an ideal of being elegant. Rather, that the girl reacts when sensing mother's entry in that kind of state because mother becomes different, distanced, and hard to grasp for the girl.

M: "Actually, I like Tina much better than Christina – though I like Christina, too. But there's something about that Christina name that I dislike. I don't know what it is … There's something harsh about it. (With embarrassment): Tina is simpler, it's softer and friendlier, but not as beautiful or elegant as Christina".
A: "These two names also seem like two forces inside of you. You're an elegant woman, a 'Christina' as it were, but the way you sometimes look at your girl is a bit stiff or harsh. You're also warm and nice with her, with a touch of 'Tina' so to speak, but you think such traits are simple and worthy of contempt. The two forces, Christina and Tina as we call them, seem to be at war. I think you fear you've lost Tina in two ways: within yourself and in your contact with your little girl".

Another way of expressing mother's dilemma is that she struggles to uphold a narcissistic shield which, however, constantly threatens to crack. In these moments, her despondency is easy to see. This could be linked, as in the ensuing intervention to the girl – which of course is overheard by the mother – that she gets frightened when "cosy-Mum" is vanishing.

A (to Tina): "When you're crying, Tina, is it because you're searching for your simple Tina-Mum but cannot find her?"

Here, I point at the mother, and Tina becomes very interested in my finger movements. Mother holds the girl so that the two can look *en face* at each other, but Tina looks at me.

M: "In the beginning, I thought she was too beautiful to be called Tina. It was too simple! On the other hand, for me being Christina-like means to be ambitious and to constantly staying in contact on Facebook with family, friends, and colleagues. It's too much!"

A (to Tina): "Something prevents Mum from enjoying breastfeeding you, Tina, and to let go of checking her cell-phone. (Tina is looking steadily into my eyes). What if she could just sit for half an hour looking into your blue eyes? Our job is to help Mum become simple! And maybe we'd need to help you as well, Tina, to become more seductive so that Mum dares becoming simpler. When you're screaming, that doesn't work. Mum gets tense and withdraws into her Christina-shell".

Referring to the discussion in the chapter's beginning, this intervention shows that I see both Nathalie and her daughter as patients. Mum needs to become simple, to relish her daughter's beauty. Also, Tina needs to enthral her mother. I would not use the word "responsibility" for a little baby, yet I think it is essential to address the baby about her activity or agency. Certainly, this is to divert some of mother's guilt, but another aim is to speak to Tina as a person with directions and intentions. Perhaps, her serious look indicates that she grasps the earnestness of my address.

In this sequence, Tina oscillates between looking happily into my eyes as I address her and twisting her body in some distress. Once, when Tina gets into her distressed mode, mother has an idea.

M: "It struck me that when she is screaming, like now, I see her as more Tina-like. When she is cute, nice and quiet, then I feel she's Christina-like".

This passage shows mother's confusion about what the two partitions, in Tina and in herself, entail. "Tina" encompasses a sweet, sensual, and cosy girl – but evidently, also a screaming baby. Being "cute, nice, and quiet" is unwelcome from the "Tina-perspective" since it quenches the baby's sensuality. But, it is appreciated from the "Christina-perspective" because such a baby is behaving well and is easy to handle.

B: "And her screaming makes you paralyzed. Inside of you, a big and mighty Christina power is rebuking you to do something with that terrible screaming girl. All the while you're unhappy because you want to comfort her – but you can't".

A while later, Nathalie and I enter a sensitive subject: her anorexia in adolescence and the parents' divorce. I suggest that perhaps her parents', as well as her own, demands on her to behave properly and look perfect could be sorted into the Christina category. Nathalie has described a feigned and strict quality of the parents' relationship. I can see it paralleled in Nathalie's behaviour when Tina is screaming and mother gets constrained and pulls herself together. At this point in our conversation, the girl becomes distressed again and starts screaming, still without yesterday's piercing quality. Mother tries to comfort her, but Tina goes on screaming and avoiding mother's eyes.

It is rather common that when two adults get immersed in speaking about the baby, he or she becomes distressed, loses attention, or starts fretting. It reflects, I suggest, the baby's feelings about loss of contact.

A (to Tina):   "Mum and I were talking about Granny and Grandpa. Maybe you felt that we dropped you and that Mum became more Christina-like, harder to reach for you. I can understand that, Tina. But you've only got one mother, and you've got to get Tina-Mum and Christina-Mum together inside of you".

Once again, an intervention pointing both to Tina as being subjected to our abandonment and to her capacity as a little, yet socially competent, human being who can signal her desire for contact in various ways.
The girl is still yelling, though with some brief moments of looking at Mum.

A: "You, Tina, has got to connect with Mum's Tina part because it's so nice and cosy. But you're so scared of Mum when you only find Christina in her. Yes, she does have that part inside of her, but I know she's also struggling to reach you and to comfort you".

This intervention has multiple points. It acknowledges Tina's longing for contact with Mum, as well as her agency in relating to Mum. It also recognizes her fear when she encounters the "Christina part" in mother, an "unheimlich" (Freud, 1919) situation. In Bion's words (1970), it corresponds to when "the absent fulfilment is experienced as a 'no-thing'. The emotion aroused by the 'no-thing' is felt as indistinguishable from the 'no-thing'. The emotion is replaced by a 'no-emotion'. In practice, this can mean no feeling at all, or an emotion, such as rage" (19). Evidently, Tina's yelling expresses a lot of emotions, among which I most easily identify despair, rage, and panic.
The girl is calming down slowly. I suggest to Mum that her Christina part is like an armour covering her Tina part locked inside of her.

A: "It's difficult for you to be spontaneous, Nathalie. (To Tina): Mum gets stiff when she's trying to comfort you. (To Mum): Can you listen to this without taking it as an accusation?"

Guilt is potentially ever-present and needs to be identified as soon as possible.

M:	"Yes. When she is screaming she is not perfect, and I do want her to be perfect".
A:	"I wonder, Nathalie, if you are also cross with Tina".
M:	"One can't be angry with a baby like Tina".
A (to Tina):	"It's not dangerous if mother is angry with you, Tina. And it's not dangerous if you're angry with Mum, Tina".

If these words were taken out of their context, they might seem irresponsible in neglecting the risk of parental violence. Here, they are voiced by an analyst who is confident that Nathalie is not violent with her baby. The idea is rather to convey that emotions per se are not perilous.

The girl is still screaming now and then, interspersed with periods of peace of mind.

A:	"It's interesting that today, Tina, you are screaming but not peering. You need to start looking at Mum, she's very good, you know, this Christina-Tina-Mum of yours. But she's also cross with you, I think. And she's afraid of it because she feels one mustn't be cross with little babies".

Tina calms down, Mum is rocking her. Tina looks at me, calms down, but then yells again.

A:	"Now the fear returned. We'll have to take it easy and work on this. There's no other way. This is hard on you, because we take this thing seriously and you don't get the breast instantly".

Interventions come and go, as do periods of calm and upheaval. Patience is just as important in parent–infant work as in any other treatment mode.

M:	"No, and besides I breast-fed her just a little while ago!"
A:	"Right, Tina, I don't think you're hungry. You've got a ghost inside, that's the problem. A terrible thing, this Christina ghost".

Tina calms down further.

M:	"Aah, had I only given her a name instantly! Everything would have been much easier. Tina, you've got a very tiresome mother". (Thoughtful and sad, Nathalie looks steadily at her daughter.)
A to Tina:	"Now you're calmer, like you've entered into yourself. It seems nice. Mum thinks she's tiresome, you see".
M:	"Very tiresome!"

A: "You, see (making the hand gesture), Mum has a little Tina inside, and
          a big Christina outside of it, but sometimes little Tina peeps through
          (I let one finger peep through my closed hand). I wonder if you, Tina,
          have noticed this in Mum. Now you're following my fingers. And now
          you stretch out your hand as if wanting to reach me. Then you tend to
          look away from Mum, and that's very hard on her. It's the worst pun-
          ishment, right?"

M: "Yeah!! But she does look at me also, and then I feel confirmed by her".

What kind of therapy was this?

Let me begin with our central questions. *What* kind of psychotherapy was this, *why*
did I work this way, and *who* was/were the psychoanalytic patient(s)? Defining
therapy briefly, we could say that it is a procedure in which a therapist addresses a
patient about his or her unconscious intentions and fantasies. The aim is to help her
become acquainted with them and connect them with other aspects of her person,
life history, and present relationships. The clinician also conveys commitment, attention, and a non-judgemental attitude. This double helix of promoting insight
and conveying acceptance constitutes psychoanalytic therapy. Does the vignette
exemplify such therapy? I tell Nathalie that her Christina armour covers her Tina
part which cannot come out, and that it is hard for her to be spontaneous, and I ask
if she can listen without feeling accused. I also link her present sadness and worries
with how she felt as an anorectic teenager. Arguably, I am doing psychoanalytic
therapy with Nathalie.

What about Tina? Do I interpret her unconscious representations? Yes, as when I
say "Yesterday, Tina, you peered at Mum while you were screaming. That gave me
the idea about your two Mums, and that one of them is scary to you and that's why
you peer at her. Like children watching horror movies". This is a complicated interpretation of primal representations (Salomonsson, 2014, p. 51) that I suggest are
clashing inside Tina, one gentle and warm, the other harsh and scary. I also suggest
that Tina avoids her mother's eyes because she fears they can activate frightening
representations (Salomonsson, 2016, 2021). Psychoanalytic therapists formulate
such interpretations to patients of conflicting representations and their influence
on behaviour. They would also presuppose that the patient understands the literal
content of such interventions. However, Tina is 3½ months old and does not know
what "scary" or "peer" mean. We seem to run into a dead end if we claim that I was
doing psychoanalytic therapy with Tina as well.

One way out would be to claim that it is only the mother who listens to and un-
derstands my words and then changes her behaviour with her baby. Thus, the only
therapy patient is Nathalie. But, before closing the case, let us reflect a bit more.
What is Tina listening to? Certainly, not to the literal content of "scary" or "peer".
On the other hand, she does listen to the *sound* of my words. One might object that
I might as well have said "blabla" to her. But that objection would overlook that
Tina also pays attention to my facial movements, gestures, tone of voice, rhythm

of speech. I would even add that she has some notion of my sincerity, vitality, creativity, and attention. In words closer to her age level: "This guy is okay". If we focus on the first group of semiotic markers, we realize that my interpretations are built up of multiple modalities of signification, similarly to an opera that consists of more than the song plus the lyrics (Golse, 2006). Words like "scary" or "horror movie" convey minute, differential voice inflexions and bodily movements, and I think Tina reacts to them.

Had I said "blabla" while varying my voice to pretend my attention, interest, and creativity, Nathalie would wonder what I was up to, and Tina would notice my insincerity, too; not while screaming but when in a more listening mode. To take a prosaic example: Think of a mother comforting her baby while learning that her husband had a car accident. She continues soothing the child, but we would be unsurprised if the baby starts fretting. To my mind, babies are more sensitive to parental insincerity than to openly expressed sadness, anger, or fear because the former creates a double-entendre, a rift between the verbal and the non-verbal messages. In the words of the Swedish Nobel laureate poet Tomas Tranströmer (2006):

From March 1979 (The Wild Market Square)
Weary of all who come with words, words but no language
I make my way to the snow-covered island.
The untamed has no words.
The unwritten pages spread out on every side!
I come upon the tracks of deer in the snow.
Language but no words.[1]

The poet is tired of everyday babbling and yearns for a more primordial and sincere communication. He finds it on an island of the Swedish archipelago, where he discovers deer tracks. They constitute a language without words, an experience that calms the weary poet. De Saint-Exupéry (1946) has formulated a similar mistrust of verbal language, as when the fox teaches the Little Prince to tame him or create a bond: "Sit down a bit from me, in the grass. I'll look at you from the corner of my eye and you'll say nothing. Language is a source of misunderstandings". Verbal language tends to create confusion, especially when we only consider its lexical, discursive (Langer, 1942) aspects and bypass its rhythm, tone, gestures, prosody, etc.

Still, to reiterate the claim that only the mother understood my words, it is true that when she heard me speak to Tina about her "two Mums", Nathalie was helped to intuit what might go on in her daughter's mind and that Tina's yelling was not just an agonizing symptom but also an expression of a struggle in Tina's mind. Britton (2000) suggests that if maternal containment fails, the infant's "unformulated fear of death" is transformed into nameless dread. When fear does not become identifiable, something even worse occurs: "the uncomprehended has become the incomprehensible" (62). Therapeutic work in PIP can be described as a process, in which the incomprehensible transmutes via the uncomprehended into something that can be endured, lived, or grasped. At the beginning of therapy, I suggest mother and daughter suffered due to unbearable affects like anguish, depression and screaming, but also because the situation was incomprehensible and Nathalie's containment had foundered. Interpretations to Tina thus had two recipients. The mother listened, reacted, reflected, and sometimes comprehended. Tina witnessed my effort at formulating what I guessed was going on in her mind. What touched her was not the intellectual message of my intervention but the calm and composure embedded in it, that is, the "language but no words".

Why was this kind of psychotherapy chosen?

The second question concerned why I worked this way with mother and daughter. There is an easy answer: because both of them suffered. Tina was obviously distressed. At her older siblings' preschool, the staff had noticed her yelling when mother came to pick up her older children. They called Tina "the fire alarm". Thus, a treatment that included Tina was mandatory. Yet, such treatment could have focused on mother's conflicts with herself while giving her advice on how to handle Tina. Many babies and parents receive such help provided by Child Health Centre nurses (Lojkasek, Cohen, & Muir, 1994). But Tina and Nathalie had already received such help – without any results. We needed to go deeper and recall a passage from Winnicott's writings: "There is no such thing as an infant. Whenever one finds an infant one finds maternal care, and without maternal care there would be no infant" (1975, p. XXXVII). When Winnicott formulated the close interdependency between mother and baby, his point was that both observable and unconscious aspects of mother's and baby's relating are closely intermingled.

Winnicott's words force us to ask: A baby is screaming like a "fire alarm"; so, where is the fire? We could say it is in the mother. She has internal conflicts between being warm, affectionate, and spontaneous, or stiff, frosty, and conventional. This "war" is confusing to Tina, who cannot read her mother. She can only notice that she can't reach Mum as she would like, or that Mum can't comfort her in a pleasant way. She can only communicate her despair through a harsh, piercing, and unbearable fire-alarm-like yell, which tightens the mother's already padlocked conflict between the two personality parts named "Christina" and "Tina".

If there is no such thing as an infant, there is no such thing as an infant's mother. The two are tightly connected in what Melanie Klein described as "a close contact between the unconscious of the mother and of the child" (Klein, 1975, p. 301). I will here leave aside the question of whether it is appropriate to speak of the unconscious in a baby. I will merely argue that the internal worlds of baby and mother communicate in ways that sometimes seem evident and coherent and sometimes, as at the beginning of this therapy, disquieting and incomprehensible. The PIP therapist's challenge is to find out how to reach and affect mother and baby. In treatments where the baby is the primary object of concern, PIP often starts with a baby focus and address like the one presented here. After a while, often surprisingly soon, the baby has left the "war zone" and calms down. If therapy then has clarified that the mother has concerns beyond her role as a baby mother, one can preferably proceed with personal therapy with the mother. This was the case with Nathalie, and many other mothers that I have encountered.

Who was/were the psychoanalytic patient(s)?

This chapter has merely touched on severe epistemological problems, as when I have written about "addressing a baby" or that "the baby seemed to listen to what I was telling her". I have addressed these challenges in several publications (Salomonsson, 2014, 2017, 2018). Yet, with all respect for the arguments against calling the baby a patient, I suggest that the notion of entering the baby's state of mind is not only an epistemological problem but also an emotional barrier. When it comes to everyday questions of how to comfort a baby or to decide if she is sad or hungry, we have no big issues. We simply do what all generations have done before us. In contrast, when it comes to discussing distressed babies in ways that might expand our understanding of what goes on in their minds, dialogues tend to run up against a wall of disbelief, doubt, intransigence, and an attitude of eyes-wide-shut. That is, one sees what goes on in the dyad but fails to acknowledge that it might have a psychological content. In Tina's case, nobody would deny that she is screaming, but not everyone would take a further step and ask what her behaviour might signify. In other words, there seems to be a resistance against attributing psychological content such as drive, conflict, and defence in mother *and* baby in distressed dyads.

As the students objected to my intervention with Peter, I was baffled that they did not note his change of mind and behaviour afterwards. They might look upon it as a serendipitous or a trivial event, but such dismissals make me respond: "Then give me a better explanation than merely calling it 'chance' or 'irrelevant'". That presentation did not enable us to discuss deeper these questions. This chapter, in contrast, contains a detailed display of two 15-minute sequences from a PIP therapy of two sessions per week that lasted ten months. The claim that mother and daughter both took part in it has been supported by an examination of what went on in the session, and how Tina and Nathalie reacted to my interventions and their changes of behaviour. The observant reader will have noted that neither Tina nor Nathalie changed promptly due to any specific intervention. It was more a process of seeds being sown by me and for them to reap at their own pace. In that sense, *the climate of containment was more beneficial than the content of any specific interpretation.* In my view, this distribution of weight differs from adult psychotherapy only by degrees and not by character.

Considerations of space has forced me to leave aside one important topic; the countertransference. In PIP, it is often intense and taxing, and the therapist's ability to bear feeling helpless, confused, provoked, and desolate is continuously put to test. It is also a most important instrument for detecting concealed affects and conflicts behind various symptoms and behaviours in mother and baby. I refer to further discussions by Avdi et al. (2020), Emde (1990), Lebovici (2000), Salomonsson (2021), and de Rementeria (2011).

Tina is today a 9-year-old girl whom her mother describes as strong-willed, spontaneous, open, and loving with Nathalie and other members of the family and of the circle of friends. Perhaps, this demonstrates her temperamental propensity to be courageous and resolved not to accept relationships that she feels are muddled and incomprehensible. Yet, this cannot be the only explanation for her positive development. The deadlock at the beginning of therapy, with a yelling baby and a helpless mother, needed to be handled by something beyond mere consolation or wait-and-see attitudes. It needed a thorough examination of how each of them seemed to experience the horror of the situation, and to suggest ways of coming out of it. For this to come about, I suggest parent–infant psychotherapy with the two patients was indispensable.

Note

1 By Tomas Tranströmer, translated by Robin Fulton, from THE GREAT ENIGMA, copyright ©2006 by Tomas Tranströmer. Translation © 2006 by Robin Fulton. Reprinted by permission of New Directions Publishing Corp.

References

Adamson, L. B., & Frick, J. E. (2003). The still face: A history of a shared experimental paradigm. *Infancy*, 4(4), 451–473.

Anzieu-Premmereur, C. (2017). Using psychoanalytic concepts to inform interpretations and direct interventions with a baby in working with infants and parents. *International Forum of Psychoanalysis*, 26(1), 54–58.

Avdi, E., Amiran, K., Baradon, T., Broughton, C., Sleed, M., Spencer, R., & Shai, D. (2020). Studying the process of psychoanalytic parent–infant psychotherapy: Embodied and discursive aspects. *Infant Mental Health Journal*, 41, 589–602. doi: 10.1002/imhj.21888

Baradon, T., Biseo, M., Broughton, C., James, J., & Joyce, A. (2016). *The Practice of Psychoanalytic Parent-Infant Psychotherapy – Claiming the baby* (2nd ed.). London: Routledge.

Bion, W. R. (1970). *Attention and Interpretation*. London: Karnac.

Blandon, A. Y., Calkins, S. D., Keane, S. P., & O'Brien, M. (2008). Individual differences in trajectories of emotion regulation processes: The effects of maternal depressive symptomatology and children's physiological regulation. *Developmental Psychology*, 44(4), 1110–1123.

Britton, R. (2000). Hyper-subjectivity and hyper-objectivity in narcissistic disorders. *Fort Da*, 6(2), 53–64.

de Rementeria, A. (2011). How the use of transference and countertransference, particularly in parent–infant psychotherapy, can inform the work of an education or childcare practitioner. *Psychodynamic Practice*, 17(1), 41–56.

de Saint-Exupéry, A. (1946). *Le Petit Prince (The Little Prince)*. Paris: Gallimard.

DiCorcia, J. A., Snidman, N., Sravish, A. V., & Tronick, E. (2016). Evaluating the nature of the still-face effect in the double face-to-face still-face paradigm using different comparison groups. *Infancy*, 21(3), 332–352. doi: 10.1111/infa.12123

Conradt, E., & Ablow, J. (2010). Infant physiological response to the still-face paradigm: Contributions of maternal sensitivity and infants' early regulatory behavior. *Infant Behavior & Development*, 33(3), 251–265.

Emanuel, L. (2011). Brief interventions with parents, infants, and young children: A framework for thinking. *Infant Mental Health Journal*, 32(6), 673–686.

Emde, R. N. (1990). Mobilizing fundamental modes of development: Empathic availability and therapeutic action. *Journal of the American Psychoanalytic Association*, 38(4), 881–913.

Feldman, R., Granat, A., Pariente, C., Kanety, H., Kuint, J., & Gilboa-Schechtman, E. (2009). Maternal depression and anxiety across the postpartum year and infant social engagement, fear regulation, and stress reactivity. *Journal of the American Academy of Child & Adolescent Psychiatry*, 48(9), 919–927.

Field, T. (2010). Postpartum depression effects on early interactions, parenting, and safety practices: A review. *Infant Behavior & Development*, 33(1), 1–6.

Fraiberg, S. (1980). *Clinical Studies in Infant Mental Health*. New York: Basic Books.

Freud, S. (1895/1950). Project for a scientific psychology. *SE* 1, 281–391. London: Hogarth.

Freud, S. 1919. The uncanny. *SE* 17, 217–256. London: Hogarth.

Golse, B. (2006). *L'être-bébé* (*The baby – a Being*). Paris: Presses Universitaires de France.

Keren, M. (2011). An infant who was born with a life-threatening skin disease: Various aspects of triadic psychotherapy. *Infant Mental Health Journal*, 32(6), 617–626.

Klein, M. (1975). *Envy and Gratitude and Other Works 1946–1963*. London: Hogarth and the Institute of Psycho-Analysis.

Kloesel, C. & Houser, N. (Eds.) (1998). *The Essential Peirce, vol. 2: 1893–1913*. Bloomington, IN: Indiana University Press.

Langer, S. (1942). *Philosophy in a New Key* (3rd ed.). Cambridge, MA: Harvard University Press.

Lebovici, S. (2000). La consultation thérapeutique et les interventions métaphorisantes (The therapeutic consultation and the metaphorizing interventions). In M. Maury & M. Lamour (Eds.), *Alliances autour du bébé. De la recherche à la clinique* (*Alliances around the baby. From research to clinic*) (pp. 223–243). Paris: Presses Universitaires de France.

Lieberman, A. F., & Van Horn, P. (2008). *Psychotherapy with Infants and Young Children – Repairing the Effects of Stress and Trauma on Early Attachment*. New York: The Guilford Press.

Lojkasek, M., Cohen, N. J., & Muir, E. (1994). Where is the infant in infant intervention? A review of the literature on changing troubled mother-infant relationships. *Psychotherapy: Theory, Research, Practice, Training*, 31(1), 208–220.

Mesman, J., van IJzendoorn, M. H., & Bakermans-Kranenburg, M. J. (2009). The many faces of the Still-Face Paradigm: A review and meta-analysis. *Developmental Review*, 29(2), 120–162.

Norman, J. (2001). The psychoanalyst and the baby: A new look at work with infants. *International Journal of Psychoanalysis*, 82(1), 83–100.

Paul, C., & Thomson Salo, F. (Eds.). (2014). *The Baby as Subject: Clinical Studies in Infant–Parent Therapy*. London: Karnac.

Salomonsson, B. (2014). *Psychoanalytic Therapy with Infants and Parents: Practice, Theory and Results*. London: Routledge.

Salomonsson, B. (2017). The function of language in parent-infant psychotherapy. *International Journal of Psychoanalysis*, 98(6), 1597–1618.

Salomonsson, B. (2018). *Psychodynamic Interventions in Pregnancy and Infancy: Clinical and Theoretical Perspectives*. London: Routledge.

Salomonsson, B. (2021). Gaze avoidance in parent-infant psychotherapy: Manifestations and technical suggestions. *International Journal of Psychoanalysis*, 102(6), 1138–1157.

Tranströmer, T. (2006). *The Great Enigma. New Collected Poems* (R. Fulton, Trans.). London: New Directions.

Tronick, E. (2007). *The Neurobehavioral and Social-Emotional Development of Infants and Children.* New York City: W. W. Norton.

Tronick, E., Als, H., Adamson, L., Wise, S., & Brazelton, T. B. (1978). The infant's response to entrapment between contradictory messages in face-to-face interaction. *Journal of the American Academy of Child and Adolescent Psychiatry,* 17, 1–13.

Tuters, E., Doulis, S., & Yabsley, S. (2011). Challenges working with infants and their families: Symptoms and meanings – two approaches of infant–parent psychotherapy. *Infant Mental Health Journal,* 32(6), 632–649.

Winnicott, D. W. (1975). *Through Paediatrics to Psycho-Analysis.* London: Hogarth and the Institute of Psycho-Analysis.

Part II

Children on the edge

Domestic and social violence, abuse and deprivation

Kerry Kelly Novick and Sara Flanders

Introduction I: Children and trauma today

Kerry Kelly Novick

What is the role and relevance of our discipline in the face of massive and rapid material, social, and cultural change and its impact particularly on those under 25, who now constitute half of the world's population?

An important focus of attention is the experience of children subjected to deprivation, violence, and abuse. Opening our lens to the widest angle, we find from recent United Nations reports that more than 357 million children in 2016 were living in a conflict zone – that is one in six of the world's children. Children in war zones are subject to killing and maiming, to recruitment and misuse for acts of war, sexual violence, abduction, attacks on schools and hospitals, and denial of humanitarian access to basic needs.

Many children living in poor areas of big cities around the world might as well be in a war zone, given the levels of violence, unpredictability, neglect, abuse, social discrimination, and so forth. And then there are the children whose very homes have the character of a war zone, with domestic violence and threats the norm. In the United States, 50 women are murdered every single day in domestic violence situations. However deep and compassionate our understanding of the predicament of the adults in these situations may be, the fact remains that the children are the worst casualties. If they survive at all, their development is distorted and their futures foreclosed.

The factors leading to violent actions are manifold and spring from all levels of development. What our clinical work shows us, however, is the centrality of the experience of helplessness and rage. Helplessness is an intolerable condition, from which people seek immediate escape. Externalization is a way to avoid the feeling of helplessness that comes with being overwhelmed from inside or outside, an escape from incipient trauma. Without sturdy internal or external supports, a readily available option is a response based on a closed, omnipotent solution, leading to the sequence – helplessness, externalization, internalization, and attack.

DOI: 10.4324/9781003216360-6

"Soul blindness" is not seeing another person as a separate individual, valuable in their own right. Once love and respect for each person are swept away, the other can be objectified and dehumanized, and then the psychological violence of externalizing parts of oneself on to another person becomes possible. A child can maintain attachment by taking in the externalizations and identifying with the aggressor, turning the violence on himself and others. Soul blindness is a condition for externalization and other assaults, ranging from bullying in school to child abuse to ethnic cleansing.

As we learn of the stories of abused children in treatment, or children orphaned or brutalized by war or refugee status, or children marginalized by poverty, racism, or prejudice, we as psychoanalysts consider the inner landscape of the minds of the children, how they populate their representational worlds on the basis of their traumatic experiences, how they bring these necessary solutions into their treatments or their functioning in the world. We are searching for ideas about what can be specifically relevant and therapeutic in a psychoanalytic clinical response, which can in turn lead us to a fuller and deeper understanding of what child and adolescent psychoanalysis has to contribute in the face of these most terrible modern challenges to children's physical and psychic survival.

I think the title "Children on the edge" is meant to evoke the image of children pushed to the point of teetering on the brink of death, oblivion, or madness – this is apt and indeed many children are vulnerable to these terrible outcomes. One author extended the metaphor to characterize "children on the edge between their suffering and their resilient strength". The authors describe the precarious journey they took together with their little patients to negotiate that knife-edge of rocky terrain.

In some ways the analyst is also on that knife-edge, struggling to ward off helplessness and terror in the face of the scale, pervasiveness and intensity of violence and abuse of children. Let's think for a moment about what we can call upon in that effort:

First, we have to accept responsibility. We must recognize that violence is part of a psychological and social system of externalization, blame, and attack. In such a closed system of defensive functioning, solutions are quick and easy – hence the appeal of violence. In an open system, we acknowledge complexity. Most human behaviour is complex and multi-determined. This is a specific contribution child and adolescent psychoanalysts can bring.

Violence demands multi-modal intervention for effective change. When a child is violent, no one person or institution is to blame. We are all responsible. Lasting change will require input from everyone – from the child, the family, the community, teachers, schools, police, courts, the medical and psychological professionals, academic and clinical research, the legal system, and legislators at all levels.

Second, we must each act despite the complexity. Anything we do, in and out of the consulting room, will have some effect. Whenever we refuse to go along with teasing or discrimination or denigration; whenever we insist that two children or adults find a way to resolve differences; whenever we demand that principals or administrators or organizational leaders use their authority to back up teachers or agency workers or junior colleagues; whenever we give and expect respectful interchange with peers, colleagues, parents and children; whenever we make the effort to help someone else; whenever we try to understand someone very different from ourselves – the list is endless. All of these actions in fact have a double effect. They impact each child and they also encourage similar actions in others. Social intimidation has its opposite in social inspiration. Anna Freud talked about psychoanalytic training as a source of inspiration.

Third, we must intervene early and keep at it. The sooner psychoanalysts get involved, the more effective we can be. The more we actively pursue a place at the table for multidisciplinary interventions, the more relevant those interventions will be. The parent who has learned not to shake her baby will teach him to take good care of himself, which will equip him to stand up to bullies. Early intervention is humanly, socially, and financially economical. The sooner we all work to create a culture in which no one feels it is more comfortable and acceptable to stand by and do nothing, the sooner we will never have to feel that what we provide is too little, too late. We can work toward a world in which all children have a safe and expansive space to play and grow, away from the edge of the cliff, and where changes in the world can be absorbed and mastered in the service of creativity and fulfilment.

The chapters in this section describe interventions that brought young children back from the brink, treatments in which the therapists were able to journey with their patients into the borderland of violence and terror and, together, find their way back to a safer world. These papers bring us into a dark place but also suggest and demonstrate that psychoanalytic treatment can offer hope.

Introduction II: Trauma in treatment

Sara Flanders

All the cases explored in this section focus on young children who, in their young lives, faced extreme trauma: Cassie, suffered a radical separation from a violent and dysfunctional family, Linda is born into intergenerational and family trauma, and Lisa, a 5-year-old girl experienced paternal sexual abuse and an acute parental conflict. Each analyst describes the profoundly challenging, tumultuous impact of the patients who nonetheless received from their psychoanalytic psychotherapists informed and sensitive attention to the baffling unknown of the young children's internal worlds. Noticeably, the therapist of the most developmentally damaged child, Linda (Joyce) was not an experienced psychotherapist, but a trainee. We see her nonetheless learning from her experience, guided like the others, by a belief that there is meaning in the most confusing and distressing, even repellent symptoms presented by the young patients. The therapeutic work described in each case is inspiring in the determination and courage of the therapists' attempts to understand. And all children are shown to benefit significantly from the brave, imaginative and intelligent work offered to them.

Cassie

The therapist, Simon Creegan, on meeting his 5-year-old patient, is rocked by the uncanny swagger of the little girl he meets. When he shuts the door of the consulting room, she "spins around, kicks (him) hard, spits, gives a mocking laugh, and walks away". He writes, "I am left exposed, mentally and physically, assaulted, my sense of security ruptured, and a bit outraged". Simon Creegan shows us here, and throughout, how he used his emotional experience, taking the full impact of the child's aggression, then using his countertransference, and his psychoanalytically informed sensitivity to understand the workings of this child's mind. He begins by offering recognition of her felt states, and we watch the patient move, from violent action to symbolic, communicative capacity, benefitting from interpretations offered with tact, but based on an impressive knowledge of the emotional needs of a child. Flinging pens violently around the room as she too spun around, she enacted what looked and felt like a volcano erupting. Creegan writes, "Through an action experience Cassie provided a compelling communication of how it feels to be enmeshed with a violent and unbounded object; beta element-lava spewing forth from a dangerous volcano-breast".

Linda

In contrast, Angela Joyce writes of a much more developmentally damaged 3-year-old, a child whose communicative capacity was much more disorganized, wildly regressive, and baffling to her trainee psychotherapist. Not long experienced, not grounded in an elaborate theory, the psychotherapist nevertheless attempted to stay attuned to Linda's chaotic behaviour. She had far fewer psychoanalytic concepts to support her understanding, but she struggled to make sense of the feelings awakened in her, supported by a commitment to search for the meaning, however elusive. She was supported of course, by a more experienced child analyst. But it is she who is on the receiving end, it is she who sticks it out.

There is emphasis in Angela Joyce's commentary on the developmental help that the therapy supports, over and above understanding of conflict and phantasy. She weds Anna Freud's notion of developmental help, as opposed to interpretation of conflict and phantasy, to the theory of the setting, the facilitating environment (Winnicott), the significance of the survival of the therapist's concerned attention. She shows the trainee psychotherapist lapsing more easily than the seasoned therapist into extra therapeutic engagement, as when the little patient's reference to a phantasy of "cheesy Pizza" awakens in her the notion of a referral to a dietician, diverting her away momentarily from her task as the emotionally receptive psychotherapist. But when she could identify the affective state of her patient, staying with the therapeutic project, she facilitates the patient's very considerable emotional, cognitive, and physical growth. The affective and attentive holding led certainly to the patient's developing a narrative, achieving a symbolic capacity to communicate to her developing psychotherapist.

It should be noted that in this case, and Simon Creegan's, there is supportive parental work, in Linda's case, a very damaged mother, and in the previous case, the foster mother of Cassie.

Lisa

Mariangela Mendes de Almeida's patient is very different, a smart and articulate little girl of almost 5 years, whose mother brought her for therapy to attend to her daughter's anxiety, and the effects of sexual abuse by the child's father. The context of her referral for therapy included legal, social services, and psychological services, together providing legal and social support to the independent provision of a therapeutic space. In the provision of that space, there is implicitly respect for the sensitivity of the child's subjectivity.

The pressures on maintaining such a space are vividly illustrated in the narrative offered, the girl's mother leaving a waiting room, going upstairs to listen at the consulting room door, overcome with intrusive anxiety and guilt, perhaps provoked by the child's own noises at the door on her side of the consulting room. The therapist herself struggles with the identification of the privacy of the treatment with the secrecy framing the abuse itself. With great sensitivity she attends to the child's communication, interpreting the child's symbolic play and her drawings in a way that is aimed at helping her to contain the experience, not repeat it. She shows finally, in her non-intrusive interpretative contributions that it is possible to contribute to the development of such elaborative capacity in the patient that the familiar compulsion to repeat sexual trauma can yield to a "benign cycle" of psychic growth. Quoting Selma Fraiberg, she states, "history does not need to be fate".

That might be the theme of all the chapters in this part of the book.

5

Cassie

From violent eruption to gathering thoughts

Simon Cregeen

Introduction

A young child, small in stature and with unusual features, walks into the therapy room, with a casual air, apparently confident and secure in their own being. However, there is a hyper-alertness, as if scanning for predators. I follow and close the door. In an instant the child spins around, kicks me hard, spits, gives a mocking laugh, and walks away, eyes watching me closely, a knowing, triumphant smile. I am left exposed, mentally and physically assaulted, my sense of security ruptured, and a bit outraged. There is a shamelessness which takes my breath away.

Cassie was age 5 when we first met and I saw her for five years, mostly twice weekly, in a UK, National Health Service context. The neglect and violence which Cassie suffered in her birth family are horribly familiar and troubling. The work I am describing builds on psychotherapy with severely deprived children by child psychotherapists over the past 40 years, initially described by Boston and Szur (1983). Long-term work for such children can be difficult to establish and sustain within NHS services, but with creativity and negotiation it is widely provided by members of the Association of Child Psychotherapists. In the UK, this represents the most significant body of psychoanalytic work being undertaken with children, adolescents, and parents.

Britton has described how, 'when family breakdown has occurred the child may or may not be homeless but he is psychically unplaced' (1983).

My patient Cassie was psychically homeless and dominated by an object which generated explosive fragmentation. I could never be sufficiently alert to deal with her spits, hits, and kicks, phenomena well described by Canham (2004). In her most malevolent states, Cassie behaved like a sprite, darkly. However, there was a need to differentiate those times when Cassie's tyrannical aggression aimed to attack my mind and any chance of us thinking together, from those times when her omnipotent relating was in the service of survival (Symington, 1985).

Working with children in such states is demanding. In terms of what the child requires, Boston and Szur (1983) make clear that 'it seemed most important that the therapist should survive and show some strength, in contrast to the fragile figures of the child's inner world and past experience', whilst Rustin (2001) describes

DOI: 10.4324/9781003216360-7

three essential factors for the therapist managing work of this nature – 'good external and internal support ... freedom to recognize that time is needed for this work' and 'turning to my own clinical imagination, to be willing to take risks, and not to know the outcome in advance'.

I hope to illustrate how psychotherapy can contribute to the development of space within such a child's mind, the growth of a capacity to identify with good objects, and to a sense of belonging. The development of mental equipment enables the child (in Bion's terms) to 'suffer' rather than evade the pain and frustration encountered in bringing together experiences and thoughts. Such developments, if they arrive, are dependent on there being a robust network around the child and family, what Britton has termed the 'reconstituted family circle' (1983). The child psychotherapist serves an analytic function in relation to this network through regular liaison and consultation.

Britton's (1998) emphasis on the oscillation between paranoid-schizoid and depressive position states provides a helpful model of the mind in constant flux, with conflicting constellations of anxieties, feelings, and phantasies. With this in mind, I will describe something of Cassie's dominant state of mind early on in our work, the middle period, and the state of mind which was in the ascendancy towards the end. I will finish with a brief discussion.

Cassie

At age 2 and a half, Cassie, of Eastern European and British dual heritage, was taken into emergency care after being beaten by her mother, who was out of control due to alcohol and drug use. Cassie's father was absent and out of contact. When the couple were together, there was shared substance abuse and violence, and significant neglect of Cassie's needs. Cassie was the youngest of a number of siblings all of whom were living elsewhere.

When I met her, Cassie had been in multiple care placements and educational provisions. She had some developmental difficulties. She was violent towards herself, her peers, her carers, and to animals. Proximity seemed to create a sense of danger, and any movement towards intimacy was perilous.

Cassie would hurt herself whilst looking directly at her carer, seeking to push helplessness and horror into them, and seeming to gain a feeling of power and perverse satisfaction over the object. Associated with this, Cassie appeared to not feel her own physical pain or, perhaps more likely, suffered it masochistically. She attacked herself in numerous ways but particularly on the skin of her lips, and the quick of her fingers, bringing blood and open sores. Cassie urinated in a standing position, and declared herself to be a boy. This was issued as a statement of fact, rather than one of choice or inclination. She may have believed that to be female was dangerous, both as aggressor and victim. Faeces were smeared and hidden. There seemed to be no receptive object into which to project.

Cassie appeared not to know who she was or what she felt, and would mimic others who were in distress or had an obvious vulnerability – a girl wearing a leg brace led Cassie to limp and complain of her own sore leg. More extremely, she sometimes threw herself off a height, or would smash her arm into something hard in a desperate effort to become the physically injured child. I think this revealed not only states of adhesive or projective identification, but also an imperative in Cassie to smash and grab another child's vulnerable state of being, and with it the possibility of forcing her way into an object in order to get the necessary care and protection of parental figures.

Cassie was often caught by the seductive pull of a perverse enactment linked to a gang state of mind, which Canham (2002) has described as 'anti-life, anti-parents, anti-thinking'. At these times, a state of symbolic equation dominated (Segal, 1957). Evacuative projective identification was her dominant mode of relating. In other moments, Cassie wanted her pain and distress noticed and responded to. Her carer, social worker, and teacher had each observed moments of softness with others, a desire to be helpful, and a pressing need to be included. Cassie's curiosity hadn't been killed off, nor had her desire to be part of a group. However, a defensive structure characterised by tyranny, triumph, and contempt for dependency often got in the way.

My impression was that Cassie had introjected what Williams (1997) has conceptualised as 'omega function', a consequence of which is, 'explosive rage experienced by the child who is not being offered containment, but is used instead as the receptacle of projections he cannot deal with'.

Cassie was a long way from having developed a secure psychic home. Rather, her internal world appeared dominated by objects which were cruel, abandoning, and intolerant of vulnerability. She had discovered that, whatever the cost, identification with narcissistically destructive objects brought a form of survival and some relief – others could have the humiliation, desperate uncertainty, and depressive pain. This can be seen as a defence against terrifying nameless dread (Bion, 1962a).

Throughout the work, there was regular contact with the network, including Susan, Cassie's carer, who was a distant member of the extended family. Susan was not obviously suited to her role; she kept her distance from services and appeared without emotional curiosity. At times there was a worrying sense of secrecy. However, Susan provided the steadiness Cassie needed, and didn't get overwrought by the disturbance that she sought to project. Although Susan's emotional inaccessibility was a clear deficit, this had to be balanced against the fact that the placement sustained over many years, and Cassie developed during this period. Such balanced judgements within networks, and the painful compromises involved, are an inevitable part of the provision of substitute family care for damaged children.

Clinical work – early period

Cassie's terrors were vividly illustrated in this drawing of a bizarre, threatening figure.

The emphasis is on the head, dominated by horns and protruding shapes, and the mouth appears to be sewn-up, alongside a phallic nose or tongue. The figure

appears aggressive, ill-conceived, a monstrous assemblage. This is an object with insufficient distinction between internal and external, and conveys no sense of a receptive mind. This terrifying figure was alive in the transference. Cassie told Susan that she was worried about coming to see me, 'I don't want Simon to take me away … there are children behind all the doors'. She was referring to the small wooden lockers in my room where each child keeps their therapy things.

Cassie's phantasy seemed to be of a Simon-object who would not only remove her from the security of her relationship with Susan, but who held children hostage and subjected them to unmitigated terror. In the transference, I was a figure who would lure children into my dark world, and use them as receptacles for my own psychotic anxieties and cruel ambitions.

In the same session, Cassie created the first of a number of 'volcanos'. The initial one involved pens and paper and a picture of sorts was created, but this was a volcanic eruption more than a visual image. Pens made fast and fleeting contact with the paper and were then flung around the room forcefully and erratically. Cassie was whirling around, chaotic and without care for herself, me, or the room. It was as if Cassie was in the volcano and the volcano was in Cassie. The state of the room evidenced the level of fragmentation.

Through an action experience, Cassie provided a compelling communication of how it feels to be enmeshed with a violent and unbounded object: beta-element-lava spewing forth from a dangerous volcano-breast. Cassie's identification with such an object can be understood as a desperate response to the imagined terrors of being imprisoned in my lockers. Throughout this, Cassie seemed held together through an aggressive excitability, including her grim delight at my obvious concern and unsettlement. I made a few observational comments of what I thought might be her felt experience, and I named some of the elements.

Cassie settled a little, and responded by saying, 'fire … blue smoke everywhere'. This indicated some sense of reality – the danger and something obscured. I spoke of what she was showing and telling me. Cassie took another piece of paper and drew another volcano, this time in an ordinary way. She'd moved from evacuative action to a desire to communicate. The second volcano also had 'fire and smoke' and then, something astonishing – she drew 'an egg' sitting on top of the volcano, at its mouth. After drawing my breath, I wondered what happens to the egg in such a dangerous place. Cassie answered plainly, 'it gets burnt'. There was a pause and she added, hesitantly, 'I think the chick inside is okay'. Although the eggshell appeared intact, I felt unconvinced that Cassie really believed that the chick was safe.

Later, she poured water endlessly between containers large and small, a fire engine attended a doll's house fire, and she initiated a to-and-fro ball game between us. At the end of this session, Cassie enquired, 'who are the other lockers for?' That is, whose things do they contain, in contrast to who has Simon imprisoned in them.

I think Cassie was communicating something not only of her post-birth experience with a violent parental couple, but also one of pre-natal distress, the 'burn' of *in utero* agitation within a mother abusing her own body. We might understand the volcano as representing the inside of the mother, within which the egg grew, and from which her chick emerged, as well as the volcano as a post-birth, life-threatening, unpredictable breast-mother upon whom the chick-baby has no choice other than to depend.

Within the time frame of one session, Cassie showed how she could move from chaotic action to symbolic thinking, along with play in which I was to be an active companion, and where water could be employed as an antidote to the destructiveness of fire. As the session progressed, I think Cassie had gained a sense of my capacity to take in her experience, not fall apart, not retaliate, and not perversely collude with the violence of a volcano state. I had been able to gather things and name them, and this helped meaning to accumulate (Britton, 1998). Cassie seemed to take this in as evidence that I had a mind which was not too easily destroyed, and that I was interested in her emotional experience. I was neither obliterated nor abandoning. In Bion's terms, this could be thought of as Cassie having an experience of a pre-conception of a receptive and resilient object mating with a lived realisation of one (Bion, 1963).

This sequence was an early indication that Cassie's mind wasn't fixed and, despite all the anxieties, she could tolerate her defences shifting, thus enabling her to make realistic observations and use of an object.

Clinical work – middle period

One particularly painful and alarming enactment, often repeated, was when Cassie would hold her hand underneath increasingly hot running water, whilst watching to see what impact this had on me – could I bear it, and when and how would I act? I was being presented with an invidious choice of either colluding with a sado-masochistic enactment, or intervening, with the prospect of a struggle, being attacked by Cassie, and then mocked as frightened and pathetic.

However, there were also developments – in terms of Cassie's play, the making of books full of drawings and written feelings, and games of football between us, always to the rules of the Football Association of Cassie! There was a growing sense of her having an internal world peopled by characters with whom she had differentiated relationships. Cassie told me to, 'hush, I want to make myself think about that'. Her writing moved from separated letters in pencil to joined-up writing in pen. That is, from separate and temporary elements, not necessarily connected with one another, to symbols which are linked and have some steadiness. At school, she was eager to learn, and this development was now in motion.

Cassie's books seemed to be a way of naming, owning, and locating these experiences and relationships within herself, and in a form able to be shared with me. She was now actively organising her experience. Cassie couldn't talk much about her books, but my acknowledgement of her personal internal experience, in a non-intrusive way, was clearly important to her. We could also think that the book structure represented something of the growth of a container: contained structure within Cassie, the development of an internal world in which different object relationships and associated phantasies could be formed, allowed to live, and be investigated.

I'll describe something of her development by reference to some session material from this period.

Cassie arrived and wanted to 'make a mirror ... so I can see what I am feeling'. Cassie compared our forearms and the veins visible on hers and on mine, as if considering what makes us distinctively different from one another, and specifically in terms of what we are made of. Then, rather than making a mirror as such, she carefully made a drawing of herself. This had not happened previously in sessions. Cassie was anxious about it, 'I look like a zombie ... I look weird'. Despite her misgivings, Cassie then told me her picture was 'of me and my feelings', and she was evidently proud of what she had created and shared with me. However, as she looked at it, with both interest and puzzlement, Cassie observed, 'looks lonely'. She couldn't say anything more about this.

She soon followed with a request to play hide and seek, but first she would 'make a detector... a telescope'. As she did this, I spoke of all she was doing, and noted how the telescope was a man sort of thing, perhaps for a daddy-Simon, to help me 'detect' her, to find her? Cassie agreed that the telescope was for me to use in the game. As we played hide and seek, I interpreted that she was seeking proof that I wanted to find her, that I had the right equipment to do this, and had a picture of her in my head, in my thoughts, even when she felt that we were far away from each other. Cassie agreed. I added that maybe this helped with the lonely feeling. There was no reply.

In addition to the comments I made, I think the telescope represented Cassie's understanding that I have my own view of her, linking across separateness and difference, with the possibility of triangulation and mental space being created (Birksted-Breen, 1996). Cassie shows two ideas about being seen, first through looking at herself close up in a mirror, and second my looking at her from a distance through a telescope. There is a suggestion of two contrasting types of gaze, perhaps associated with maternal and paternal positions.

Cassie's comment about 'a feeling' suggests a relationship to another object, that is, 'I have a feeling about something/someone/some situation'. She then looks at what she has drawn, and this looking leads to qualities being seen – weird, lonely. I think here Cassie is identifying with an object who knows she is a girl with feelings, including that of being lonely. In order to know about feeling lonely, there has to also be a 'not-lonely' girl. In this exchange between us, maybe Cassie feels she is not lonely in relation to me, but rather that I am with her, alongside her. This allows her to know her loneliness, or rather the girl she is when she feels lonely, and to be interested and a bit puzzled about this emotional state. In this moment, Cassie is able to find out something new about herself by being in the presence of an object, both externally and internally.

Linked with the above is Cassie's observation of the drawn image of herself as 'weird' and 'zombie'. Her growing awareness of the separateness of others, and thus the possibility of being seen by others differently to how she sees herself, brought anxieties about what others make of her, what do they see? And how does this affect how she sees herself? I think there was a growing awareness in Cassie of the ways in which she was different to others, most notably her peers, and how this difference might be one source of loneliness.

To bring the description of this period of work to a close, I think this next drawing indicates something of what Cassie had achieved within herself by this point. This is Cassie and her carer. The writing underneath says, 'Susan was holding my hand to keep me safe across the car park'. Some form of psychic home had been found.

Clinical work – later period

Cassie used Play-Doh to flatten, cut out, and mould what she said was 'a wedding cake'. I wondered who for? 'You and … are you married? You've got a ring', Cassie said, somewhat accusingly. I said she was thinking of me and a wife, a wedding, and wanting to know about, or be part of this somehow. This comment was too much for her, and led to a more manic state and more insistent cake-making. Once things had settled a bit, I said that maybe Cassie felt she had to be in charge of the wedding, and of how a wife and I might come together.

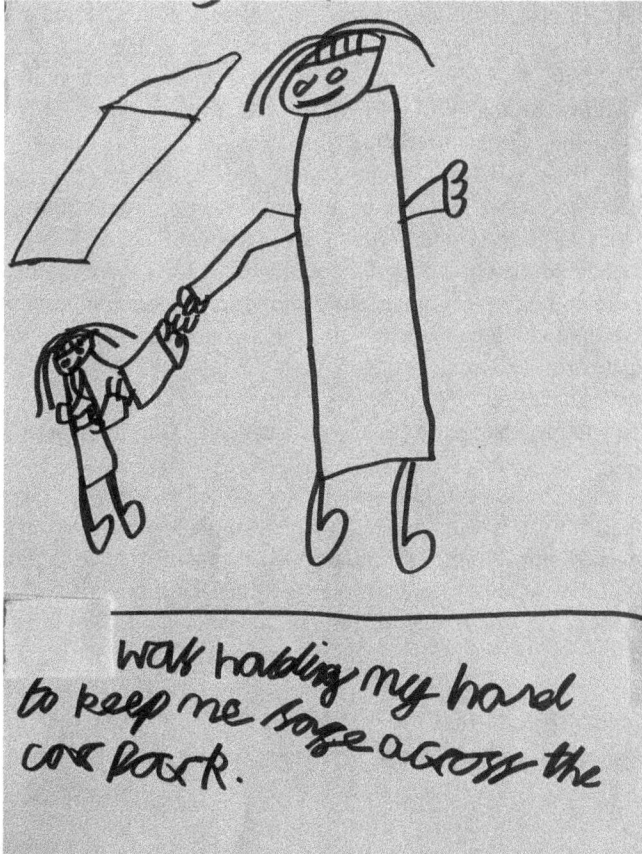

was holding my hand
to keep me safe across the
car park.

Cassie responded by setting out three plates and dividing the cake up, with the triumphant comment, 'Not much for the wife! ... She's not hungry'.

I interpreted that Cassie thinks that 'the wife' ('Your wife!' Cassie interjected) gets enough of me already, and doesn't deserve more. I said that I thought Cassie was saying she wants more of me, and she thinks this can only happen if my wife has less of me, and is made to wait.

Cassie went to the sink and drank copious amounts of water, followed by climbing on top of the filing cabinet, then down, and measuring herself against it. I interpreted her thinking that the only way she could have enough of me, to feel really full inside, was if she was as big and greedy as my wife. Cassie, slightly downcast, responded, 'It's a week until I see you again'.

I said how she felt left without enough of me, and pointed out that in fact her next session was tomorrow. I added that when she feels so hungry for me, and is worried she won't get anything, she loses what she does have of me; it feels to her like my wife gets it all. Cassie looked seriously at me, seeming to take this in.

The following day, Cassie and I made cakes again, and she said, 'we'll put the cakes together', which she did. I spoke of how she was interested in how she and I join up. When I suggested this was a bit like a couple, Cassie shouted at me, 'you're married, again!' I tried to help Cassie think about the possibility of room for a wife *and* room for Cassie. She again denied my wife any cake, then swiftly moved to the vertical window blinds and broke all the plastic chain links which hold them together, leaving the blinds un-tethered.

I said that she feels so frustrated, she wants to be big like my wife, not small, and it makes her feel so jealous to think of me and my wife like a mummy and daddy joined together. Cassie responded, 'how do you know that?'

Cassie now had an idea of a parental couple, one which she imagined as forever feasting on cake and on one another. She seemed to be having a passionate experience of the Oedipal challenge in relation to this couple, along with all the associated feelings, desires, and anxieties.

Some months later, a few weeks before a planned reduction from two to one session per week (due to changes in my work situation), Cassie created the drawing below.

Unusually, she labelled the elements, explicitly showing how things are connected. Cassie told me it was 'a tree', with 'a nest', and 'a snake … a python'. Behind this was 'a sun … blue sky', and in the right-hand corner, 'a bird'. Cassie said, 'I started off with an S shape but then it turned into a snake'.

I said how the S may be like S for Simon, and how she feels I have turned into something dangerous, like a python. How perhaps Cassie was letting me know that

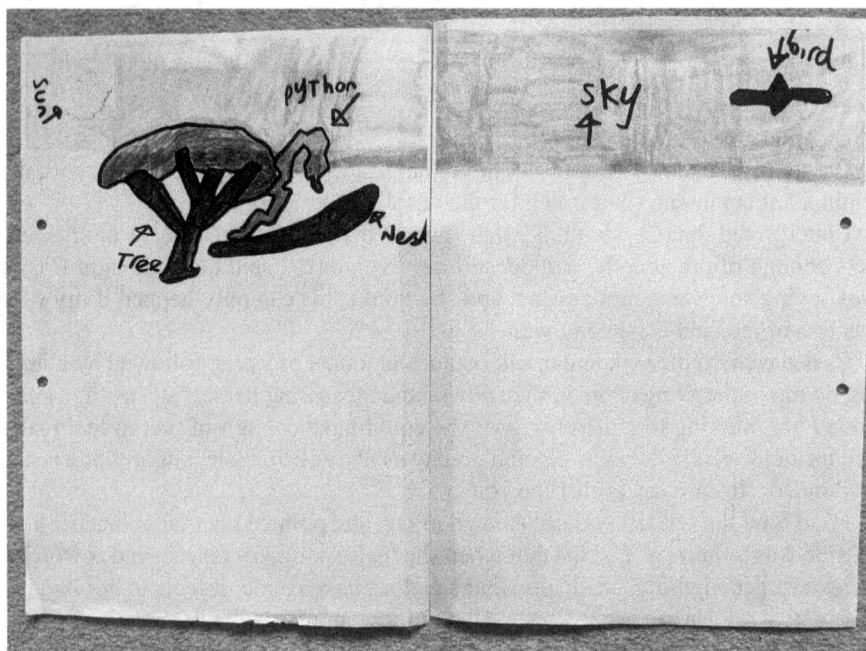

her feeling that she had a safe place with me, like a nest, was suddenly upset by my taking away her Tuesday session. Cassie carried on quietly colouring.

I said that maybe she felt I was like the snake – she thought she could trust me but now feels I've betrayed her, and hurt her feelings, and this makes her worry whether she is safe with me. Cassie was looking intently at me, quiet, and coloured some more. After a short while, I added that I thought she was frightened that I was robbing her of something precious, something of our closeness.

Cassie didn't speak but initiated a game of football. Untypically, this was not a competitive encounter but a gentle passing of the ball. There was a feeling of intimacy, of being in something together.

Poignantly, Cassie noted how my couch was very slightly pushed to one side of its usual position. I said that seeing the space at the side made smaller was like the loss of the Tuesday session; that I thought she was sad at this, and worried would she be getting less space inside me, and will we still be close? Cassie remained quiet.

I think Cassie here has a concept of a Simon who is solid like the tree, and that I can be trusted to take in this drawing and think about what it means, including her fear of being consumed or cast out by a python-me. However, she is anxious that with the loss of a session, her place inside becomes less solid, less trustworthy.

By the end of her psychotherapy, Cassie was bringing material about herself and her 'boyfriend' at school, along with a girl into whom badness, disgust, and exclusion were projected. I was also an excluded third (of another generation) and referred to with some disdain as an 'old man'. Her identity as a female appeared more secure, and she was sitting down to urinate. An idea of triadic relating had developed, albeit with an idealised coupling, with anything unwanted pushed into excluded others. Violent enactment had significantly diminished, and aggression was mobilised more ordinarily in the service of developmental conflicts, including Oedipal struggles.

Discussion

Cassie's early declaration, 'I am a boy' was not, I think, primarily associated with gender confusion so much as a desperate bid to survive; an evacuation of everything female in favour of the male. In the early transference relationship, I was often related to as if I was a helpless little girl, my femininity held in contempt, with Cassie behaving in a phallic and muscular way. Perhaps for Cassie there was an unconscious belief, derived from lived experience, that to be a girl, to be like mummy, inevitably determined that you would be in the line of fire, you would explode with fire, and you would become the fire.

The times when Cassie's mum was relating to her as an undefined thing, rather than as her infant daughter, must have been terrifying. By declaring herself a boy, perhaps Cassie sought to evade a trans-generational fate which Faimberg (2005) has described with her concept of the trans-generational transmission of narcissistic links and family cultures.

In her nature, Cassie seemed to be a child unimpaired by too much envy or grievance. Despite her grossly damaging early experiences, she was often more open to the gains of dependency than the apparent certainties of pseudo-self-sufficiency, and was able to tolerate frustration sufficiently to enable thinking to grow.

I suggest that children such as Cassie are constantly monitoring and closely observing the object's fluctuating capacity to bear and contain their projected pain, psychotic fragmentation, and unknown experiences. The therapist's capacity to tolerate the counter-transference is linked with the patient's experience of being provided with what Britton terms 'sanctuary' (1998). The therapist needs to receive, work through, and name these emotional states and psychic qualities. This helps to transform the patient's un-metabolised experience. As Britton says, '… the experience of the emotion gives meaning to the word' (1998).

With a shrinking of narcissistic identifications, and a growth of introjective processes, there is development of phantasy life and symbol formation, and thus the possibility of meaning making. This is central to developing one's capacity to know one's object, and to being known by them. Rusbridger (1999) suggests that the 'whole process of engendering, disguising, attacking, and tolerating meaning' is directly related to the working through of the Oedipus complex. The patient's response to creativity within their own mind, the analyst's mind, or between the two of them, is associated with the parental couple's intercourse, and there is an oscillation between moments when this can and cannot be tolerated.

For children whose parental experience is dominated by violence and neglect, developing a loving and creative couple in mind is a formidable challenge. The child suffers a profound lack, *and* is required to manage gross intrusion of parental pathology. This seriously distorts the child's sense of generational boundaries, brings enforced disorganisation, and promotes confusion of self and objects to a terrifying level. The child's identification with such objects may be the only possible way to survive. Additionally, as Rustin has described (1999), such children carry 'multiple families in mind'. These children have crowded minds and there is no 'back of the mind' space.

When the child can tolerate their therapist using his mind to think, the child has an experience of an intercourse between different parts or objects in the therapist's mind. The therapist's interest is then experienced by the child as being rooted in emotional curiosity, what Bion termed an enquiry in K, rather than experienced by the child as the object's provocative and attacking intrusion, minus K (Bion, 1962b). Such a thinking process may be experienced by the child as the coming together of a parental couple, and as a help towards uniting the child's psychic world (Britton, 1989).

Ending

In 'Notes on memory and desire' (1967), Bion states, 'Progress will be measured by the increased number and variety of moods, ideas, and attitudes seen in any given session'. This proposal provides a useful balance to the current dominant trend for behavioural measures of clinical outcome. I hope I have given some indication of such progress within Cassie. One form of evidence is the development of dimensionality in her drawings. The first image is a thing, a beta-element, the second is like an illustration of an event, the third suggests a dream image.

In her final session, Cassie was telling me all she'd like to take away with her from the therapy room. She eventually settled on one thing, 'the key to my locker'. This was said without trickery or insistence.

I understand it straightforwardly as Cassie's ambivalence regarding the ending, in having to take leave of me and her locker, but I think it conveys something more: that Cassie was communicating how a feeling of mental space had opened up between herself and her object, there was space within her object, and space within herself. This development allowed Cassie to conceive of a relationship with another person in which she could come and go with freedom.

References

Bion, W.R. (1962a). A theory of thinking. *Int. Journal of Psychoanalysis*, 43(4–5).

Bion, W.R. (1962b). *Learning from Experience*. Karnac, Heinemann: London.

Bion, W.R. (1963). *Elements of Psychoanalysis*. Heinemann: London.

Bion, W.R. (1967) Notes on memory and desire. *The Psychoanalytic Forum*, 2: 272–273, 279–280. Also in, Bott Spillius, E. (1988) *Melanie Klein Today: Volume 2 : Mainly Practice*. Routledge: London & New York.

Birksted-Breen, D. (1996). Phallus, penis and mental space. *Int. Journal of Psychoanalysis*, 77: 649–657.

Boston, M. & Szur, R. (Eds) (1983). *Psychotherapy with severely Deprived Children*. Routledge & Kegan Paul: London.

Britton, R. (1983). Breakdown and reconstitution of the family circle. In, Boston, M. & Szur, R. (Eds). *Psychotherapy with Severely Deprived Children*. Routledge & Kegan Paul: London.

Britton, R. (1989). The missing link: Parental sexuality in the Oedipus complex. In, Britton, R., Feldman, M., & O'Shaughnessy, E. *The Oedipus Complex Today: Clinical Implications*. Karnac: London.

Britton, R. (1998). Naming and containing. In, Britton, R. *Belief and Imagination*. Routledge: London.

Canham, H. (2002). Group and gang states of mind. *Journal of Child Psychotherapy*, 28(2): 113–127.

Canham, H. (2004). Spitting, kicking and stripping: Technical difficulties encountered in the treatment of deprived children. *Journal of Child Psychotherapy*, 30(2): 143–154.

Faimberg, H. (2005). The telescoping of generations: Listening to the narcissistic links between generations. Routledge: London.

Rusbridger, R. (1999). Elements of the Oedipus complex: Building up the picture. *British Journal of Psychotherapy* 15(4): 488–500.

Rustin, M. (1999). Multiple families in mind. *Journal of Clinical Psychology and Psychiatry* 4(1): 51–62.

Rustin, M. (2001). The therapist with her back against the wall. *Journal of Child Psychotherapy*, 27(3): 273–284.

Segal, H. (1957). Notes on symbol formation. *Int. Journal of Psychoanalysis*, 38: 391–397.

Symington, J. (1985). The survival function of primitive omnipotence. *Int. Journal of Psychoanalysis*, 66: 481–487.

Williams, G. (1997). On introjective processes: The hypothesis of an 'Omega function'. In Williams, G., *Internal Landscapes and Foreign Bodies*. Duckworth: London.

6

The child analyst as a "new developmental object" to a developmentally delayed young child

Angela Joyce

Clinical psychoanalysis has long been challenged by patients, adults, and children whose ordinary developmental needs have not been adequately met, resulting in major deficits in their personality functioning as well as concomitant disturbances as these deficits interplay over time with developmental challenges. Children like this come with multiple diagnoses – e.g. ADHD, ODD (oppositional defiant disorder), attachment disorders, conduct disorder with explosive, destructive behaviour, inappropriate sexualised behaviour etc., and frequently threaten to overwhelm inadequately equipped child mental health clinics. They have often been offered multiple short-term interventions that have changed nothing and more than likely are prescribed psychotropic medications of one kind or another. Anna Freud described these children as "atypical" or having an "underlying primary deficiency" – and perhaps in modern parlance, they might be thought of as having emerging borderline personality disorders of one type or another. Their development is severely compromised by a multiplicity of factors, often chief amongst which has been their unstable family environments, with severe traumas of neglect, maltreatment, and loss. They reflect disturbances in ego development, object relations, and superego formation, are often impulsive with poor affect regulation and a profound level of mistrust of those caring for them; they might be referred because of uncontrollable aggression, be immature for age or developmentally delayed, have no sense of danger, difficulties concentrating, and unaffected by punishment or praise, and so on. This chapter will explore, through a clinical case, the technical and conceptual challenges and particularly the kinds of interventions child psychotherapists and analysts might make in order to promote both developmental progression and resolution of psychic disturbances.

Linda (aged 4.9 years) was referred by her GP to the local Child Development Centre wondering if she was autistic. A mixture of the waiting list and some recognition of the family history of trauma, led to an assessment for psychotherapy, certainly not at that point regarded as the treatment of choice. The child psychotherapist (I will refer to as CP) who assessed the child and who subsequently worked with Linda, noted her extreme deficits: ordinary developmental milestones had not been reached or were late; there were delays and distortions in her eating, toileting, language, learning, play; she behaved like a young toddler who had not

DOI: 10.4324/9781003216360-8

yet developed, making repetitive baby-like noises, had little expressive speech, had been seriously delayed in her ability to reach milestones such as rolling, crawling, and walking; she could be selectively mute, often incontinent of urine and faeces and engaged in repetitive actions that made people suspect that autism lay at the cause of this presentation. She had a lack of interest in playing with peers although she was observed at school being carried around by older children as if she was a very young child. Of further concern, Linda was described as seeming to focus on one activity for a very long period of time or watch TV for extended periods of time, not aware of her environment or people around her, suggesting dissociative processes.

The assessing psychoanalytic psychotherapist CP, also noted the collusive, en- meshed but rather hostile relationship Linda had with her mother Sarah, where it seemed there was very little even dyadic *functioning which would indicate a modicum of separateness, and Sarah seemed heavily invested in maintaining Linda in a baby-like state. Sarah described herself as often staring into the distance in a dreamy state, likening herself to her daughter in this way. Despite the presence of Sarah's (recently acquired) partner, there was an absence of paternal functioning in the family that could facilitate any evolving separateness in the mother–child relationship.*

The assessment shockingly revealed that, born to a late adolescent mother (Sarah), this little girl's birth had been followed by her mother having three mis- carriages, one stillbirth, and one young child death from Sudden Infant Death Syn- drome (SIDS), all in Linda's first three and a half years. So, Linda and Millie, her two years elder sister, were the two surviving children out of seven. Sarah (mother) by this time was in her mid-20s. As well as suffering these repeated losses, Sarah herself had a childhood marked by adversity: parental separation, alcoholism in her mother, multiple partners and children from many liaisons, and poor socio- economic conditions. Sarah, aged 16 years, had been moved to supported housing by the local authority but very quickly began to have her children. The man with whom Sarah had her first two children, Millie and Linda, was convicted of sexu- ally assaulting an underage girl and subsequently imprisoned around the time of Linda's birth. Thus, Linda was born into an intergenerational family system char- acterised by neglect, loss, abuse, and to a mother who subsequently lost all her later babies. There is high probability that Sarah was unable to provide emotion- ally contingent care for her young child Linda in the context of her own ongoing experiences of catastrophic loss (Green 1980). Very likely she was only able to go through the motions of care in an emotionally dead way – "her heart is not in it" (ibid., p. 151).

The effects of Linda's developmental delays on the way she was in her life – her relating to herself, to others, at home, in school, and now at a clinic, could all be regarded as inauspicious for a psychoanalytic intervention, and indeed the original referral had not been for such a treatment. However, many psychoanalytic clini- cians have been prepared to see how far their discipline can be of help to such children, particularly as such a high proportion who are referred to child mental health clinics come with similar traumatic stories of their early history and family background. These phenomena have long been recognised within psychoanalysis as challenging the way we work. The original neurotic patients that stimulated Freud and his followers to develop psychoanalysis, led to a more or less agreed set of psychoanalytic techniques, largely centred around the verbal interpretation of unconscious conflicts in the mind of the patient that manifested in the transference relationship to the analyst. The emphasis was classically on conflictual, internal psychic reality. However, the impingement of relational trauma, including the kind evident in this case, was also recognised, if somewhat contentiously (Ferenczi 1913), as powerfully significant in the creation and functioning of a person's internal world. In the 1960s already the literature invoked the "widening scope of psychoanalysis" (Freud 1954), and earlier the impact of World War II in the UK stimulated psychoanalysts such as John Bowlby and Donald Winnicott to investigate and theorise the developmental consequences for children who had suffered all manner of adversity in their young lives. Ferenczi in the 1920s and 1930s had recognised that early trauma in the aetiology of later disturbance required technical modifications in the analytic work, also stressing the challenges to the analyst's countertransference of such work. His propositions were not well received by his contemporaries and in fact Martin-Cabre (2001) points to the disappearance of discussions about countertransference and regression for nearly three decades after Ferenczi's death. However, pioneers like Bowlby, Winnicott, Anna Freud, and others led the way in adapting classical psychoanalysis to meet the clinical needs of a population of children for whom the verbal interpretation of unconscious conflict in the treatment situation was not sufficient for the therapeutic task. Additionally, in more recent years, there has been an increasing amount of interest in the impact of early relational trauma on the developing child across disciplines, and within psychoanalysis there has been considerable focus on the fundamental processes of the construction of mind (for example, Green 1980; Botella and Botella 2005; Ferro 2005; Levine, Reed & Scarfone 2013). The investigation into how raw sensory experiences are represented and transformed in the mind into elements that are then used as feelings and thoughts available to consciousness has been one of the most productive areas of psychoanalytic theorising and clinical practice in the last 40 years. It is an area which has drawn upon hitherto differing psychoanalytic explanations in a creative combining of theorising, and which underscores the relational context of all human development. These conceptual and clinical developments have followed the opening up of psychoanalytic treatment to cases that previously would have been regarded as unsuitable for such treatment and through this has enabled psychoanalytic understanding of early trauma to be deepened and elaborated.

Linda clung to her mother (Sarah) when initially brought to the clinic, Sarah saying with great certainty that she would not go with CP (child psychotherapist) on her own. This only slightly veiled injunction to her daughter not to leave her was met very quickly with Linda doing the opposite. She did join CP in the therapy room, and although for many weeks she was silently watchful, she did start to "play". The kind of play this nearly 5 years old insisted upon at this point was a game of "pairs" – a card game where the player(s) match the cards together. Usually, it is a competitive guessing game with at least two people involved but it took until the third meeting for Linda to silently indicate she wanted CP to join her. She placed the cards methodically so that the pairs just touched each other overlapping slightly in the corner, "only just", as CP verbalised. The non-matching cards were put to one side. Linda then rather recklessly and without reference to CP climbed precariously to shut an open window and also shut the curtains so that it was dark. CP noted that Linda had not asked for her help and then thought to herself that it felt like being inside a womb. Linda proceeded to line up the cards so that their long edges now touched each other but were not overlapping. A moment of panic followed when she thought she had lost the box in which the cards belonged. CP was able to find the box but Linda then seemed to "disappear" into a dreamy space, apparently gazing at the clock but was actually quite unresponsive for several minutes, when she "came round" and she then wanted to pair the cards again. Despite also noting the way she was excluded, CP felt very engaged with what was going on in the room in contrast to the previous assessment session when she had felt bored and unconnected.

This description of the very early contact between Linda and her therapist captures both the predicament of this young child and the therapeutic challenge of the work. Breaking the apparent injunction to remain within the maternal orbit, Linda brought this game of pairs to her initial sessions and very precisely indicates the possibility of the wish and need to control her contact with the other person. Whether this contact insists on sameness, or connection that might lead to a sense of linking across separating boundaries is not yet clear. But given that Linda, aged nearly 5 years old, is functioning in many ways like a young toddler barely into her second year of life, this seems to be a scene in which a young child brings her actions within a potentially relational frame requiring and allowing for elaboration and the creation of meaning, the building blocks of mind. Her object hunger seems palpable, sufficient to propel her into the therapy room and away from her mother in the waiting room. Her therapist CP charts her own affective and imaginative responses to Linda's activities: she is bored, or not, engaged but at the same time alert to being excluded, not sought out to be of help, but also interested in the image that came to her own mind that the consulting room now felt like a womb in its darkness. Here we have the beginnings of the possibility of what Winnicott called imaginative elaboration, and Bion called reverie, and more recently Botella and Botella (2005) have suggested the analyst's state of regression or "regredience" in giving some representation, figurability, to the patient's state: the capacities of the adult mind to give meaningful form to infantile experiences (Wright 1991) that are fundamental to psychic development. For children who have not had this as part of their primary relationships, the therapeutic task then surely must encompass its provision.

Linda's therapist, CP, often found herself assailed by different feelings that she found exceedingly disturbing and hard to manage. Early on in the work she often felt intensely bored as Linda repeated the card game of "pairs" many times, evoking a powerful sense of deadness associated with being required to pair-up, be the same, surrender difference. Linda was a "hungry" patient however, and quite quickly brought simple somatic expressions which were received by CP as indicative of bodily states that hadn't been elaborated into recognisable feelings: a facial expression, tear-filled eyes, "accidents" when she wet herself or farted smelly farts, reluctance to leave at the end of sessions – and then often only when she had made a mess with the contents of her box – which aroused contradictory feelings of interest and compassion as well as irritation, disgust, and repulsion in CP. Linda's activities in the sessions became slightly more enlarged arousing more contradictory responses in her therapist. She moved on to using the Play-Doh like a very young child, now expressing pleasure in the feel of the moist, sticky texture as she smeared it around the table. She would squeal like a young pre-verbal toddler, repeating CP's word "sticky" as if only now learning the word and putting it together with the sensation. In another session as Linda licked her hands to remove the stickiness after using the Play-Doh, CP found herself feeling disgusted, and then tired and clockwatching, only halfway through the session. She was irritated with what she thought was a falsity in Linda's laugh, and feeling Linda wanted to manipulate her therapist with this seeming pleasure. She had to struggle to manage her own tone of voice as she then noted a frozen quality in Linda's look and tone. She felt frustrated and then guilty as she struggled to control her sense of disgust and aggression watching Linda smearing the Play-Doh and licking her hands, as she looked at the clock and found it was only three minutes since she had last looked at it. Later Linda came very close, intrusively into her personal body space, too close for CP's liking, stirring up a feeling of being trapped and "totally overwhelmed" annoyance. She wished the session would end. When Linda took herself away to look in her box, perhaps sensing her therapist's feelings, CP felt relieved that there was some distance, but the poo-ey Play-Doh was everywhere and she felt she couldn't bear it any longer. It was only when she noticed that Linda had slopped water on the calendar in her box that CP could retrieve her own thinking space and put together her feelings and what she might be picking up from Linda: they were to have their first half-term break the following week. As Linda tidied up by rubbing the cleaning cloth on CP's hand, arm, and on towards her face, CP felt desperate to get away, she tried to put into words what she imagined Linda was feeling – that she was very annoyed that she wasn't coming to see CP the following week. At this moment for the first time CP also then felt compassion for Linda's mother.

As CP struggles with boredom, disgust, interest, compassion, desperateness, then putting these elements together to think about a meaningful sequence, we see her aliveness as she encounters Linda's responses to the new setting which offers a "new object" (Hurry 1998) experience of emotional attentiveness. In CP's mind, these evoked states have potential meaning and although she is assailed by the wish to escape, she sticks it out, attending in her mind to the psycho-somatic expressions of her patient. It is clear here at the beginning of this treatment that Linda has very little capacity for elaborated self-states, of feelings and thoughts that could be put together to create a representational narrative, expressive of that self.

In CP's adult mind, these encounters with Linda stir up responses that are familiar to her and which she is able, with a struggle, to put together meaningfully, and which hold the possibility of Linda's self being conceived of, represented, in her mind. Whether we invoke notions of projective identification to describe the processes in the encounter between patient and therapist whereby CP's experiences are understood to be projected from Linda, landing so to speak in CP's mind, would depend on the conceptual framework used. However phenomenologically the analytic "field" (Baranger & Baranger 2008; Ferro 2005) does include these feeling elements and their associated images in the therapist's mind, not only what might be inferred as belonging to Linda. Ferro's development of "field theory" in psychoanalysis (2005) helpfully denotes those elements of the session with which we are concerned: "narratives, narremes, proto-emotions, sense-impressions and the apparatus for elaborating and managing all of these" (2005, p. 8). These are the basic building blocks of mentation, and the elaboration of potential meanings of our myriad experiences. Linda came into treatment with severe deficit in the area of the apparatus for elaborating, representing, and managing the integration of sense expressions, feeling states, and little indication that her somatic sensations were imaginatively elaborated in her psyche (Winnicott 1949).

The clinical concept of a "new developmental object" emerged out of the Anna Freudian tradition where child analysts were faced with the limitations of classical psychoanalytic interpretative techniques with some of the children referred for treatment. This was in parallel to a similar discourse in the US with the work of Hans Loewald (1960). Anna Freud's views had been that once these early deficits and disorders are established in development "they are part of the personality, no longer readily available for conflict interpretation, but needing other techniques. They do not respond solely to interpretation of their original causation. One has to do something more if development is to be in any way freed" (Edgcumbe 1995, p. 22). Edgcumbe notes that there was a move in Anna Freud's thinking over the decades of her work from initially conceptualising two forms of therapy, sharply distinguished in terms of technique, to her later works where she saw them as intertwined in most analytic work with children. Other kinds of intervention (originally referred to as "parameters" within the ego psychology tradition in the US) were tried out and eventually came together as "developmental therapy" (Hurry 1998). These interventions included the verbalisation of affective states by the therapist in the context of the child's inability to put words to feelings; the clarification by the therapist of internal and external dangers too frightening to the child to recognise and integrate; the setting of limits and boundaries to help create a structure of self and other in more behavioural terms as well as other interventions (Edgcumbe 1995).

Within the independent tradition of British psychoanalysis, most particularly in D. W. Winnicott's work, similar technical developments emerged for similar reasons. Winnicott's distinction between different levels of psychological disturbance (Winnicott 1960) led him to emphasise the particular role that elements of the psychoanalytic setting played for certain kinds of patients. For some, and I think Linda would be included here, interpretation of psychic conflict would be irrelevant because that assumed the development of a "whole person", that is the establishment of a coherent sense of self which was integrated and related to internal and external reality. Instead, those aspects of the setting which he saw as fundamental to this treatment would be the reliability and consistency of the setting offered, including the capacity to bear the intense affects often induced in the analyst in response to the patient (Winnicott 1947).

The repeated experience of a therapist who can bear the kinds of feeling states within the analytic setting here described, and find meaning in them, aims to meet the fundamental needs of the child which, for whatever reasons have not been available to them before. Although this area has been a contested one within psychoanalysis as it has been so associated with the notion of the "corrective emotional experience" (Alexander & French 1946), nevertheless in contemporary psychoanalytic discourse the idea that some patients need or take from their analytic treatment elements that are fundamental to psychic growth has gained more credibility. Thus, providing a child such as Linda with therapeutic interventions that constitute new experiences promoting psychic development is understood as within the remit of psychoanalytic treatment.

The recognition of these aspects of psychoanalytic treatment reflected the extension of its aims and shifted attention within mainstream psychoanalytic discourse to incorporate non-interpretative techniques and interventions. It has been accompanied by a much greater sensitivity not only to the analyst's countertransference but to the functioning of the analyst's own mind in the analytic endeavour. In this case of Linda, and the work with children who have suffered early relational trauma, maltreatment and/or neglect, the often-used analogy of the mother–infant relationship for analytic work points to the question of what exactly is to be provided when it is "primary experience" that has been missing and is now required. Although Winnicott wrote about recognising that in the Oxfordshire scheme for evacuated children the therapy was often done by the "cook, by the regularity of the arrival of food on the table, by the warm enough and perhaps warmly coloured bedspreads …" (1984, p. 200), within the psychoanalytic setting these elements surely are represented not by the actual food cooked but by the symbolic food offered through the presence of the analyst, her reliability, consistency, and receptivity to her patient's states of being, and then what she does with what is received in her mind. For Winnicott, some patients, and some patients in states of regression to dependency, the couch *is* the mother's lap, the analyst's words *are* the needed food (Winnicott 1954). Here we are in the territory of pre-symbolic functioning, proto symbols, or even raw sense data which become the constituents of symbolic representations. For a child like Linda where there has not been sufficient psychic development to allow for regression, those elements of basic psychological development were needed in the treatment as psychic "food", nurturing development.

How the receptivity of the therapist, putting her own sensations, feelings thoughts together in response to the encounter with her patient actually serves the psychic growth of that patient, also has needed to be elucidated. In addition the variety of aetiological factors (neglect, maltreatment, losses, etc.) give rise to similar presentations which might hide important distinguishing aspects of the internal problem in the patient (Music 2009). For example, a significant factor in Linda's earlier life (pre-3 years of age) was that her mother had suffered repeated losses through a stillbirth, a baby who died through SIDS, and three miscarriages. It would not be excessive to presume then that she was psychically preoccupied with these deaths to the detriment of her emotional availability to Linda as a baby and toddler. This is the territory that Green wrote about in his famous paper "The Dead Mother" (1980), where the de-cathexis of a young child by a mother preoccupied with her own trauma, produces voids in the fabric of the developing psyche. These empty spaces are devoid of fantasy content, vacuums that draw in storms of affect to fill them but are essentially in a deathly identification with the dead mother. The detail in the referral where Sarah described herself sitting for long periods, staring in vacant states similar to what was observed in her young daughter, captures this probability as a significant aetiological factor in Linda's developmental delay and accompanying disturbance. Furthermore, Sarah's evident wish to keep Linda as her baby, although to some degree conflictual, must have been a factor in this situation. The "neglect" of Linda's emotional states that were inevitable in this situation would have a different character to one where a mother's more "straightforward" hostility to her child can lead to neglect or maltreatment. The acute ambivalence suggested in Sarah's simultaneous clinging to and hostility towards her daughter had its own valency in Linda's developmental problems.

Green's work in the area of the dead mother complex can also help us think about the absence of elaborative, imaginative play. Early experiences of a simultaneously too-present and too-absent maternal object contribute to the situation where instead of richness of fantasy and affective life, the bases of playing, the framing structure in the internal world is empty. He says that

> the object which is always intrusively present, permanently occupying the personal psychic space, mobilises a permanent counter-cathexis in order to combat this break-in, which exhausts the resources of the ego or forces it to get rid of its burden by expulsive projection. Never being absent, it cannot be thought. Conversely, the inaccessible object can never be brought into the personal space, or at least never in a sufficiently durable way. Thus, it cannot be based on the model of an imaginary or metaphorical presence.
>
> (Green 1975, p. 41)

Green's work, and others in the French tradition, has broadened attention within psychoanalytic discourse to incorporate the significance of psychic voids, empty spaces, gaps, indicative of traumatic intrusions into the fabric of the psyche. Green extends Winnicott's interest in the consequences for the young child's development of an intrusive and/or absent maternal presence, which is helpful for our purposes in understanding the limitations in Linda's capacity to play. Transitional space (Winnicott 1952/1971) is that notional psychic territory where the mingling of the "me" and "not me" alongside the separateness of self and emerging other, constitutes the frame for elaboration and meaning making. It is recognisable in early development as the baby's interest in physical objects, rattles, soft toys, etc. frequently includes an attachment to a particular one – indicating emotional investment in it – what Winnicott called the first "not-me possession" (ibid., p. 35). It is used by the baby at times of separation – for example, at bedtime or when mother is away. It is fundamental to the development of the capacity for symbolisation and emphasises the necessity of the facilitating presence of the maternal object in reality. As Gail Reed describes, "The emphasis is on the role of the object as mediating the development of meaning and therefore on the too-long absence of the object as presaging the failure in meaning" (Reed 2013, p. 21). It is not just the maternal physical presence that is needed but more particularly her emotional presence and attentiveness. We might also propose that shared enjoyment and pleasure are essential elements for psychical representations to build up of the maternal object such that they become a rich internal resource for the young child. In this account, it is not internal destructiveness which leads to an absent or dead internal object but the absence, real or psychical of the external object upon which the internal object is based. Restrictions in the development of transitional space then becomes a therapeutic challenge and an aspect of the aims of such treatment and the contribution of the therapist in this regard is to facilitate the emergence of transitionality. Green talks about it in terms of the "analytic object":

> the analyst makes great efforts, which lead him to form a picture in his mind of the patient's mental functioning, *he supplies what is missing in the patient* [my italics] … But in the end the real analytic object is neither on the patient's side nor on the analyst's, but in the meeting of these two communications in the potential space which lies between them, limited by the setting which is broken at each separation and reconstituted at each new meeting.
>
> (Green 1975, p. 48)

Linda could not play in any truly imaginative way. Her "play" at the beginning of this treatment was physical activity – the pairing of cards, for instance, but its meaning most probably could be better described as full of possibility that had not been psychically realised. It remained at the level of sensorimotor activity. However, as suggested earlier, the context of this new relationship with her therapist provided new opportunities for this activity to become open to affective and meaningful elaboration and representation, eventually the constituents of symbolisation. She had abandoned the card game of pairs and was using the Play-Doh as described above, messing and smearing it seemingly with pleasure.

Linda's use of her body was not confined to games with only proto-meaning. She had never attained toilet mastery and wet and soiled her pants as though they were nappies: "accidents" were frequent. She "played" with the Play-Doh repetitively over these sessions but despite the apparent pleasure, and her therapist putting words to the activities such as describing the texture – sticky, or her affect – enjoyment, Linda nevertheless became severely constipated, necessitating hospitalisation for a temporary solution. This can be understood as a somatic expression of the dilemma she was now in, offered a new experience of an adult mind able to resonate her emotions and to give them form (Wright 1991), and her commitment to her constipated, stuck, and unmoving development. On her return to her therapy after the hospital admission, CP was puzzled to note that their shared pleasure in the reunion was such that she (CP) "forgot" to mention Linda's absence and its cause. *In fact, Linda, who before she had gone into hospital had begun using the small doll figures in the doll's house, creating simple but realistic stories of life at home, was determined to continue what she had been doing before. She created a family scene where CP was to be "mum" who served breakfast of "cheesy pasta". In an example of how difficult it might be to find the right "wave-length" with a child who is moving rapidly between different developmental capacities, CP questioned the menu, consciously thinking to herself that Linda's mum needed to see a dietician as such food would be bound to contribute to constipation. Her tone must have conveyed some negative affect as shortly afterwards CP smelled urine and Linda had an accident – not constipated now but enuretic, her sphincter control perhaps giving way under the pressure of felt disapproval.* Having such an "accident" may have different meanings, but it seems here that Linda sought her therapist's approval and pleasure in the creation of a narrative of home life that could lead to more complex pretend and symbolic play. What happened instead is that the "forgetting" perhaps indicated CP's unconscious identification with a "forgetting" maternal object, not able to sustain connection with the emotional meaning of absence and the gap, and then a too-literal understanding of the potentially meaningful play with which Linda so enthusiastically engaged her therapist.

The anal-level actions remained a significant aspect over the following months, including mess, "accidents", dirty hands, and the countertransference feelings of repulsion and disgust. In addition, however, there were early signs of the pleasure in mess giving way in reaction formation (Furman 1992) to pleasure in cleanliness and a dislike of mess and dirt. CP was challenged to bear her myriad affective responses and not enact them in countertransference identification with those toxic aspects of the maternal object. But these elements of her responses – for example, disgust, are usually in the developmental "field" in a young child's ordinary gaining of toilet mastery. Parents and caregivers often have to struggle with feelings of disgust in helping a young child take control of their bodily functions and the child has to manage their ambivalence, as what might early on feel to be a precious part of their own body becomes something smelly and dirty which has to be got rid of. This is an aspect of the psychoanalytic setting for the treatment of a child like Linda for whom these usual early developmental milestones have not been achieved but are in train. It is a challenge for clinicians and CP was no exception. Perhaps we can think about the responses of disgust and revulsion reflecting an unconscious communication from Linda of how she felt in her psyche-soma; that somewhere she felt she was a disgusting, repulsive little girl and this is what she challenged her psychotherapist to encounter and deal with. It certainly was a pervasive aspect of CP's affective responses for a long time in the therapy.

Linda's object hunger was unabated and she increasingly brought through playful activities themes that were alive with potential meaning. One of those themes was a repeated story of a birthday party for one of the doll figures which never really happened; the guests never arrived, or the cake didn't get made. Linda's affective tone in elaborating these narratives was largely dull and unquestioning. It was as if she was enacting her reality rather than playing with possibilities. The birthday celebration was probably heavy with painful associations alluding to not only her own birth, but her dead baby brother, the stillbirth foetus who never became a living sibling and the ghosts of the other possible siblings in the three miscarriages. It was in a relational context however which was increasingly pleasurable as this therapeutic pair increasingly enjoyed their shared company. This positive affective atmosphere is an essential part of the therapeutic alliance, ultimately enabling painful and difficult elements to emerge and be recognised and worked with. It took fully seven/eight months for Linda to be able to bring her rage and anger directly into the work with CP.

Linda brought a toy to a session which she had found in a charity shop. It was an animal figure which turned out to be a unicorn. She was very excited to have found such a treasure. CP was aware of Linda's increasing confidence in the sessions, although this still felt precarious. Linda tried to describe the unicorn and particularly its horn. However, as her expressive language was still very unclear, CP took some time to understand that she was saying it was like a microphone. Linda became cross, throwing down the toy hard onto the floor. CP acknowledged her frustration at not being understood but this didn't assuage her anger. She proceeded to tip her box and its contents onto the floor. CP put words to her angry feelings which then seemed to help Linda recognise her state.

This is an interesting sequence in the session: although Linda's diction was such that she could not easily make herself understood, nevertheless what she was trying to convey was an achievement – her ability in that moment to see sameness and difference simultaneously – one of the basic building blocks of symbolisation. The unicorn's horn could be a microphone. Her rage in the transference was to a maternal object who couldn't "get" the infantile struggle to establish this fundamental differentiation and the play with the possibility of metaphor and articulate it.

As Linda's therapy continued it seemed clear that her development had been kick-started. There is complexity in the therapist's contribution to this, as I have been arguing, as her interventions needed to be tailored closely to Linda's developmental needs. We have already seen how precarious that can be with the risks of unconscious countertransference identifications giving rise to enactments. Linda's delayed language was of particular note; not only had she a poor vocabulary but her poor expressiveness frequently gave rise to misunderstandings as this last example demonstrates. CP had to make sure that the words she was using were simple enough to be understood by Linda, often observing that it was like talking to her own toddler daughter, elaborating Linda's sounds and giving words to proto thoughts, ideas. The unelaborated sensorimotor activities gradually became narratives of stories, initially linked to her everyday life as is the case when very young children start to pretend play; the ordinary developmental course concretely reproducing real experiences and then moving on to symbolised complexity of meaning in transitional space. The presence of the facilitating object in the therapist was crucial: Linda had a companion in CP; indeed, we might say a playmate, whom she increasingly invited to participate in the storylines, frequently assigning her the parts of the characters in the stories, or simply giving a place to witness and learn about Linda's life from her. What was essential was CP's responsivity to Linda's "spontaneous gestures" (Winnicott 1962, p. 353; Hopkins 2018). That responsivity essentially comprised of CP's emotionally alive elaboration of narrative that was increasingly symbolised in Linda's identification with her developmental object. CP's interventions gave words to the affective and imaginative manifestations in the room, and the complex interactions Linda played out with doll figures, sometimes taking the story into the transferential relationship, mostly leaving it in the enactment of the play. Here Linda's growing capacity to bring these stories reflected a variety of aspects of her ego development, not only language, but increasing complexity in her emotional life and ability to modulate those states, greater agency as a young child whose development was not so at odds with what could be expected, greater capacity to invest in relationships with her peers, and increasing capacity to take ownership and management of her body.

It must be mentioned that alongside CP's treatment of Linda (three times per week over a period of three years) initially in a community-based child mental health clinic and subsequently within her school setting, Linda's mother also developed a parallel relationship with CP. This was not a therapeutic treatment nor indeed conventional "parent work". However, it reflected Sarah's own object hunger that she used the opportunity for contact, e.g. small passing conversations in the waiting room, text messages, occasional review meetings, to take what she herself had been lacking. It was a significant aspect of her support of the treatment her young daughter was receiving and from which she also benefitted.

Discussion

The role of the adult mind in "feeding" these aspects of the young child's development and its particular significance in analytic psychotherapy has been well captured by Ferro in his expansion of Bion's work on maternal reverie (2005). Ferro says "the qualities of the other's mind must have the capacity to receive, to leave in abeyance, to metabolise, to return the elaborated product to the subject and in particular to 'transmit the method'. This is achieved by returning the product in unsaturated form and allowing the subject's mind as it were to learn its trade in the workshop of the other's" (p. 16).

This is close to Winnicott's propositions about the psyche as the "imaginative elaboration of somatic parts" and transitionality, and Enid Balint's concept of "imaginative perception". She defines "imaginative perception" as "what happens when the patient imagines what he perceives and thus creates his own partly imagined, partly perceived, world" (Balint 1988/1993, p. 103). Imaginative perception is also a quality in the analyst in their encounter with the patient. To imaginatively *conceive* of the patient is fundamental to getting to know them deeply and in my view is a feature of the analyst's capacity for transitionality. I want to emphasise the psyche-somatic nature of this and in this particular case we can see how challenging and at times assaulting this was in the therapist's countertransference.

Ferro carefully articulates the process whereby the adult mind imaginatively conceives of the child's situation. He sees this as "totally creative, original and artistic" and I would add if it has been missing in the child's ordinary family life then it is incumbent on the therapist to do this. Inevitably it involves struggles and is not a linear process, involving much to-and-fro, but it requires a large measure of internal freedom in the therapist to imagine, try out things including images, feelings, ideas without having to know prematurely or "explain" in the form of interpretations. Fundamentally, it requires the capacity to bear the impact of voids, absences, and also emotional storms that comprise this territory. These are both personal and technical capacities in the analyst necessary in order to be a "new developmental object" for children with severe developmental delay.

It is possible to bring different theoretical accounts together in elucidating the processes whereby a child such as Linda with complex developmental delay and disturbance can be helped. It is not that the therapist sets out to provoke demand from the patient which is then met in the treatment as in the original protocols of "corrective emotional experiences" (Alexander & French 1946). The variety of adaptations to classical psychoanalysis that have been made across different traditions can be thought of as addressing the ego developmental needs of these kinds of children, abandoning the idea that complex interpretations of internal psychic conflict was the distinguishing feature of psychoanalysis.

Acknowledgement

I want to thank my supervisee (Isla Clarke) who I identify as CP in this chapter, for her generous permission to use her clinical material from the treatment of this young child. CP was in the later stages of her training at the Independent Psychoanalytic Child and Adolescent Psychotherapy Association (IPCAPA) training, part of the British Psychotherapy Foundation.

References

Alexander, F. & French T. M. (1946) *Psychoanalytic Therapy*. New York: Ronald Press.
Balint, E. (1988/1993) Creative Life. In *Before I was I, Psychoanalysis and the Imagination*. J. Mitchell and M. Parsons, Eds. London: Free Association Press, pp. 103–108, 1993.
Baranger, M. & Baranger, W. (2008) The Analytic Situation as a Dynamic Field. *Int. J. Psycho-Anal.*, 89(4): 795–826.
Botella, C. & Botella, S. (2005) *The Work of Psychic Figurability*, London: New Library of Psychoanalysis.
Edgcumbe, R. (1995) The History of Anna Freud's Thinking on Developmental Disturbances. *Bul. Anna Freud Centre*, 18(1): 21–34.
Ferenczi, S. (1913) *First Contributions to Psychoanalysis*. London: Hogarth, 1952.

Ferro, A. (2005) *Seeds of Illness, Seeds of Recovery*. London: New Library of Psychoanalysis.

Freud, A. (1954) The Widening Scope of Indications for Psychoanalysis: Discussion, in *The Writings of Anna Freud*, Vol 1V 1945–1956, pp. 356–376. New York: International Universities Press, 1968.

Furman, E. (1992) *Toddlers and Their Mothers: A Study in Early Personality Development*. New York: International Universities Press.

Green, A. (1975) The Analyst, Symbolisation and Absence, in *On Private Madness*. London: Hogarth and the Institute of Psychoanalysis, 1986, pp. 30–59.

Green, A. (1980) The Dead Mother, in *On Private Madness*. London: Hogarth and the Institute of Psychoanalysis, pp. 141–173, 1986.

Hopkins, J. (2018) Meeting Winnicott, in *Donald Winnicott and the History of the Present*. A. Joyce, Ed. London, Karnac, pp. 45–48.

Hurry, A. (1998) *Psychoanalysis and Developmental Therapy*. London: Karnac.

Levine, H., Reed, G., & Scarfone, D. (2013) *Unrepresented States and the Construction of Meaning*. London: IPA & Karnac.

Loewald, H. (1960) On the Therapeutic Action Of Psychoanalysis, in *Papers on Psychoanalysis*. New Haven and London: Yale University Press, pp. 221–256.

Martin-Cabre (2001) Winnicott and Ferenczi: Trauma, and the Maternal Analyst, in M. Bertolini, A. Giannakoulas, and M. Hernandez, Eds, in collaboration with A. Molino, *Squiggles and Spaces: Revisiting the Work of D.W. Winnicott* Vol 2. London: Whurr, pp 179–180.

Music, G. (2009) Neglecting Neglect: Some Thoughts About Children Who Have Lacked Good Input, and are "Undrawn" and "Unenjoyed". *Journal of Child Psychotherapy*, 35(2): 142–156.

Reed, G. (2013) An Empty Mirror, in H. Levine, G. Reed, & D. Scarfone, Eds, *Unrepresented States and the Construction of Meaning*. London: IPA & Karnac, pp. 18–41.

Winnicott, D.W. (1947) Hate in the Countertransference, in *Collected Works of D. W. Winnicott*, Vol 3. New York: Oxford University Press, pp. 59–68, 2016.

Winnicott, D.W. (1949) Mind and its Relation to Psyche-Soma, in *Collected Works of D. W. Winnicott*, Vol 3. New York: Oxford University Press, pp 245–258, 2016.

Winnicott, D.W. (1952/1971) Transitional Objects and Transitional Phenomena, in *Collected Works of D. W. Winnicott*, Vol 4. New York: Oxford University Press, pp. 35–43, 2016.

Winnicott, D.W. (1954) Metapsychological and Clinical Aspects of Regression, in *Collected Works of D. W. Winnicott*, Vol 4. New York: Oxford University Press, pp. 185–200, 2016.

Winnicott, D.W. (1959) Classification: Is There a Psychoanalytic Contribution to Psychiatric Classification?, in *Collected Works of D. W. Winnicott*, Vol 5. New York: Oxford University Press, pp. 445–460, 2016.

Winnicott, D.W. (1962) The Development of the Capacity For Concern, in *Collected Works of D. W. Winnicott*, Vol 6. New York: Oxford University Press, pp. 351–356, 2016.

Winnicott, D. W. (1984) Residential care as therapy, in *Deprivation and Delinquency*. C. Winnicott, R. Shepherd and M. Davis, Eds. London: Tavistock publications, p. 221.

Wright, K. (1991) *Vision and Separation between Mother and Baby*. Northvale: Jason Aronson.

7

Psychoanalytic intimacy as an alternative to psychic suffering for children on the edge

Mariângela Mendes de Almeida

Introduction: Opening thoughts

Clinicians who value Kleinian and post-Kleinian contemporary clinical developments, particularly those who have had the privilege of working with the live matter of primitive states of mind in children and infants, have been showing how "in the field of psychic effects of traumatic experiences which have not yet reached a representation, we must find alternative ways of listening and interpreting" (Souza, 2016). Analysis, in this view, has been "a field where a containing object is built, as an experience of acknowledgement and hope—an experience that may not have been found in the relationship with the initial objects" (Souza, 2016).

Bringing French tradition into contemporary psychoanalysis, Roussillon (1991) in dialogue with British contributions mainly by Winnicott and Bion, describes how the analysand tries to communicate to the analyst something that has not been heard, seen, or felt in his subjective history, or at least not in a sufficient way to be fully owned by the subject. In this situation, the unconscious does not refer to what was noticed and repressed, but to what did not find a subjective place to inscribe itself. For him, the analysands come not simply to ask for recognition of what has remained dead material in their history, they come to turn non-represented content into something possible to hear, see, or feel, inviting the analyst to share and reflect what is waiting for subjective appropriation, that can thus be born for psychic life. He associates this with the Kleinian concept of projective identification which is expanded by Bion (1962) as the most primitive modality of communication, ordinarily taking place since the very early processes in every parent–infant relationship.

In this chapter, I intend to highlight our daily, powerful, and delicate microscopic work within the transferential field with children on the edge between their suffering and their resilient strength, considering their own internal objects and internal world configurations in their dynamic dialogue with the surrounding relationships.

Lisa: struggling with abuse

Lisa is a smart and articulate little girl of almost five years, whose mother came to me due to concerns with the emotional effects of sexual abuse of the girl by her father, in a context of intense relationship difficulties between the parental couple,

DOI: 10.4324/9781003216360-9

already separated (mother had got pregnant after one month of relationship and they only lived together for four months).

When I started seeing Lisa, there was already a parallel child protection care process going on with the case, with social work procedures being applied regarding the need for reducing and regulating the girl's visits to her father, which were only happening with professional assistance.

There was already a team involved with social services and psychological assessment procedures connected with court evidence and disclosure of paternal abuse, besides maternal pressure involved, which had also an abusive quality for the child.

My independent psychoanalytic role was to offer a therapeutic space for the child, considering of course the complexity of the abusive network, but trying to go beyond its overdetermination, to be able to also contact the child's inner and intersubjective experience not only as the identified abused child. I took the stance of looking at her inner self through the child's eyes, through her play and through the countertransferential impact she had on my ways of seeing her and of containing her needs. I could feel from the potency of her playing material how she was struggling with the ambivalence felt towards her caring figures, on the one hand, close bonds that she valued and considered, on the other hand, threatening and pressurizing links, with mutual denigration.

The child herself offered her own lenses to look at her inner paternal and maternal figures and how difficult it was for her to feel the integration of a parental couple in her mind, which could allow her to experience her child self in play and in relation to her peers. We will be able to see in the clinical material how we, as therapists, are led to feel the emotional quality of anxieties to which the child herself is exposed, and at the same time are called to represent the projected fears she has to face to be able to inscribe them in a subjective place.

Although the child's therapy was made possible by the mother who was the one to bring the child and organize the payment through the child's health insurance, the child protection team had close contact with both father and mother, allowing that the general network could contemplate working on the child's interest and also allowing me to work with the child's inner representations. This helped me to work with the child's and mother's projections, most of them demanding processing of uncomfortable qualities of feeling intruded upon or intruding, protecting or controlling, merging, or neglecting as powerful elements in psychic care.

The need for psychotherapy emerges when Lisa starts not wanting to go to school, getting involved in little fights with friends, "lying", reporting to the mother that she is ashamed of the girls (for example, going to the bathroom with them). As part of an advanced process of gathering legal evidence of abuse, the mother is quite committed to check and "register" the child's experience with the father to be able to keep him away from the child (for example, recording the child's spontaneous statements during mother–child dialogues after Lisa had been staying with him). He has always had regular contact with Lisa, despite Lisa's demonstration of difficulty in going to her father's house. He lives with his own mother, very close to Lisa's mother's place. Lisa chats with her mother (in specific detail) about situations in which she is with her father and his girlfriend related to alcohol abuse and trips to motels.

Close to Lisa: psychoanalytic play as an alternative intimacy

When we get to the consulting room, I find little rolls of pieces of paper on top of the cupboard-sink, with Lisa directing my look to them with a cheeky face. I wonder, considering her cheeky way, whether she may have brought them and left them there for me to find. However, I also find myself wondering: had I been so careless to the point of not noticing that they were there before? (I identify this with emotional concerns related to seeing/not seeing and blaming oneself for not having seen, very common anxieties in parental care confronting abuse configurations). *There was some seriousness and something very genuine in Lisa's discovery, as if he she was really surprising herself by seeing the paper rolls for the first time.*

In this atmosphere of surprise and playfulness I open the papers, small notepad sheets, and notice a series of drawings of little balls in a row, initially two, then in the next sheets, increasingly three, four, five. Under the little balls are wavy lines, in increasing quantity and size, suggesting a written message quality, as well as, especially in the first sheet, a little face-like image with the balls as the rounded eyes and the first wavy/snaky line as the mouth. It strikes me that the sequence of sheets gradually shows a coordinated increase in the quantity of elements and size. I comment that it looks like there's a face and a message there that is growing and growing. Have we found a secret message from a little girl, telling us something she wants us to notice and needs help with? Something is growing, growing, and she wants us to understand the message and help her. She makes a larger roll with her notepad sheets and new sheets from the consulting room, and sings along, in a very lively way, after trying successfully to remember the song: "the toad also has a son, also has a son, also has a son! The toad also has a son, also has a son, called tadpole. The son is called tadpole, is called tadpole, is called tadpole. The toad lives in the water, tadpole lives in the water. The toad also has a son, also has a son, called tadpole".

I talk to her: the toad and the tadpole are from the same family, huh? The tiny tadpole has a Mom and has a Dad too. There is a Daddy toad. The little girl in our message also has Mom and Dad, like Lisa, who has a Mom and a Dad too. It may be that the message of the little girl Lisa is for us to help her to understand these things that happened with Dad and Lisa, which made the little girl become sad, confused, upset, without understanding how things are with this Dad.

An insect/little mosquito comes along in the air. Lisa tries to keep it away with the paper roll, says it's the "penelongo"—daddy long legs (pernilongo/penelongo: long legs/long penis). I say she's trying to defend herself from this penelongo that bothers her, that has bothered her and that came close to her body in a way that scared her and that she didn't understand. She says: "It bites us". I say: sometimes, grown-ups do things we don't understand well, even Daddy may have done things that upset and hurt because they are things that grown-ups do with grown-ups and not with children. Lisa is confused, because it's her Daddy, as the toad is the tadpole's Daddy. She wants to get to know this Daddy more, as a daughter, but is also afraid of getting close to him.

The mosquito "penelongo" goes near the wall and Lisa goes after it with her roll, talking in a squeaky and exalted voice, moving her hands and legs in an increasingly restless way while "hunting" the penelongo, throwing her roll in the insect's direction. She asks me to help her to throw her messages towards the penelongo and I say that the little girl Lisa asks me for help so that she can show that she doesn't like this penelongo that does things that hurt, she wants the message to reach him so that this penelongo Daddy can understand what she feels and stop doing these things.

While throwing the roll several times, she jumps and goes towards the door when returning from the jump, making a noise as if forcing the door. It comes to my mind that it may seem from the outside that she's trying to get out, hitting and forcing the door, and her mother, having already expressed concerns about what happens inside the room and the therapeutic space, may be possibly impacted, although the sound-atmosphere of play might also be felt from outside. I find out later that the mother had climbed up the stairs and was "listening". She comments when we leave, that she was worried about the noises at the door. "I'm a mother".

In that context, is Lisa's play of jumping close to the door a desperate and healthy communication or a compulsive repetition perpetuating the abusive chain? The scene may be seen as a reproduction of the atmosphere of turmoil in internal objects, ambivalently claiming communication and seeking help when facing abuse, but at the same time, evoking an abusive, invading reaction from supposed protecting elements, in an endless repetition of an abusive chain. In my countertransference, I had to deal with feeling myself "abused" by the possible suggestion—through the noise and bashing on the door—of us doing something in the room that might be threatening the child.

At the end of the session, Lisa wants to take the roll with her message and the consulting room sheets of paper with her. I comment that she wants to take to her mummy this message that she is trying to understand and defend herself from these things that happened with Dad. When she comes down, she puts the roll on her mother's lap and I comment, while her mother mentions that she was worried about the noises at the door, that Lisa played a lot, even jumping near the door, talking about things that bother her and that if she wants, she will also show her mummy these messages she's made.

I thought about Lisa's conflicting feelings: wanting her mother to hear, repeating the excitement of an intimacy, leaving her mother out, or wanting her mother to come in/listen and protect her (from something that she had not been able to protect her from before?). Reflecting upon Lisa wanting her mother to hear us in the room, repeating the excitement of an intimacy which may be dubious and ambivalent to the child is one of the main challenges to people who face abuse. She may be guilty about leaving her mother out of this "playful" and secretive contact with a dear meaningful figure, but at the same time she wants her mother to come in/listen and protect her, both from an intrusive relationship but perhaps also from her excitement of keeping mother away.

The rhythmic noise at the door, the child with me in the room, make me feel in the countertransference as if we are like the couple in the primary scene and the mother is the excluded child, with Lisa, taken by great excitement, putting herself in the place of the mother with the father in the oedipal relationship. At the same time, she may be communicating, to all of us who can hear or feel, the despair, the painful impact and the harshness of an abusive relationship.

This meaningful clinical scene had a huge impact on me as an emblematic configuration. The mother's intrusive curiosity about what was going on in the room and her need for control made me feel that I was being pushed under a pressure to comply with a parental self and merge to an adhesive part of mother's personality, which felt as extremely threatening to allow the other/the child's self to grow and experience her own exchanges. Both the child and I could feel the risk of losing our own borders. At the same time, I was meant to be in the place of the "bad" one, torturing the one which had to be freed from the danger inside. Fusion and ambivalence between being the abuser and the saviour were mixed producing an invitation for a paralyzed state of mind. I could feel in my skin, the tension and anxiety that was probably producing the overexcitement and the ashamed constraints to which the child was exposed to.

I was concerned about the doubtful possibility of restoring parent–child links, and the re-establishing of parental hierarchies. I felt the impact of blurred differences between parents/adults and children, resulting in the pressure for abusive relations repetitions, for example, when listening to mother's communications or reading the transcribed recorded reports she handed me of inquisitive conversations between her and the child regarding the abuse. I saw myself in a position of having to continuously attempt to metabolize contents of perverse excitement. We had to struggle to differentiate child and parents in a parental hierarchy confused by the infantile needs within the parental couple, while keeping alive the space for their daughter to remain a child. Lisa, rather than only being the child who has always been protected from abuse or defended herself through abusing others, could have friends and enjoy many aspects of an ordinary development with pleasant interchanges.

We had to face many traumas, the abuse itself, the maternal guilt for the failure in protection with its compensatory reactions and hyper-focus on sexual issues, the fear of acknowledging one's own perceptions against other people's wishes or expectations and the internal turmoil around how to conceive an experience that on the one hand has to be kept as a secret, and on the other, has to be reported and described in details with some possible developments that go beyond one's own relational landscape. What is one's own experience in this context, how to represent it, how to communicate it? An adult patient, having gone through a similar experience in childhood, which was very diffused in her mind, and which made her avoid thinking about her relationship with her currently distant father, and permeated all her current partnerships, brought to her analysis of seven years the image of a compressed "little package" which she and I could carefully and gradually unwrap.

By microscopically describing Lisa's play and our dialogue in the above vignette, I expect to have been able to give a hint of what the struggle to make sense of a situation like this may be. In our playing and talking about her drawings, body movements, and creation of paper figures, we could show the therapeutic relevance of allowing internal representations to take shape and to be shared within a relationship that offers itself to contain and think about complex aspects of experiences, both pleasant and unpleasant ones. With our ability to think about our own reactions towards projections and appeals for repetitions of abusing and abused quality, and in talking about these contents in a metabolizable way, as demonstrated in the clinical illustration, we hope to contribute to the traumatic repetitive chain being discontinued and substituted by a less repetitive and more creative and benign cycle of psychic growth. As Selma Fraiberg et al. (1980) have inspired us to continuously witness in our clinical work with children, parents, and infants, history does not need to be fate.

Final considerations: against being swallowed by void, the power of building up internal representations

I hope to have demonstrated how psychoanalytic work, relying on our detailed attention to our patients' internal world and objects, and to our own internal responses to the object relations that take place in the clinical setting, can allow traumatic contents to be worked through, thus reducing their powerful effect of transmission through present and future relationships. In a microscopic, gradual and seminal way, we can facilitate that children can address the particular contents of their own anxieties. Different facets within their internal objects, dynamically related, can be revealed, so that trauma does not remain a non-differentiated block which then grows and grows in secret and forbidden areas of silent emotional knowledge on the edge of an unrepresented void.

While experiencing and re-experiencing trauma, inner strengths can be swallowed in an endless battle with continuous rebirth of devouring forces, but these strengths can also transform fates from within by symbolic and representational communications of inner truth. The horror of trauma in its repetition and dreadfulness was addressed with Lisa, but we could also see its possibility of being overcome, considering the inner struggles described in this psychoanalytic encounter and our dialogues within this paper. My contact with Lisa also represents vividly what moves us in the countertransferential dilemma of exposing such powerfully painful and delicate intimacies, with the wish that our communications with attentive listeners and readers can resonate as a truthful therapeutic aim and psychoanalytic learning to be shared.

References

Bion, Wilfred, *Learning from Experience* (London, Heinemann, 1962).

Fraiberg, Selma, Adelson, Edna, and Shapiro, Vivian, "Ghosts in the Nursery: A Psychoanalytic Approach to the Problems of Impaired Infant-Mother Relationships", in Fraiberg, S (Ed.) *Clinical Studies in Infant Mental Health: The First Year of Life* (London, Tavistock, 1980).

Roussillon, René, "A Função Limite da Psique e a Representância". *Revista de Psicanálise da S.P.P.A.*, 14, 2(1991), 257–273.

Souza, Audrey Lopes de, "Construindo formas de comunicação: revendo o conceito de interpretação representação na clínica do não representado". *Revista Brasileira de Psicanálise*, 50, 3(2016), 60–75.

Part III

New realities, new challenges

Catalina Bronstein

Introduction

During the last few years, there have been several issues that have greatly impacted on the work with children and adolescents. The development of the internet created exciting new possibilities for both children and adolescents, who could now have easy access to new sources of knowledge, as well as to quickly contact friends, make new friends from around the world, exchange opinions, and satisfy their interest and curiosity on a wide range of subjects. But the internet can also be a source of anxiety and can contribute to children's and adolescents' difficulties. Websites inciting self-harm and suicide, the possibility to expose young people and bully, seduce, and/or intimidate them have contributed to states of depression, suicidality, and self-harming practices. Websites related to pornography, beauty, food intake, and to issues related to body transformation and sexuality are visited by millions of children and teenagers who feel lost, confused and often isolated. Anxieties about FOMO (fear of missing out) can paralyze adolescents. At the same time, openness in matters related to sexuality and gender can be also helpful and are welcomed by many adolescents who have doubts and are confused about these issues. In the last years, there have been many changes in the way that sexuality is viewed, particularly in connection to identity and gender issues. The internet plays a very important role in this respect as adolescents can easily find sites where they can share their experiences with other adolescents. The web also offers an intermediate space – in some of the chapters it is described as a 'transitional space' – for adolescents struggling with the developmental task of separating from parents, a space where they can remain both dependent on the object but looking at possibilities to establish a different relationship with reality, including the reality of their own body. Others use it to defend themselves from claustrophobic anxieties such as part of the defensive 'no-entry system' as described by Gianna Williams.

Children and adolescents have become very adept at navigating the web as the role of the internet and remote access hugely increased in the last two and a half years when the COVID-19 pandemic prevented children and adolescents from

DOI: 10.4324/9781003216360-10

going to school, going out to play with other children, and to socialize in general. Phantasies about the possible death of parents could be now felt to be a more real and palpable possibility. Children and adolescents felt forced to modify their lives to protect adults. Young children's development suffered from the lack of contact with other children, impinging on their language development. Older children and adolescents could not go to school or university and had to rely on the use of computers. The pandemic forced therapists to have to quickly adjust to the challenge of having to continue providing psychotherapy by remote means. Here too, the use of the internet played a very important role in the continuity of treatment. We could say that we all had to adapt to this situation but there were also important losses to contend with. The pandemic has not yet finished. We are still struggling to survive amidst the fear of death and the huge impingement on our ordinary way of life. One could say that we are still living within this traumatic episode and even though it will be mainly in the years to come when the whole impact will be able to be assessed, the thoughts that we have now will hopefully be a helpful contribution to a more fuller understanding of the effects of the pandemic.

Sara Flanders's chapter explores the role of psychotherapy in working with two adolescents who are caught up in the virtual online world. Following the developments proposed by Moses and Eglé Laufer on the fundamental task of adolescence to accept and integrate the adult sexual body, Flanders underlines the narcissistic vulnerability of adolescents when dealing with the contradictions imposed by their post-pubertal state in their conflict between their need for parental help and their need to separate from parents who have now become intensely incestuous objects. Flanders describes how in their struggle with the intensification of the drives and with conflictual object relationships adolescents turn to the wider culture, to peers, to the external world, this including the world wide web (both light and dark). It is in this world of cyberspace where explorations, playing, dreaming, as well as losing themselves in it, can offer ways of reworking identity. Flanders proposes that at its best is a transitional space. It can also be a temporary escape from reality with the potential dangers of adding to the pressure, to self-destruct, and to withdraw from reality. In an evocative way, Flanders describes the psychotherapy with a girl called Samantha who presented herself as 'they', not 'she'. This was very early days in the change of pronouns, now commonplace. Samantha had great difficulties in acknowledging her feelings, in tolerating a sense of the unknown without quickly needing to reach for the validation offered by the internet with which she was in constant connection. Flanders shares with us her painful experience of being with this girl, who felt a horror about her adult body, even about the words 'sexual body' and who took refuge in a virtual world which was now contributing to a greater sense of disembodiment and withdrawal. The sessions were equally violently rejected. Flanders then introduces another adolescent girl called Iris who even though she too withdrew from the embodied world of others, could sustain psychotherapy and use the internet in an interactive way, as a bridge to the world. Iris had a traumatic history, marred by her mother's psychosis and by being excluded from a child's ordinary world, of a connection to her father, school, friends, and relatives. Flanders describes Iris's therapy and the engagement with a game – *Warcraft* – which proved to be a connection to Iris's father. We can follow the vicissitudes of a very painful session that illustrates Iris's intense conflicts as they are lived out in the transference relationship and an illustration of the important role of the setting, the walls of the consulting room that functioned like the frame of the computer game, as a bridge, rather than as a delusional world.

Susan Donner discusses the different types of impact of cyberspace in that it can both promote growth and development as well as contribute to a more depressive, deadening experience. She proposes that examining the use of cyberspace and technology in patients can give therapists a better perspective of their patient's unconscious phantasies. She stresses that cyberspace can become a tool for creativity, growth, and development, a potential transitional space to help the developing ego. But, following Meltzer, cyberspace can also become a sort of 'Claustrum', more like a psychic retreat. She reminds us that it is only if there are good, internalized objects that the infant can make use of transitional objects. Donner explores in greater detail what is meant by the word 'transitional'. Following Sugarman and Caldwell, she highlights the role of transitional phenomena in facilitating and reworking the internalization of primary objects and how this can be seen in the adolescent's use of technology. But, and following Marzi's ideas, cyberspace can be also seen to connect to a damaged and damaging claustrum, full of claustrophobic anxieties. Through the analytic treatment of a 14-year-old boy who had a very difficult childhood and who was addicted to internet porn, and with her deep understanding of her patient's unconscious phantasies, Donner shows us the movement in this boy from a claustrum of destructive phantasy to a reworking of overwhelming infantile experiences which led to a more progressive and creative development.

Carlos Vasquez highlights the changes in our technique brought about by COVID-19. He explores the difficulties of having to modify our practice, cancel the personal encounters with patients, and to have to use remote methods. This is even more significant in the treatment of children and adolescents as movement, action, play, bodily communication is an intrinsic part of the way they communicate and express themselves in therapy. Carlos Vasquez describes the use of a video game in therapy – *Minecraft* – that creates a 'virtual world' and can be played in two different modes: survival and creative. Despite all the difficulties inherent in establishing a session via remote means, of playing a computer game rather than having free play, this method still proved to be a creative way of accessing unconscious phantasies and anxieties and helping children. Vasquez explains how through identification – projective identification – with the characters in the game he could experience some of the embodied and proprioceptive sensations that he might have experienced if the two of them would have been in the same room. Vasquez's detailed description of his work with a 6-year-old boy called Mario allows us to see the establishment of a space for thinking and playing where Mario started joining in and wanted to share the same virtual space. Issues about closeness and anxiety and about Oedipal conflicts became quite evident and could be worked through. Vasquez shows how the vicissitudes and choices made in the game can be helpful but he also points out the difficulties inherent to the use of these games. He stresses that electronic devices and the internet can be also very inaccurate devices to carry important loaded communications as the glitches in the game can make the connection to the therapist more difficult to sustain. It is interesting to follow Mario's development of a greater flexibility and trust, becoming more able and willing to explore, without as much fear as before. Around the Easter break, he even blew a goodbye kiss to his therapist. It is worth underlining the importance of the creation of a shared space between the therapist and the child patient, one where the communication of psychophysical states can happen.

Gianna Williams and Leontine Brameijer explore the links between a pathological 'no-entry system of defences', the fear of intrusion and the current pandemic. Gianna Williams's profound understanding of the nature of primitive anxieties concerning body orifices informs her theory on the disturbance behind the 'no-entry' system of defences. The fear of intrusion into the body orifices could be often seen in anorexic patients. Williams suggests that these patients were prone to suffer from huge fears during the pandemic. Brejamijer presents two current cases where we can see the profound impact of the pandemic as it is felt by the two adolescents as a dangerously intrusive agent. Both girls created a defensive system to try to control the intrusion, with different levels of pathology, clearly aggravated by their destructive unconscious phantasies. Claire, a 19-year-old girl, suffered from extreme anxiety that centred around intrusion. She suffered a breakdown and had to be admitted to hospital. In her therapy, she communicated her great fear to be intruded upon and kept quite a rigid control needing to carefully watch her therapist that alternated with dissociative states which followed her therapist's interventions. COVID-19 regulations meant that the therapy had to be continued over the phone. An exaggerated fear of having been infected became pervasive, even when she did not have much personal contact with anybody. The analyst could see the connection between the adolescent's fear of intrusion and possible death and the early experience of having been in an incubator which could not be recalled. Lynn, a 14-year-old girl, had also an early hospitalization as a baby. As Brameijer sees it, she developed a defensive hyperkinetic type of self-containment against a sense of 'nameless dread'. After her parent's separated, Lynn, who also suffered from anorexia, started to attack her body causing deep self-harm, swallowing razorblades and batteries and repeating a cycle of self-harming that led to a medical intervention to repair the damage and to more self-harming. When COVID-19 struck Lynn found the telephone calls with her therapist too hard. Lynn was convinced she had been infected with the virus and was in a panic. Brameijer vividly describes the tormented state of these two girls who already suffered from a no-entry system of defences, and how their fear of intrusion got exacerbated by the Covid pandemic.

All these evocative and thoughtful chapters illustrate the new challenges and difficulties that confront child psychotherapists and child analysts today and the need to further our psychoanalytic understanding to overcome them.

8

New challenges for adolescence
The virtual world and the gendered body

Sara Flanders

The challenge of adolescence

No one escapes the crises of adolescence, there is even the opinion that no one escapes the trauma of adolescence, inasmuch as the changes of puberty, the upsurge of drives, and the transformations of the body cannot be anticipated (Gutton 1998). The feeling of continuity, the feeling of the self's "going on being" (Winnicott 1949) that gift of early experience and then the product of emotional and physical growth, is challenged by a radical discontinuity. At puberty, the body, which had been the foundation of emotional, intellectual, and social development, suddenly erupts (Lombardi 2017; Ferrari 2004; Anzieu 2016) and presents itself to the mind, now a weakened and disoriented mind, newly fragile in its foundations, for hard psychological work.

We agree with the Laufers (Laufer and Laufer 1984) who have written that the fundamental task of adolescence is to accept and integrate the adult sexual body, that all other developments of adolescence follow from this fundamental change, this call made by the changing body, on the mind for work (Freud 1905). Every adolescent is under pressure, as hypothesized by Freud, when he stated that it is only at puberty that the strands of infantile sexuality must come together, coalescing into what he then termed the "final normal shape" of adult sexuality. His daughter Anna first emphasized that this integrative task falls to an ego weakened precisely by the transformations in the body to which it must adapt (A. Freud 1936). The narcissistic vulnerability of the adolescent lies in this consuming contradiction: The helplessness before the inexorable changes, the intensification of the drives, the transformations of the body, taking place as the parents, to whom the adolescent habitually has turned at moments of helplessness (Gutton 1998), become highly charged, intensely incestuous objects from whom the adolescent must separate in order to become, as Raymond Cahn writes, a "subject" (Cahn 1998). In this context, Anna Freud describes the chaotic and desperate state, whereby the adolescent

> escapes the danger [of total narcissistic withdrawal] by convulsive efforts to make contact once more with external objects, even if it can only be by way of his narcissism, that is, through a series of identifications. According to this view,

DOI: 10.4324/9781003216360-11

the passionate object relations of adolescence represent attempts at recovery –
another respect in which they resemble the state of psychotic patients whose
disease is about to take one of its periodic turns for the worse.

(A. Freud 1936, p. 171)

Anna Freud was one of the first to link the process of adolescence with the processes associated in psychanalysis with psychosis, periods when the self is flooded
with overwhelming newly potent drives. In adolescence, the ego struggles to find a
way of defending itself, but importantly not defending itself so completely that reality is lost and the potential for relationship is also lost. The hallmark of this struggle is the diffuse, chaotic reaching after identity so notable in adolescence. Today's
adolescent turns to a wider culture than the family, to the external world, to peers,
to popular culture, to the new frontier, the world wide web, the light and the dark.
In the brave new world of cyberspace, it is possible to lose the self completely in a
delusory world, or, more commonly, find an alternative place in which to explore,
to play, to dream, not only to seek, but actually to find representations that amount
to developmental help towards a new reworking of the old identity (Erikson 1968).

Gender and desire mediated by the internet

At its best, it is a transitional space (Winnicott 1971), a field of play that is separate, free from palpable physical intrusion. It confirms a barrier that excludes the
parents, whose protection is now aversive, coloured with incestuous meaning, a
painful and conflicted loss, what Freud deemed the most difficult of losses (Freud
1905). An alternative experimental space, the world of the internet, offers temporary escape from the pressures of relating to reality. The field of play is framed,
boundaried, like the framed space of any artistic event. It can be entered, used
(Winnicott 1969), even surrendered to, in a willing suspension of disbelief (Coleridge 1817) without replacing reality. Yet in adolescence there is an urgency, a life
or death edge to the search for an embodied path into adulthood (Laufer and Laufer
1984). There is a danger, that the loss of the *modus vivendi* which served the adolescent up to puberty is too sorely challenged by the changes in the body (A. Freud
1936). The pressure brought to the world of the internet is too extreme, psychotic
in intensity. At its most dangerous, the adolescent can be offered there a world
into which to retreat (Steiner 1993), retire, self-destruct, attack eventually links
to reality as manifested in the body, links to embodied others, and to the reality of
the process of impending adulthood (Turkle 2018). For the very fragile adolescent,
the realities of the body can be dispersed into a discourse that functions like Victor
Tausk's "influencing machine" (1933).

The transgender discourse

The transgender discourse, which provides a field for discovery and validation,
also opens the way to action, an action very attractive to some adolescents at sea

in a confusion, bordering on psychosis. The discourse can tell you how to be, even how to change and control the body which has been in a state of transformation. Several years ago, which seems now a long time, in terms of the now much more nuanced gender discourse, I was interested to take on, for twice-weekly psychotherapy, an adolescent girl who, after considerable exploratory work in prolonged clinical diagnostic meetings, agreed that she was interested in and would accept the opportunity to consider more deeply her stated wish to reject her feminine body, to operate on it, to change it ... but to what? I did not realize in the beginning how much I would be competing with the internet, nor how little leverage I would have.

On first meeting her, an attractive, shorthaired girl in a trendy black leather jacket and jeans, I was struck by the tiny voice with which she spoke, however articulately and in earnest. There was something inescapably "little girl", in her short coloured nails, her tiny voice. Towards the end of the first meeting, at which we arranged times to meet, I asked her if she had any questions for me. With more assertiveness than I expected, she stated, rather than questioned, that she would like to be known as "they", not "she"... not "he" either, for that matter. I was totally taken aback as this grammatical position, those few years ago, was not one that I had heard before. She explained that this was a new position, this was an invention of a new movement. I believed her, though it also seemed very extreme. It seemed to me then that the seizing of linguistic authority took hubris to new levels, briefly I wondered about some collective psychotic omnipotence. I felt annoyed with myself, I had actually invited her to ask me if she had any questions, and I was faced with something totally unanticipated. I searched in my mind for a way to open up a dialogue, to regain my own equilibrium, to try for shared understanding. My countertransference was split very markedly, and I felt under pressure. I commented that "they" was plural, it usually referred to more than one person. She said no, not two people and in history there was a precedent: In Chaucer's time, the "indefinite third" was used frequently. At the invocation of Chaucer, my mind reversed, my associations, which did not resonate with the notion of the indefinite third, were awakened with the warmth I feel for Chaucer, the great 14th-century, deeply humanist writer.

Chaucer shows his pilgrims on a journey together, telling stories that link their wishes, their realities, their past and present, their social and sexual life, with the stimulation of the others on the same trip. Samantha was trying to do the same. Another bit of literature came to my mind, one which has long impressed me, the cry from the heart of the troubled and unmothered adolescent of Carson McCullers' *Member of the Wedding* (1946), who, as her big brother and his bride take off on their honeymoon, pleas for them to "Take me", stating with the poetry of pain, "They are the we of me". Problems of separation and differentiation, the adolescent task, are condensed in the young heroine's poignant, powerful voice, struggling to negate the inevitable, the facts of differentiation and separation. I heard my prospective patient's tiny voice, amplified by allies she had found on the internet, and I was moved. Through that sense of emotional connection, I felt hope. But that emotional connection was probably what my patient finally did not want. She was already defending herself powerfully from just such an unnerving experience.

I was not able to hold this patient in the psychotherapeutic space, however much I struggled, and was sometimes able, to open up my mind to hers, help her enter the therapeutic space, the play space, to use it to explore the meaning of her refusal of her developing female body. In her way, my patient tried too, and I think what she found was that the analytic space I provided, which of course, included me, could not contain the terrors that broke out as our exploration continued, could not provide the illusion of "pure control" that the internet gave her (Lemma 2010)

The first indication of the depth of the difficulty, which I only briefly noted to myself, took place in the first session, after I acknowledged the long time she had spent with her diagnostic consultant, implying she might be missing her. She protested, she had no feelings about her, though she could acknowledge a "kind of pattern" which now changed. I later noted in the margins of my records, a passing query about autism. I did not pursue it, even in my own thinking. In retrospect, I think this was the first very important message to me of her difficulty with feelings, attachments, and particularly any embodied attachment, as well as her withdrawal from the realm of the symbolic. But I did not take it so seriously at this first session; adolescents who are referred to psychotherapy after a period of exploring their issues are often cut off from feelings of loss, partly out of anger at having to change to a new therapist. I was heartened by her wish to think about a "child self" that she said she was not in touch with, but she did her best to contact. I was charmed by the way she addressed this child self, as if another person was in the room. I appreciated her eagerness to reveal herself through the definitions, by which she ordered her world: "pescatarian", "vegetarian", "straight edge", finally "trans bi". She said she was not depressed, because she had read a definition of depression, she agreed, she would not "appropriate" that word. She disapproved of appropriation, a word I had introduced. All the labels she claimed for herself seemed to have their validation on the internet, with which she was, I quickly gathered, in almost constant connection. I did not quite appreciate how close the words were to things, concrete objects to be clung to. She confirmed that she had no memory of feeling uncomfortable as a girl, or boyish, in her latency years. She did say that she liked wearing clothes that were all the same colour, "khaki".

I thought of our sessions, at least in retrospect, as a kind of journey through archipelagos of concrete images, words, and what she did not like was when there was a sensation of the unknown, when it seemed as if we left some safe verbal or conceptual port, and moved into unknown territory. In retrospect, I have thought that these moments occurred when her allegiance to her "trans bi" identity was in danger of being threatened, when we were faced with the sea of change which in fact describes the adolescent experience ... a process that has to be tolerated for adaptation to take place (Ladame and Perret-Catipovic 1968). I think she then longed for the keyboard, "the order of pure decision" (Lemma 2010).

Well into the three months we met, she announced that her mother said she should tell me about her wish for a hysterectomy. I said that she wished to remove what was specific to her adult sexual body, the capacity to have a baby. She responded almost physically to what I said, palpably recoiling, turning white with horror. "Honestly," she said eventually, "something about this conversation" was bothering her very much, she was feeling almost unwell. It was, she agreed, the words "sexual body", and she then confirmed that it was her adult body, she would not be able to have children if she were to have the hysterectomy. She did not want to have children. And this was a conviction she identified as recent.

The conversation shifted, away from the intolerable adult body, to cyberspace, where, it was clear, she did not encounter physical sexual bodies (Turkle 2018; Lemma 2015). I felt sad, as she talked of the *SIMS* games on her computer which she had enjoyed for a number of years, games in which there are characters, pixilated and abstract, with which she could play. She described how she could invent stories, where characters grew up, married, had children. She could create a world, as D. H. Lawrence said, of the novel, "a world fit to live in". I do not know if it was only me feeling sad at the recognition that in her virtual world, playing the *SIMS* game she had now given up, she had been able to imagine a real life. She did not disagree with my observation that the importance of the game world was its disembodiment (Turkle 2018).

She came to few sessions after this, though she was explicit about the degree of withdrawal that had ensued, she gave up school entirely, including the important exams which would have taken her to university; she withdrew to her bedroom, ate tiny amounts of her "lactovegetarian" diet, and by the end of the third month of our therapeutic journey, slept all day and engaged with her computer at night, when her parents were home in bed. She broke down completely. She had, she said, as if in dismay at what was happening to her, become aversive even to her beloved cats, she could not bear to be touched at all, even by her own towel after she took a bath, she would stand, arms extended, letting the water evaporate. All physicality was violently rejected, as were our sessions.

Discussion

I think Samantha made of the transgender discourse discovered on the internet a defensive network which gave a language or in her words, "made a pattern" that helped her to feel safe and recognized. But it did not function like play, like a dream (Freud 1900). It was not a transitional space (Winnicott 1971). The screen circumscribed a retreat (Steiner 1993) and the words and images, were the last objects she could cling to, as she faced the uncharted terrors of irrevocable change. Words and images were things, stripped of the penumbra of meaning and the acknowledgements of the resonance of symbolic functioning. They were not symbolic, more like the branch Aulagnier describes the autistic person clinging to when the world is in danger of falling away (Aulagnier 1985). Adolescent change had morphed into the falling away of the world, reality, sanity as the sexual body was repudiated. Years after the fact, I have learned that autistic features appear more prevalently in the transgender population (Di Ceglie 2018; Bonfato and Crasnow 2018) and particularly amongst those who become gender dysmorphic in adolescence.

Samantha was left, relating only to the internet, haunting the trans bi network, significantly, never entering into it, never risking the dangers of exchange. Her therapy with me, standing as it did for the reality of embodied change, had attacked the delusion which was the "patch" she had clung to as a last-ditch defence against total withdrawal (Freud 1924). By the end of our encounter, it did not function in this way. Samantha seemed well and truly confirmed in a psychotic withdrawal, the internet discourse was no bridge to reality, not even a patch of delusion that allowed her to stay linked to her life. It functioned as a total system with which she blocked out reality altogether. In her history, as she told it to me, the virtual world had not always been fostering rigidity and delusion, her games once had the feeling of a play space. But under the pressure of adolescent change, the internet world of transsexual discourse functioned as an impermeable barrier, effectively offering a total escape from the world, reality, her body.

Cyberspace: the bastion becomes a bridge (Baranger, Baranger, and Mom 1983)

In contrast, another young patient, who dropped out of school and withdrew from the embodied world of others at the same age as Samantha, was able, unlike Samantha, though with acute conflict, to sustain a psychotherapy, and to use the internet as a bridge back to the world. Different from Samantha, she could just, with intermittent withdrawals, endure the conditions of therapy, and survive the encounter with an embodied therapist. Her engagement with the internet was interactional, she played games, with groups, after some time in therapy, she entered into conversations, and her engagement with other players increased as her therapy progressed. She was not a voyeur. She dared to interact with it, to test the reality of the others involved with it. But like Samantha, she had broken down at the age of 18, withdrawn from school, peers, and academic preparation for university.

The challenges Iris faced growing up were externally much more obvious and acute than those which may have affected Samantha, whose history remained a mystery, but whose parents never reported any early trauma nor could she recall one in childhood. Growing up alone with a paranoid mother, Iris had been the recipient of powerful projections (Gianna Williams 1997). She remained vividly in touch with this heritage, and was often palpably taken over by it (Paul Williams 2004). She was clear, as she described her past, that her capacity to read her mother's psychotic needs had been a crucial factor in her growing up. At the same time, she established a defensive strategy against the paranoid accusations that invaded her when her mother's equilibrium was disturbed. She needed a screen more than most, and a relationship with the world was kept alive by various programmes or games, the foundation for what would become a path back to reality after her breakdown as an adolescent.

When Iris had been a toddler, around the age of 2, her mother gathered her up and walked out the front door of the home she shared with Iris's father, removing herself and her daughter from home, disappearing, from all but a maternal grandmother, with whom she kept in touch. She cut her daughter off ruthlessly from a past Iris would struggle to piece together in a psychotherapy consciously driven by a need to make history out of recurrently relived, past trauma (Baranger, Baranger, and Mom 1988). The mother's florid paranoia, first manifest in the demonization of the father, eventually excluded most of the ordinary world of childhood. As a young child, Iris was allowed classes, in art, drama, some intermittent contact with other children, but not school. From the age of 2 to 13 she attended two weeks of ordinary school, that at the age of 7. Most importantly, there was no contact with the father, who failed to find them. As her story has unfolded, the evidence has grown, to the effect that Iris's mother became more paranoid as Iris grew older. She became more and more reclusive. By the time social services intervened, alerted by concerned neighbours, Iris herself had become the pair's sole link with external reality. She described receiving the delivery of groceries on the doorstep, posting payment through the letterbox. Iris has spoken of her mother's preference for little girl clothes, shoes too small, a baby's bath for many years, an avoidance of help with hygiene, after she began to menstruate. It seems clear to me that development of Iris's sexual body inflamed her mother's paranoia, made real the loss of a baby whose separateness she could not tolerate. Her daughter's puberty therefore constituted a trauma for the mother as much as the daughter. Iris's permanent infancy might be understood as the delusional "patch" preventing Iris's mother's collapse into a psychotic withdrawal (Freud 1924). She was never able to reunite with her daughter after Iris had been removed from home. So mentally and emotionally invaded by the long years of isolation with her mother, Iris has since struggled with her own development, her own femininity, her own sexual body. What of her aversion to ordinary life belongs to her mother, so invasive of her internal world? What to herself? Are they the same, or are they different? She often found herself terrified of near-psychotic symptoms, hallucinatory experiences, fearing them as manifestations of the paranoid schizophrenia with which her mother was finally diagnosed. And of course, the absence of the father in her childhood contributed mightily to her internal confusion.

Iris was offered therapy with me for three years, three times per week, in an adolescent therapy clinic. I met in Iris, when first introduced, a wildly anxious girl on the cusp of her 19th birthday, her foot tapping anxiously, the shame of needing help acutely evident in an edgy defensiveness, an agoraphobic dependency on her father close to the surface. He had brought her to the consultation. Her only contact with the outside world seemed to be through the internet, I was not sure how. The rejection of any steps toward real-world engagement was lifted only in her agreement to seeing me, crucially supported by the relatively constant relationship with her father. Her father, who had missed out on her childhood, was very invested in trying to be of help to her development and her therapy. He was also, and with reason, wary of the force of her negativity and the fragility of her equilibrium, so clear from her breakdown. Trying to arrange therapy proved a struggle. She refused to come to my consulting room, thereby limiting her therapy to two times, rather than three times per week, as recommended and initially agreed upon by her. She opted to see me in an institutional setting, where I worked twice a week, and where a paternal function was more concrete, where the "brick mother" (Rey 1994) was more containing, there was less of the dreaded emotional experience of being left alone, trapped and isolated with a demanding maternal object/therapist (Gianna Williams 1997). At the early stages of her therapy, as far as I came to know, her engagement with the internet was limited to playing a game called *Warcraft*, interestingly a game her father had once played. Eventually, she would meet, then reject the first game-playing group she connected with, but she would move on to others. This movement, from game playing to interaction beyond the gaming project, to physical meeting and social interaction was repeated several times, her father at one point finding himself hosting a visitor from halfway around the world. He could stretch himself, allow his adolescent daughter to enlarge his world as she enlarged her own, a dramatic reversal of the mother's intolerance. As for the games themselves, Iris sometimes shared with me the intricacies, including her various roles, of whatever game she was playing, but throughout her therapy it remained her world, her separate world, and an important guarantor of her privacy. Like the reported dream of last night (de Moncheaux 1974) her experience of games were hers to share or not share, and she grew to enjoy her role as expert and teacher in the realm to which I was a foreigner, a novice, an immigrant. Perhaps she profited from the fact that I had no inclination at all to become a gamer myself. I was, however, very interested in her relation to it, intuitively respectful of the boundaries their existence reinforced, but often worried by the thought that she might retreat permanently into them. However, Iris' use of the internet was varied, ultimately, progressive, different from Samantha's, who never let me into whatever she was perusing on her computer, nor did she use it to connect with any others, nor to mediate the anxiety of being overwhelmed by the encounter with me.

Several months after Iris settled into twice-weekly psychotherapy within the "brick mother", the adolescent centre, but well before she shared with me much information about her game playing, and before she risked meeting any member of a group of gamers, she came to a session during which time her supportive father was abroad on holiday with his girlfriend. I had wished that he had not left Iris on her own so soon after therapy started, he had been so helpful in the establishment of treatment, occasionally bringing his daughter when she showed reluctance to come on her own. On the other hand, I appreciated the pleasure, relief, and appropriateness of his having a life of his own with a partner. Iris too had been worried about this separation and we were able to talk about the fears, the wishes, often expressed with great masochistic attacks on herself for being afraid of being alone, or of feeling confused. She had no tolerance of mixed feelings, experienced as mess, as bad. But we could arrive at some idea of her conflict. She did not want to be on a train with them, claustrophobically shut in to an imagined train compartment, but she was also very frightened of being alone, a starkly drawn image of fundamental adolescent conflict (Gutton 1968). However, despite her fears, and mine, this period went remarkably well: At a session previous to the one I will discuss, Iris had acknowledged with pleasure and surprise how well she was doing in her father's absence. Anticipated with dread, but accompanied by a capacity to think, Iris took some relatively big emotional steps. She was pleased to say that she had taken a new initiative, she had dared to cook, to fry a couple of eggs; I had not realized how many things one might expect as ordinary were extraordinary for her. She had taken a shower, and she had not had to guard against a paranoid anxiety that her father would, for example, barge in on her, something he had never in reality ever done, but she lived with a dread of intrusion that was pervasive and concrete. She came on her own to sessions. She even brought a dream, of an invasive swarm of cannibalistic cicadas, which we were able to reflect on a little. I felt very encouraged by what seemed amazing progress in her relation both to reality, to an ownership of her body and its boundaries, and at the same time, to a dream life.

Toward the end of her father's holiday, she announced, again to my surprise, that when he got back from holiday he was going to be so upset that she was better, he was so looking forward to his new job, which would enable him to work from home, and therefore to bring her to her sessions. I thought this was a blatant projection of the possessive internal mother, the internal mother who did not allow her to go to school, have friends, grow out of the baby bath, wear shoes that fit, that were not too small for her growing feet. I did not consciously connect with the mad oedipal mother who had crazily forbidden any contact with the father, an overdetermined element in the traumatic potential that would unfold. I took her revelation in the transference; I said that she was worried about father/me being disappointed if she grew more autonomous and less like a child. However much I thought this transference interpretation to be called for, even crying out loud for interpretation, she took it as a violent and indigestible intrusion (Lombardi 2017; Aulagnier 1975). I was rewarded with first panic, then a barrage of negatives, in palpable desperation, she turned every clarification I tried into an insult of her mind. Spitting with rage, she shouted, sarcastically "You know better, you are the only adult". Taken aback, I nonetheless persevered: Perhaps she felt I was jealous of her having attended, during this period, a session with the support worker in the same institution where the therapy was taking place, in order to try out an activity, some form of occupational therapy. (She had rejected three-times-a-week therapy with me, which could only have been done outside the institution.) Suddenly she changed completely: "Oh don't say you are angry with me, please don't be angry". The hostile and superior tone completely shifted, as she pleaded with me, and then, as quickly, reversed again, attacked herself verbally, "Oh, I am bad". The projections were flying, I struggled to field them, to fathom what was going on, when, finally, to my horror, she ferociously banged her head on the wooden arms of her chair, not once, but twice or three times. It was the most explosive session I remember ever being in. Horrified, struggling with my own panic, I asked her with a kind of imperative concern to stop banging her head. She stopped. She got up to go. It was not yet time. I asked her then to sit down, and feeling very battered, very aware that I had precipitated and then intensified this storm with transference interpretations, I said that I thought we could see that "there was a very fragile line or boundary, after which anything that felt like her getting better or doing well was damaging to someone". I aimed to distance myself from the interpretation, make it more abstract, I could see that I had provoked a traumatic explosion. I barely knew what I meant, though I had a vivid feeling that I had crossed a line. As I spoke, trying to calm an enflamed situation that I did not really understand, she turned to the wall behind me, she stared at the white wall, her eyes wide open, as if she was seeing something. I turned to look at this wall, I thought she was hallucinating, although she has never confirmed that she was. The moment was so vivid, it was as if I too thought something might be coming alive, through the blank white walls of the consulting room. I had tried to gather my wits, to survive (Winnicott 1969) as her therapist, to say something that kept our link alive, but my tone had been palpably fragile. Soon I told her that it was time. As if mirroring my slow speech, at the end of our 50 minutes, she got up to go, and she held herself against the door frame as she walked out. My faltering but still struggling voice seemed reflected in her body's movement. I believe she had taken something in, something of a reparative empathy, more evident in my voice, perhaps, than in words, something fragile, still alive but not a violent invasion. I believe it was benign, an "interpenetrating mix up" (Balint 1979), an emotional communication, mother and baby stretched to breaking point, and then, not broken, and not invaded either. Significantly, she held on to the frame of the door as she left, as if testing and then leaning on the boundaries of the space, which she could now leave, on her own two feet, as she had come. Green might think that the arms of the chair, and the door frame, both carried a symbolic connection with the holding or containing capacity that facilitates the capacity to represent, the origins of the frame, the arms of the holding mother (Green 2005, p. 161; Perelberg 2016). I remain struck by the displacement, from me, to the wall, the scene where projection moved away from mother/me and my body (Klein 1930), at the same time, staying in the room with me. It was clear we had emotionally affected each other, and survived.

I am including this extreme moment because I think it illustrates many aspects of Iris's intense conflicts, the susceptibility to being invaded, here, by my interpretation, I came too close, I was too penetrative (Gianna Williams 1997; Aulagnier 1975; Lombardi 2017). But I think it also marks a significant developmental moment in her therapy with me. She moved, within our therapeutic space, from explosive projective activity to violent head banging, to the desperate but less destructive negative hallucination (Green 1999b; Freud 1895), away from me, onto the wall, the blank screen, the barrier, the boundary, the dream screen (Lewin 1946). She did not leave the session when I said we still had some time, she stayed in the room with me. The frame (Milner 1952; Green 2005) had previously collapsed entirely in the violent action of banging her head, an action I would later learn that she resorted to as a child to ward off her punitive and paranoid mother. At the time of this session, I knew that violently banging her head had been a symptom of her breakdown. She had concussed herself banging her head while struggling to concentrate on studying for her A-level exams. I think the move to the negative hallucination (Green 1999b, 2005; Freud 1895), a displacement momentarily from me and my body, describes a move to a representational space, simultaneously a step toward a maintenance of her relationship with me, just barely the maintenance of an object she could *use*, within a boundary that could hold her and her aggression (Winnicott 1969).

She never regressed to violent action again, though the language of negativity erupted often. I believe this movement in the session also preceded her ability to make a creative use of the potential space of the virtual world.

The possibility of a framed space (Milner 1952; Green 2005, p. 161) was, I think, for this young woman, very much bound up with her need to keep out a violently intrusive present/parent/other/therapist (Gianna Williams 1997; Paul Williams 2004), and it describes a way of maintaining her sense of self without having to destroy herself or the other. The setting, the walls of the consulting room here finally, like the frame and screen of the computer game, come between Iris and the penetrating nightmare mummy/analyst, a version of which I suspect was vividly projected onto the walls of the room. I believe this movement describes a developing capacity toward a relatively healthy use of the internet, something which had been established in her latency years, before her mother closed that off too, as she approached puberty. The negative hallucination in the setting summons a self-preservative capacity which she had used creatively in her childhood but had partially lost in her breakdown, when she left school, and all real relationships with her peers. Inasmuch as both she and I survived the explosive emotional storm I have described, both she and I became safer in the embodied world of therapy. Later, she would enlarge her world of others, they too would come alive, present in her reality. She would allow herself to risk association, to move from chat rooms to reality with her fellow gamers. She would experiment with embodied connection, meet with some, eat with others, enjoy a world of proximity without invasion. Between her and me, we had found a representational path toward a fragile continuity, precisely what failed in Samantha's therapy.

As with Samantha, the world of cyberspace had a role to play in a struggle with sexuality and gender, Iris's experience so dominated by the profound terror of intrusion (Gianna Williams 1997). Cyberspace as a field of play (Winnicott 1971) allowed her to experiment with her sexual identity, inasmuch as she could use the safe place of the game to cast herself as male. She kept this from me for some time, and I would not be truthful if I did not own the fact that when she seemed to be implying that she was considering using the masculine and foreign-sounding name of her game avatar in her bourgeoning real life, I was not so happy. For the most part, she held onto an ambiguity that I hope will lead toward the possibility of integration of her masculinity and femininity. She never presented herself as confused about her body, and often revealed a joy in reporting to me of its actual growth, owning, not without some ambivalent, even terrified disclaimers, her developing feminine beauty.

Though she used a masculine avatar in games, in conversation with her fellow gamers she was herself, a girl, one of the few involved, a fact she eventually lamented. She used the representational field to pretend, most of the time, as I understood it, to enter into a battle, to risk failure, to tolerate defeat, and then try again, to learn, to graduate to higher and higher levels of making a war on a monster. The monster never had a sex, at least not disclosed in the therapy with me. But the primitive mad mother, incidentally a very well-educated mother in reality, I often pictured as a many-headed hydra, as I pictured the monster of the game. Most of Iris' fellow gamers were masculine, comrades in arms, allies, she was not left alone to fight a monster. Many she liked, from a distance, some she could admit to fancying. But, different from the experience she had with a real, probably frightened boy at secondary school before her breakdown, she remained in control of penetration, she never, while in therapy, allowed any of her fellow gamers to become sexually close. Interestingly, that first and only boyfriend was also a boy who played games. As she reported from time to time, as she recalled the historical trauma of unwanted sexual penetration, she could remember having been drawn to him, she wanted to be normal, to have a boyfriend, but her experience of sex was an assault, a terrifying making real of being taken over, her body invaded as she so often experienced her mind (Gianna Williams 1997). This actual sexual experience, along with the pressure to take in information in order to be tested at A level, had driven her breakdown. And yet, however much she initially withdrew from study and from peers, and in this she was like Samantha, she was also able to keep alive an interactional relationship with the internet which required the development of skills, competition, and interaction that eventually materialized, after some time in therapy, into real human contact, of which she was profoundly appreciative. A comparison of the relationship to food is telling, as Iris grew excited by food, relishing it, discovering a new world of gratifying sensuality, sometimes brilliantly vivid, Samantha moved in the opposite direction. In the therapy, Iris retrieved something from her childhood, and was also able to keep something of her own identity, and with me, survive the violence of interpretation (Aulagnier 1975) as Samantha did not.

In conclusion, the virtual world was not embraced by Iris as a delusional world, but has functioned as an alternative world, important because not real, used as a bridge, which she dared to tread, though she hesitated to cross. In some significant ways, she did not let go, she remained in control, though not in absolute control (Lemma 2010; Green 1999a). So with her sessions, with me, she did not quite allow herself to free associate, and she did not bring dreams to the session after the week in which her father went on holiday. The boundary between play and reality, inner and outer, past and present, dream and hallucination, could suddenly break open and frighten her, as it did most dramatically in the session included in this chapter. In this, perhaps, our experience as I have reported it would not quite be risked again. Although her preconscious capacities were very much enriched through the process of adolescent psychotherapy, there were also limits to the nonetheless impressive levels of integration achieved (Ladame and Perret-Catipovic 1968). She brought continually evolving news of her adventures in cyberspace, along with relations to other gamers, and reports of significant experiences, present and past, islands of anxiety or mastery (Freud 1920) gradually linking up into a container that gained strength. More illusion than delusion, her internet connection finally did not function as "patch" (Freud 1924) over a rent in the relationship to reality (Bronstein 2018). Her relationship with me has usually been very alert, active, and vigilant in the sessions, not quite surrendered to the moment (Green 1999a). As her "good" therapist I was often cast as a passive and appreciative audience to her telling me of her achievements. She was, of course, frequently very upset with me. However, I did not abandon transference interpretations (Lombardi 2017), though I was careful of them. From time to time, we were able to achieve something like reverie (Bion 1962), but this was rare. I hope that will follow someday, that a therapeutic alliance can be established in her adulthood which will further her capacity to free associate, to dream, to imagine a benign and pleasurable sexual penetration, and to mourn her considerable losses, chiefly, her loss of contact with her loving, if also crazy mother. For the most part, she has kept one foot in the virtual world, needing it in order to tolerate being in the embodied world/consulting room with me.

Her every move forward, of which there have been many, has been followed by a temporary retreat or reaction. This movement contrasts with Samantha's. There was only one direction in her trajectory while in therapy: After a brief period of engagement, she turned away from an intolerable reality, and away from me. We could not survive the terrors of transference, my embodied presence in the same room with her. No negative hallucination, no dream screen, no frame emerged to help us. Cyberspace became tragically a black hole into which her body disappeared, while Iris grew, literally, in inches, in shoe sizes, in stamina, and in a capacity to bear an emotional life.

References

Anzieu, Didier (2016) *The Skin Ego*. London, Karnac.

Aulagnier, Piera (1985) Retreat into hallucination: An equivalent of the autistic retreat? In *Reading French Psychoanalysis*, ed D. Birksted-Breen, S. Flanders, and A. Gibeault. London, Routledge, 2010.

Aulagnier, Piera (1975) La Violence d'interpretation: De Pictograamme a l'enonce, Paris: Presses Universitaires de France, *The Violence of Interpretation: from Pictogram to Statement*), trans. A. Sheridan. London, Routledge, 2001.

Balint, Michael (1979) *The Basic Fault: Therapeutic Aspects of Regression*. London, New York, Tavistock Publications.

Baranger, M., Baranger, W., and Mom, J. (1983) Process and non process in psychoanalysis. *IJPA*, 64: 1–15.

Baranger, M., Baranger, W., and Mom, J. (1988) The infantile psychic trauma from us to Freud: Pure trauma, retroactivity and reconstruction. *IJPA*, 69: 13–128.

Bion, Wilfred (1962) *Learning From Experience*. London, Heineman.

Bonfatto, M. and Crasnow, E. (2018) Gender/ed Identities: an overview of our current work as child psychotherapists in the Gender Identity Development Service. *Journal of Child Psycho-Therapy*, 44: 29–46.

Bronstein, Catalina (2018) Delusion and reparation. *IJPA*, 95: 1057–1074.

Cahn, Raymond (1998) The process of becoming-a-subject in adolescence, In *Adolescence and Psychoanalysis*, ed M. Catipovic and F. Ladame. London, Karnac.

Coleridge, Samuel Taylor (1817) *Biographia Litereria*. Edinburgh, Edinburgh University Press, 2014.

De Moncheaux (1978) Dreaming and the organizing function of the ego. In *The Dream Discourse Today*, ed S. Flanders New Library of Psychoanalysis. London Routledge, 1993.

Di Ceglie, Domenico (1998) *A Stranger in My Own Body*. London, Karnac.

Di Ceglie, Domenico (2018) The use of metaphors in understanding atypical gender identity analytic work, development and Its psychosocial impact. *Journal of Child Psychotherapy*, 44(1), 5–28.

Erikson, Erik (1968) *Youth Identity and Crisis*. New York, Norton.

Ferrari, A. B. (2004) *From the Eclipse of the Body to the Dawn of Thought*. London, Free Association Books.

Freud, Anna (1936) *The Ego and Mechanisms of Defence*. London, Hogarth, p. 171.

Freud, Sigmund, with J. Breuer (1895) *Studies on Hysteria, Standard Edition Vol II*. London, Hogarth.

Freud, Sigmund (1900) *Interpretation of Dreams, Standard Edition Vol V and VI*. London, Hogarth.

Freud, Sigmund (1905) *Three Essays on the Theory of Sexuality*, London, Hogarth.

Freud, Sigmund (1920) *Beyond the Pleasure Principle, Standard Edition, Vol 18*. London, Hogarth.

Sigmund Freud (1924) *Neurosis and Psychosis, Standard Edition, Vol XIX*, p. 151. London, Hogarth.

Green (1999a) Passivite-passivation: Jouissance et detresse. *Revue Francaise de Psychanalyse*, 63(3): 1587–1600.

Green, Andre (1999b) *The Work of the Negative*. London, Free Association Books.

Green, Andre (2005) *Key Ideas for a Contemporary Psychoanalysis*. London, Routledge.

Gutton Phillippe (1998) The pubertal, its sources and fate, in *Adolescence and Psychoanalysis*, ed M. Perret Cactipovic and F. Ladame. London, Karnac.

Klein, Melanie (1930) The importance of symbol formation in the development of the ego. In *Love, Guilt and Reparation*. London, Hogarth, 1945.

Ladame, Francois and Maja Perret-Catipovic (1968) Normality and pathology in adolescence. In *Adolescence and Psychoanalysis*, ed F. Ladame and M. Perret-Catipoivic. London, Karnac.

Laufer, Moses (1966) The central masturbation phantasy, the final sexual organization and adolescence. *Psychoanalytic Study of the Child*, 31: 297–316.

Laufer, M. and M. E. Laufer (1984) *Psychoanalytic Breakdown and Beyond*. London, Karnac,

Lemma, Alessandra (2010) An order of pure decision: Growing up in a virtual world and the adolescent's experience of being in a body. *JAPA*, 58(4): 691–672.

Lemma, Alessandra (2015) Psychoanalysis in times of technoculture: Some reflections on the fate of the body in cyberspace. *IJPA*, 96(3) 569–582.

Lewin, Bertram (1946) Sleep, the mouth and the dream screen. *Psych. Quarterly*, 15: 19–434.

Lombardi, Riccardo (2017) *Body-Mind Dissociation in Psychoanalysis*. London, Routledge.

Lombardi, Riccardo and M. Polo (2010) The body, adolescence and psychosis. *IJPA*, 91: 1419–1444, 43(1): 134–137.

McCullers, Carson (1946) *The Member of the Wedding*. London, Penguin, 1972.

Milner, Marian (1952) *The Framed Gap in The Suppressed Madness of Sane Men*. London, New Library of Psychoanalysis, Routledge, 1988.

Perelberg, Rosine (2016) Negative hallucinations, dreams and hallucinations, the framing structure and its representation in the analytic setting. *IJPA*, 97: 1575–1590.

Rey, Henri (1994) *Universals of Psychoanalysis in the Treatment of Psychotic and Borderline States*. London, Free Association Books.

Steiner, John (1993) *Psychic Retreats*, The New Library of Psychoanalysis. London, Routledge.

Tausk, Victor (1933) On the origin of the influencing machine in schizophrenia. *Psych Quarterly*, 2: 519–556.

Turkle, Sherry (2018) Empathy machines. In *On the Body*, ed V. Tsolas and C. Anzieu-Premmereu. London, Routledge.

Williams, Gianna (1997) The no entry system of defences. In *Internal Landscapes and Foreign Bodies*. London, Karnac.

Williams, Paul (2004) Incorporation of an Invasive object. *IJPA*, 85: 1333–1338

Winnicott, D. W. (1949) Mind and its relation to the psyche-soma. In *Through Paediatrics to Psychoanalysis*. London, Tavistock, 1975, pp. 243–254.

Winnicott D. W. (1969) The use of an object. *IJPA*, 50: 711–716.

Winnicott, D. W. (1971) *Playing and Reality*. London, Tavistock.

9

Child analysis 2.0

Jonah and the internet

Susan Donner

Cyberspace writer and speaker Alexandra Samuel divides today's youth into three groups: digital orphans, digital exiles, and digital heirs (Samuel 2015). The orphans are those who are left alone to explore the world of cyberspace, like gaming, websites, YouTube, social media, and porn. The exiles are those whose access is limited and therefore either throw themselves full force into cyberspace as adolescents or become Luddites, identifying closely with the older generations. Finally, the digital heirs are those who are guided from a young age by teachers and parents to embrace the technology, develop strong tech skills such as coding, evaluating online information, building and curating social media, and actively engage in ongoing dialogue about becoming a responsible internet user. Embedded in Samuel's categories is the object-relatedness of the process, that is, the parental views of cyberspace and technology and the parental protective role of filtering information.

As child and adolescent analysts, we are positioned to help our young patients and their parental figures think about the interface between the developing mind and the technology. And yet, with many of us as digital immigrants, as opposed to digital natives, we are in our infancy in approaching this world and helping our patients navigate it. Two psychoanalytic concepts—transitional phenomenon and claustrum—can expand our thinking about the interface of cyberspace and psychoanalysis as shown through the analytic case presented later in this chapter. Recently, a number of psychoanalytic authors, including Andrea Marzi, have taken the metaphor of the Winnicottian play space and identified cyberspace as a potential space, even a container of sorts, for mental contents: fantasies, proto-informatic elements, virtual objects and intersubjective patterns and relationships (Marzi 2016, p. xxviii). The manners, meanings, and potential creative use of cyberspace are as varied as an individual's internal objects. The aspects of the user, intersubjective and interpsychic, come alive in understanding how someone interfaces with cyberspace and the content they access passively and, alternatively, actively introduce. In this way, it might be a vehicle for daydreaming, exploration, creativity, play, and learning, in Winnicottian terms, a transitional phenomenon, or, on the other hand, a claustrum, to use Donald Meltzer's concept, a closed space of retreat, sadomasochism, entrapment, and addiction (Winnicott 1953; Meltzer 2018).

DOI: 10.4324/9781003216360-12

In Winnicott's 1953 classic paper, "Transitional Objects and Transitional Phenomena—A Study of the First Not-Me Possession," he writes about the first "not-me" possession of the infant and the wide variations in the infant's relationship to this possession. He uses these terms to

> designat[e] the intermediate area of experience, between the thumb and the teddy bear, between the oral erotism and true object-relationship, between primary creative activity and projection of what has already been introjected, between primary unawareness of indebtedness and the acknowledgment of indebtedness.
>
> (Winnicott 1953, p. 89)

Furthermore, the way an older child might

> [go] over a repertory of songs and tunes while preparing for sleep may come within the intermediate area as transitional phenomena, along with the use made of objects that are not part of the infant's body yet are not fully recognized as belonging to external reality.
>
> (Winnicott 1953, p. 89)

These phenomena occur at times of anxiety, when an object becomes vitally important for the infant for use in its defense, but can play this role "only if there are good internal objects can the infant use transitional objects, which are intermediate between internal and external" (Caldwell and Robinson 2016)

At the February 2019 American Psychoanalytic Association meetings, Lesley Caldwell gave a paper on "Parent–Infant and Adult Psychoanalysis: Re-examining Transitional Phenomena." Her main point was the frequent misrepresentation of the meaning of transitional objects/phenomena in contemporary culture. She clarified that Winnicott's use of the word "transitional" implies "movement" as opposed to "static phenomenon." In addition, she described that the identification of such an object/phenomenon is, for the infant, a "primarily creative endeavor with intersubjective and interpsychic connections but also a relation to the external world" (Caldwell 2019, p. 8). She emphasized that the transitional object serves as a substitute for the mother and therefore begins the process of symbolization. It serves, however, a dual function, both a defensive mechanism to "ward off anxiety, provide comfort, primarily in the absence of the other, with a wish to fill that gap … together with a curiosity" (Caldwell 2019, p. 37). What Caldwell emphasizes is the infant's active process of locating, identifying, and linking the internal and external. Thus, "the capacity to have a transitional object in a way that does not become a fetish depends upon a prior state of affairs between mother and baby … a good enough mother baby relationship" that the child captures in the relationship with the transitional object (Caldwell 2019, p. 26).

"A Developmental Line of Transitional Phenomena" is a chapter in the 1989 book, *The Facilitating Environment: Clinical Applications of Winnicott's Theory* in which Alan Sugarman and Lee Jaffe broadened the concept of Winnicott's transitional objects beyond facilitating the transition from omnipotence to the perception of external objects to include an additional developmental function. They highlighted that

> transitions from one stage of development to another precipitate strains within the individual due to a heightened disequilibrium between the individual and environment and these phenomena are needed in order to reduce this strain and allow for the regaining of equilibrium.
>
> (Sugarman and Jaffe 1989, p. 91)

They elaborated that "the specific nature of transitional phenomena will differ at each stage due to maturational and developmental shifts in cognitive functioning, defensive functioning, libidinal focus, affect organization and the demands of the environment" (Sugarman and Jaffe 1989, p. 91).

Thus, they emphasized the internalization and reworking of the internalizations of the primary object(s) via these transitional phenomena at these crucial periods, not just during childhood and adolescence, but, as Caldwell described, throughout the life span.

In his 2017 article, Sugarman reprised the concept of transitional phenomenon in the form of the smartphone during adolescence.

> It can facilitate the internalization of the regulatory functions necessary for the adolescent to move through that developmental stage and exit it as a self-regulating adult with an integrated and hierarchically organized self-schema or identity that involves self-agency and a capacity to be intimate with others.
>
> (Sugarman 2017, p. 146)

His emphasis on the use of the smartphone by adolescents to compensate for defects or to develop skills shined a positive light on the use of technology and its interface with cyberspace.

Cyberspace has the potential to be an integrative experience, an enabler of growth and creativity, but it also has the potential, in Marzi's words, to be a "compartmentalized transformation that narrows down to a claustrophobic experience typical of the various alterations present in the claustrum," a reference to Donald Meltzer's concept (Marzi 2016, p. 114). To review for a moment, Melanie Klein defined projective identification as an unconscious phantasy in which aspects of the self or an internal object are split off and attributed to an external object, often projected into the mother's body (Klein 1946, p. 104). Meltzer made a distinction between projective identification and intrusive identification. He felt that the former was a necessary healthy communicative mechanism by which an infant needs to control, possess and project into the mother as a containing function, directly referencing Bion's concept of the container-contained (Meltzer 2018, pp. 126–136). On the other hand, intrusive identification takes place with an infant with intense needs and fury who must violently penetrate what is experienced as an unavailable, unresponsive mother and thus, in phantasy, damages the object (Meltzer 2018, pp. 58–62). In this case, the mother's body becomes not a container but a claustrum, an invaded damaged space inhabited by claustrophobic anxieties. Without an effective father or third to protect this maternal space and/or modulate the infantile needs and affects, the infant invades and then cannot exit parts of the mother's body, the head-breast, genital, or rectum, as Meltzer described.

Marzi, in his chapter on "Cyberghosts", linked cyberspace to these chambers of Meltzer (Marzi 2018, pp. 114–115). The head-breast compartment can appear to contain intellectual stimulation or brilliance but be a dead-end of sterility, perfectionism, intolerance of ignorance, even an autistic refuge. Contrast the curiosity of exploring the internet with the flourishing of a cruel and omnipotent superego, the endless opportunities for envy and jealousy, embodied in the ubiquitous FOMO (fear of missing out) or critiques of one's own appearance, creativity, or achievements. The genital compartment, rather than a garden of sensuality and sexuality, can become what Marzi referenced from Meltzer, a "priapean religion" with the intensity and frequency of escape and gratification, which can lead to phobic and hypochondriacal anxieties. He poetically described the rectal compartment as a "true anal black hole that actively sucks the subject, in a satanic, omnipotent way, into a state of implacable addiction," and, I would add, tyranny, perversion, and sadomasochism. He is referring to the world of cyberporn with its "hyposymbolic or asymbolic states, an objectless void that is dehumanizing and annihilating" (Marzi 2018, p. 115).

Through a recent case, I propose the importance of the object-relatedness of an analytic treatment to allow a child or adolescent's mind to shift from what might be experienced as a claustrum of destructive phantasy to a more open system of play, creativity, aesthetic wonder, and progressive development. Perhaps cyberspace might be seen as another object for projection and projective identification that can assist the analyst in identifying the patient's unconscious phantasies. How a particular patient chooses to use the technology reveals much about their psychology and developmental status. In fact, the treatment might be viewed as a kind of virtual game with multiple progressive levels of interaction and even achievement for the patient and the analyst, with successful completion of each level leading to a new revelation and a new use of the technology, the analyst and the patient's developing mind.

Fourteen-year-old Jonah walked into my office with his hoodie stretched over his bent head and rounded shoulders. He punctuated his sentences with sobbing and bursts of hiccups, like a dysregulated infant. For weeks, he could not finish a phrase or sentence without interrupting himself. I was a witness to his non-stop annihilation of his verbal expression, like in a first-person shooter game. And he could not look me in the eye. Clearly, I was a potential judge who might criticize him and cause further shame and humiliation. Overwhelmed by his anxiety, panic, and academic and social paralysis, his aggrieved parents felt that his previous interventions had failed and agreed to a four-times-a-week analysis with frequent parent work.

Two months into treatment, Jonah came to the Monday session looking exhausted and tearful and recounted that he had asked a girl to come over to his house over the weekend. Soon after they started to make out, she stopped abruptly and said she didn't want to continue. He was distressed but complied. A few hours later after she left, she tweeted that she "had just kissed the grossest creature ever, dripping with sweat." Jonah was devastated and sobbed as he described the lie and humiliation, "My palms may have been a little sweaty but that was normal, wasn't it?" Over the next several sessions, he repeatedly reviewed the sequence of events and couldn't figure out what he did wrong. He tearfully recounted that he may have touched her breast, but he didn't think that merited her abrupt withdrawal and cyber-attack. Abruptly, he shut down all of his social media and cut contact with his group of friends, even his best friend who he felt was not adequately defending him. And yet, Jonah shared that he was addictively looking at Facebook, Instagram, and Snapchat postings by his friends and feeling FOMO. He would torture himself for hours and look at photos and "stories" non-stop to the point that he would get muscle spasms in his hands, perhaps a somatic representation of the excruciating pain of being left out. For Jonah, what may have started as a world of online and offline teenage play and exploration turned into a sadomasochistic nightmare of persecutory attacks. Jonah revealed more episodes of humiliation, where teachers and peers called him out publicly for his disruptive and grandiose behaviors. He and his parents labeled these incidents as examples of him being "misunderstood" or "underappreciated" but were oblivious to his initiation of provocative and contemptuous attacks.

In the consultation room, Jonah demonstrated his persecutory experiences through his need to question, doubt, mistrust, and criticize me. I focused on containing these negative bits, listening attentively and calmly and not responding defensively. I conjured Winnicott and allowed myself to "survive destruction by the subject" by tolerating his attacks without retaliation or abandonment. Eventually, Jonah and I were able to link his hypercritical judgment of me as a way of ridding himself of his feelings of disgust and imperfection and locating them in the other.

A crucial element to understanding Jonah was the gradual unraveling of his complex early history. Jonah's father was a partner in a successful public relations firm and his mother was a painter. Jonah's parents, already parents to one daughter, could not conceive another for over five years and had several failed *in vitro* fertilizations. They underwent successful surrogacy (the implanted embryo was with her egg and his sperm) with an easy pregnancy and delivery. They were devastated when Jonah was diagnosed with a life-threatening heart malformation during infancy that required emergent hospitalization and surgery. In addition, Jonah's mother suffered from depression and intense rages postpartum and during much of his childhood, targeting Jonah and his father, but not his favored older sister.

Jonah lifted his shirt one day when telling me a version of his early surgery. "I think my parents told me when I was little that it was a birthmark, but that didn't make sense. I know it is the scar from when they fixed my heart." He talked about needing to rub it like Aladdin's lamp when he wished for something, but he also described feeling ugly, disgusting, and defective. In a parent session, the parents and I were talking about those early months. I asked them when and how they had explained the procedure to Jonah. They looked at me blankly and said that he was a baby and wouldn't have any memory of it, so they told him around 3 or so that it was a birthmark. His mother added that there was nothing to discuss once it was over since it was a success.

It became clearer to me that, in this family, explanations were not necessary since separate minds, especially Jonah's, were not fully recognized. For Jonah, it became more apparent that not being seen was not just being left out, but feeling invisible or dead. He used his cell phone almost every morning to call his mother from school when he felt panicked, helpless, or sick, which happened almost daily. She dutifully picked him up immediately, did his homework with him and for him, cooked his favorite meals, and fulfilled his wishes. Even as a high school student, he would lie down on the futon in her pool-house studio and watch television and YouTube, stripped down to his swim trunks while she worked. The collapse of space demonstrated that the cell phone for Jonah was not a transitional phenomenon with creativity and movement per Caldwell but a perpetuation with his mother of the earlier facilitating environment of infancy with the mutual terror and overstimulation ricocheting back and forth from one to the other without an effectively present third.

Now, in adolescence, Jonah felt like a failure, unable to function academically, socially, or creatively compared to his talented sister and peers. Jonah retreated to a passive, depressive, narcissistic refuge where, helpless and ill, he could omnipotently control his objects with incessant demands and critiques. He even worried aloud that I would control his mind. About a year into the analysis, he was drumming with his hands during a silence in session. I asked him what that song was. He answered, "Janet Jackson's *Control*." He used his phone to display the lyrics, and he smiled as I interpreted his wish to be the one controlling his parents, his friends, and me. He spoke openly about wanting to be the one in control of everyone and everything as a way to compensate for his pathetic and diminished state.

Months later, after a successful teen travel experience, he recounted that he and a girl on the trip had sex, both for the first time, but it was disappointing. He repeated hysterically over several weeks that he was desperately confused by his lack of excitement. It took several weeks for him to tell me what was really on his mind. Eventually, turning away from me, he whispered that he was addicted to porn. He sobbed as he explained that it had been going on for years with unsupervised internet use. He was worried that the women that he was attracted to were all porn stars and that he had permanently damaged his brain. Sex with his friend was not what he imagined it would be. We looked at his outrageous expectations for women, including me, who would disappoint him and invariably be disappointed by him. He was convinced he was defective in so many ways, including his body, his creativity, his mind. He felt he could always rely on the porn images to allow him to be the judge, to control and repeat, or to dismiss in disgust or boredom. Not so in reality where he could not always be "in control."

Just before Jonah's departure for college, his father pulled him aside to show him something from work that made him proud: a secret file of clients' compromising photos and videos that he had kept from being exposed on the internet. The father asked his son to page through them at the kitchen table while his father ate a piece of apple pie. Jonah felt compelled to obey and speak about the "heroic" work intelligently. Jonah came to session the next day shaken by the experience and alternated between two assessments of his father, that he was either "some kind of genius" or a "perverted voyeur" who "couldn't give a shit about the impact of this on my mind." He worried about what it meant when his father was perusing his face and reactions to the images. He paused and quietly said, "Like he is a voyeur." He was surprised but did not want to disappoint his dad but was also excited to be treated like he was a grown-up, finally. He repeated that he liked that part but wished his dad could think about the impact on him. I asked him where his mother was during this kitchen scene. He shrugged and said, "Somewhere, another art show, it didn't matter to her." Again, I thought, the third did not protect him from the overstimulation of the claustrum, this time the genital compartment.

As I look back now, there was always a tension between Jonah's wishes to be seen and not seen that played out over the three-year period in the analytic treatment. For the first several months, Jonah sat in the chair opposite me but, only slowly over time, could he make direct eye contact with me. For several months, he tried the couch but then moved to sit on the floor to the side of the couch, so that he could talk more freely and be partially hidden. Before leaving for college, he asked to sit in my chair. We analyzed that he wanted to be in, what he fantasized, was the most powerful position and see the view from my perspective. While in college, we conducted the treatment by phone since he didn't want to be seen.

The transition to college overall was positive except for a new significant worry, that he might be impotent. Women were pursuing him for sex and, convinced he would be impotent and humiliated, he was making excuses and avoiding them. He worried that perhaps he was gay. He then revealed that he had had homosexual relations with a boy when he was 12 or so. Tearfully, he then told me that they "did almost everything." He was devastated after a couple of encounters that the boy disappeared.

In his obsessive and tormented worry that he might be homosexual, he described looking at girls and worrying that he didn't find them attractive since none of them looked like porn stars. He had researched on the internet the impact of porn on the brain and felt that maybe it had changed his brain chemistry. I commented that he had become quite confused about which images were his own desires and fantasies and which belonged to others. These cell phone sessions allowed Jonah a greater freedom to talk about his body, sexual feelings and fantasies, and sexual components in his dreams. He still was terrified of sex. I interpreted his confusion about what he was feeling when his heart rate went up—was it sexual or another kind of excitement or terror, fear of failure or judgment, or a return of the procedural memory of the panic of the early heart problem? He associated with a memory of when he was young of almost drowning in his pool and his mother being distracted and not rescuing him fast enough. In his distress, he screamed obscenities at her and she refused to speak to him for what felt like an eternity. I addressed his worry about needing me so much and being so angry and then worried I would turn away. He paused and then associated to a mirror in the girl's room. Strangely, he felt better making out with her in her room since she had a large mirror in her room where he could see himself. I wondered aloud if he unconsciously worried that he would disappear during sex and no longer be able to locate himself.

In that next session, he said that he had been thinking about not being seen and was ashamed to tell me that the previous summer he found a ChatRoulette site that allowed him to expose his genitals to other people, men and women, to see if he measured up. He explained that participants may find themselves viewing one or more people of the same or opposite sex who may or may not be to their liking and then can click the mouse and exit the chatroom into another random pairing, in essence spinning the wheel. Therefore, there was the opportunity not only for voyeurism, but also exhibitionism, appreciation, mutual masturbation, cruel criticism, and rejection. He assured me that his identity was protected. He said he was focused on preparing himself for college so he would be more confident if seen naked.

Jonah confessed that he was using the webcam while I was away for summer break. I interpreted, "While I was away, I couldn't see you when you desperately needed to be seen and this was your substitute." He sat quietly thinking. Over the next several sessions, we were able to piece together his underlying anxieties: that he worried he would be humiliated if he was not adequately "equipped" for college compared to other young men, that his sense of defectiveness would overwhelm his developing ability to soothe himself and he would need to return to his parents and to me as a failure and, most powerfully, if he was not seen or held in mind, that he might not survive.

We also explored the idea of withholding sex as a kind of power he held over the women but also as a masochistic and omnipotent solution. This way he was "in charge" of the suffering and conflict of "needing to be seen." I interpreted not just his hurt that I too might see him as a sexually incompetent little boy but also his terror from childhood that he could die from any extreme excitement, such as orgasm. He associated to his being sick or broken as a mechanism to keep his mother's attention. I wondered aloud if he felt he still needed to be ill to be loved.

Not long thereafter, Jonah announced triumphantly that he and the girl had had sex successfully several times, and he thought that the mirror in her room helped. I interpreted that the mirror allowed Jonah to watch himself during sex, to make sure he didn't disappear and to ensure that he would not be surprised with some kind of a scar. He was excited and surprised that she was complimentary about his performance and the pleasure he brought her during sex.

Jonah clearly used our analytic work as a vehicle for movement, development, transformation, and remodeling of his internal objects. In this way, it was a transitional phenomenon that moved him not just through adolescence but also through a reworking of the overwhelming early infantile experiences that became sequestered in his defensive claustrum, a retreat against death, defectiveness, invisibility, and shame. He used the analyst and the analytic situation not just to separate from home and leave for college but to relinquish the pseudo-independent world of cyberspace and cyberporn, establish his own emotional equilibrium and allow himself to have better relations with peers, family and even a girlfriend.

Cyberspace is potentially a challenge for the child and adolescent analyst, but also an opportunity. Examining the use of cyberspace and technology by patients allows for additional perspective on the patient and the analytic relationship. The revelation of Jonah's webcam site later in treatment allowed us to look at the stress of, and vulnerabilities underlying, his separation anxiety. For him, that revelation gave him a new level of self-knowledge and self-regulation. The analytic situation, as a transitional phenomenon permitted Jonah to shift from not just a digital orphan to a digital heir, but, to use Kerry and Jack Novick's (2016) concept, from a more closed sadomasochistic and omnipotent system to a more open and flexible one.

References

Caldwell, L. (2019) "Revisiting the transitional object and transitional phenomena" (personal communication).

Caldwell, L. and Robinson, H. (eds) (2016) *The Collected Works of D. W. Winnicott*. Oxford: Oxford University Press, www.oxfordclinicalpsych.com/view/10.1093/med:psych/9780190271350.001.0001/med-9780190271350-chapter-88

Klein, M. (1946) "Notes on some schizoid mechanisms." *Int. J. Psycho-Anal.*, 27: 99–110.

Marzi, A. (ed.) (2016) Psychoanalysis, Identity, and the Internet. London: Karnac.

Meltzer, D. (2018, revised edition) *The Claustrum*. London: Harris-Meltzer Trust.

Novick, K.K. & Novick, J. (2016) *Freedom to Choose: Two Systems of Self-Regulation*. New York: International Psychoanalytic Books.

Samuel, Alexandra (2015) "Opinion: Forget 'digital natives.' Here's how kids are really using the internet," www.ideas.ted.com

Sugarman, A. (2017) "The transitional phenomena functions of smartphones in adolescents." *Psychoanalytic Study of the Child*, 70(1): 135–150.

Sugarman, A. and Jaffe, L. (1989) "A developmental line of transitional phenomena" (pp. 88–129), in Fromm, M.G. & Smith, B.L. (eds), *The Facilitating Environment: Clinical Applications of Winnicott's Theory*. Madison, CT: International Universities Press.

Winnicott, D. W. (1953) "Transitional objects and transitional phenomena—a study of the first not-me possession." *Int. J. Psycho-Anal*, 34: 89–97.

10

Enforced virtuality

An unavoidable dialogue with some basics of communication within child psychotherapy/analysis

Carlos Vasquez

Introduction

The COVID-19 pandemic brought a radical change to our way of working with children. In my experience, and I guess in that of most people, psychoanalytic treatments with children carried out remotely was a very uncommon, almost unheard-of practice. In fact, Pozzi and Micotti (2020), in their literature review of the topic, found that only Sehon (2015) and Widdershoven (2017) had published papers about this. It was very difficult to imagine how one could work remotely with a child. The difficulty of remaining settled for some children with whom we work, within a video-call setting, seemed very difficult to imagine. In child psychotherapy, [1] children move, jump, hide, may want to play, to pass or throw a ball to the therapist, sometimes may run away from the room, and sometimes attack the clinician, amongst other activities that involve the necessary presence of the bodies of both the clinician and the patient.

Whilst in adult psychotherapy/psychoanalysis the main method of communication is verbal language accompanied by some bodily communication; in a child's case, one of the main things that serves the purpose of communication and interaction is action and bodily communication. It is as valuable as verbal language and in many cases is even more valuable. The child hides, for example, and the therapist seeks, maybe walking around the room. The child throws the ball, the therapist catches it and maybe throws it back. The child threatens to hit or spit and the therapist may feel scared, interpret, but must also protect themselves from a potential object or attack coming their way.

I remember one child patient who would constantly try to push me out of my seat, usually using his body weight. On several sessions, I had to sit as solidly as possible on my seat, and at the same time try to help him understand what he was trying to do, whilst he attempted to move me away. The meanings of his behaviour varied, but his relentless and challenging attempt to move me out of my seat was at times mixed with some desire to be in close physical contact with me. Sometimes, he managed to get to my seat by being faster than I was. I had to stand close to him and on top of interpreting what I thought was happening, remain close to him so that he could also feel the presence of my body, which I thought contributed to the

DOI: 10.4324/9781003216360-13

meaning or weight of the attempt to interpret his actions and recover the position he felt he needed to overtake. I usually recovered my seat only after he was sure I had *thoroughly* experienced what it was to be left without a seat and treated like a weak and humiliated person. Looking back, I thought it was important for him that I *concretely* felt in my body that someone pushed me out. He didn't feel he could just talk about it, but the concreteness of being pushed out needed to be experienced by me physically, so he felt I was *really* getting what he was experiencing.

I wonder as to whether we doubted so much about remote work with children, because we are aware of how central the communication and interaction is between the two bodies, within the context of child psychotherapy.

Video games: A possibility to continue working with children

During lockdown, Adam Duncan, [2] a child psychotherapist and adult psychoanalyst colleague of mine, commented that Ben Stambler (child psychotherapist) and himself had started thinking of *Minecraft*, an online video game, as a way of working with children remotely. I've never been a keen video-game user, but when I tried playing *Minecraft* for the first time, I could experience how realistic the game was. One could feel in the body what happened to one's character, such as the fear of drowning in the sea or the feeling of being lost when it was dark. In general, I could notice that through identification with my virtual character, my body was reacting to where my character was positioned, to what it was doing and to what the other player was doing to my character. This is something that Taylor (2002), amongst other researchers (e.g. Bailey, Bailenson, and Casasanto, 2016), has referred to as embodiment. They have studied the phenomena happening when players identify in an embodied way with a character in a video game – also called an avatar. The embodiment is a phenomenon that happens easily when playing a video game by making use of a character and therefore one's own body reacts in a similar way to the character's body phenomena.

Seeing that the game could easily elicit interactions between a 'virtually-embodied-psychotherapist-character' and a 'virtually-embodied-patient-character', and that one could easily feel things in relation to the virtual space in which one's character was located, I decided to give it a go. The other thing that I liked from *Minecraft* was that it allows players to use free play, and that this aspect of the game resembled the nature of child psychotherapy thus allowing the display of someone's imagination.

Minecraft description

Minecraft is a game where there is a virtual world, in which one can be with one or more players. The other players may be connected from anywhere in the world. The game creates a 'virtual world' with graphics that resemble Lego and therefore it feels like a game and not too real (Duncan, 2021). There are animals, plants, and different landscapes which are infinite – this means that as one wanders, the computer creates landscapes, animals, resources such as iron or gold, and also some monsters, such as big spiders or zombies. There are two modes of playing it: survival and creative. In *survival* mode, one can build and play in different ways but one could die. In this mode, one must work hard to get the resources to feed, build a house, keep oneself safe, and protect oneself to survive. In *creative* mode, one is unable to die and has access to many resources – something like a very well-resourced toy box.

As the reader may imagine, these two modes may be used by children to convey different states of mind. In my experience, children tend to use survival mode to bring dangerousness and the need to fight and defend themselves into the therapeutic setting, communicating states of mind more akin to fight-flight ones.

I'm including a picture of the game below so that the reader can form an idea of how it looks.[3]

One of the important features of using *Minecraft* for therapy is that one can set up a virtual world that is exclusively used by therapist and patient and that these creations will be stored allowing for some continuity, such as the toy box stores the child's creation, also providing continuity.

Some observations about the communication when the body is absent

As said before, in psychoanalytic treatments involving children, I find particularly important the impact the child feels they have on the clinician, usually using other ways of communicating, rather than – or on top of – the visual and verbal/auditive

level. That is, the body and action are usually at the service of communicating via projective identification, so that the patient makes sure (non-consciously usually) that they get across their emotional state to the therapist (Bion, 1959). One of the ways Bion (1959) regarded projective identification was as a baby's early way of communicating states of mind to the mother. One would hope that the mother would offer some containment of them. This is crucial from very early on in life, so that the primary caretakers are able to potentially 'read' what an infant needs physically and emotionally. The infant must make use of their whole body to transmit their psychophysical state in the hope of finding someone that can attune to it and react to it. Researchers focusing on infancy and the early interaction between babies and their main carer, have found how important it is for healthy development that a main carer can respond in an empathic way to the babies' cues. Music (2011) states:

> If a baby's signals are habitually not responded to, then what starts as a momentary coping mechanism, something that all infants have to manage, can turn into an ongoing defensive strategy. Such infants might automatically turn away from even friendly and empathic adults. Infants are aiming to avoid negative and uncomfortable experiences and optimise their chances of experiencing regulation of their affects (Music, 2001) and emotions.
>
> (p. 34)

Following Music (2011), we can see how babies make use of a whole range of cues in order to transmit their emotional states in order to get regulation from their main carer. In psychoanalytic terms, and following Bion (1959), projections are needed in order to convey their emotional state of mind to the object and thus be contained and not feel overwhelmed. This happens also in therapeutic settings. Salomonsson (2007) has given an example of how verbal and non-verbal communication interact to create the containment needed for a mother and her infant in a parent–infant analysis. Harrison and Tronick (2011) have also shown how consciously-unnoticed non-verbal, bodily cues between a child patient and their analyst have a major role in the transformations of states of mind in both, the patient and the analyst, only able to capture them with the looking back of a video recording.

The more a human being develops healthily, the less pronounced the ways of bodily communication usually become. That is, one hopes that the human being can rely less on their body as a way of communication as they develop. Therefore, children will still be at a stage in which bodily communication is crucial and responding using the body may be crucial as well, such as working with children under the age of 5 shows us.[4]

In the consulting room, action will be used by the child to communicate. Something I have found out whilst working therapeutically online is that the full blow of the communication using the whole embodied self is constrained. The communication involving smell and physical contact gets lost. Not only that, but the proprioceptive dimension of the patient's body in relation to the therapist's body and vice versa also gets somewhat lost. The patient can't sense if they feel the therapist is too close or if they want them further away. Or, likewise, if they feel the therapist is too far away, they may do something to make the therapist approach them. I think that feature gets somewhat lost, especially if one uses only a video call and therefore claustro-agoraphobic fears (Rey, 1994) or core complex anxieties (Glasser, 1992) may adopt particular manifestations, such as turning the camera off to keep distance and defend themselves from closeness.

I think that a similar phenomenon happens with the psychotherapist as a receptor of the patient's communications. Our ways of receiving the communications from the child are also curtailed. In a video call, we only use sight and sound to get the patient's communication. We can't use other senses and we can't use the whole body to communicate either, that is, where we stand or sit, in relation to the patient, for example. We don't know if what we say is heard by the patient at the volume we intend it either. The multimodal perception tends to be affected as well. At times, the image freezes, we hear something but can't see the patient saying it. The sound starts cutting and the impact of the communication arrives at the receptor in a modified way, not conveying the strength and the accuracy of it, demanding more efforts from psychotherapist and patient to repair these 'missteps in the dance' (Stern, 2009).

Both, the patient's communications and ours can get transformed or stopped by things outside our control, influencing the way the message comes across or maybe influencing explicitly the delivery or power of the projections. Therefore, I think one of the differences between remote and face-to-face child psychotherapy is in relation to how states of mind are communicated in a curtailed or affected way, making children and therapists feel that the usual ways of body-based communication may not be as effective. Thus, I am under the impression that the processes of projective identification get affected, especially with children.

However, I do think that when one includes a game such as *Minecraft*, on top of a video call, one isn't only able to include free play, but one is also able to incorporate, in a virtual way, the variable of a shared space. This is an important difference, because both, patient and therapist, identify with their characters and share space and time in the virtual setting. The possibility of playing together with the same elements reinstates body-based communication as there is a shared 'physical-virtual', three-dimensional space, albeit virtual. The notion of distance between patient and therapist (in the virtual world) gets somewhat recovered, albeit virtually. Given the fact that the game makes one feel realistically the things their character is doing, then, as said, there is a more real feeling to the interaction, because some of the embodied and proprioceptive experience is recovered by the identification with one's character. That is, if one gets too close to another, one can feel it in the body, if one gets too high up, one can feel it in the body, and so on. It incorporates a shared space–time dimension that is difficult to get through a video call.

For example, I had a child patient that was very aggressive during a video call session and seemed to want to get through to me in an aggressive way. After kicking the desk, he was looking around, seeming to look for a way to generate an effect on me. However, I thought that when realizing that he couldn't reach me physically, he started slapping himself and pulling his hair. It was only then that my countertransference changed and my fear and worry about a body being badly treated became more urgent. This made me comment in a serious and worried tone about him feeling he could only reach me by hitting himself as I wasn't physically there. He admitted to it and was then able to continue the session without hurting himself, even though he was still aggressive and had a diminishing attitude.

In general, this makes me wonder as to whether children that tend to act out more often, when only using a video call, would need to find alternative ways of transmitting the intensity of their emotional communications, given the fact that they do not feel the therapist is experiencing the real danger, for example, of a violent situation. I find that in online work, the possibility of being attacked physically, for example, is non-existent and therefore a child that needs its therapist to acknowledge a fear such as that, may have to change its usual ways of conveying this. Because of the embodiment phenomena, online video games, such as *Minecraft*, add variables which may feel, for some children, communicative enough when wanting to attack their therapist, for example, through an attack on the therapist's avatar.

In the following part of the chapter, I will present clinical material of a case to try to show how I think communication gets affected and the consequences of it. I will also try to show how *Minecraft* can be an effective tool in online treatments with children.

A case depicting some challenges and possibilities of remote psychotherapy using video games

Mario is a 6-year-old boy with whom I've been working for almost one year in twice-weekly psychotherapy. I think it shows the challenges of an online treatment, especially with children that tend to withdraw or disconnect emotionally and therefore some of them may turn the cameras off or find a way to keep the psychotherapist at a distance, which in online psychotherapy can be done very effectively. However, I also think that Mario's psychotherapy shows how there is still a possibility to work online towards creating some deeper connection with a somewhat disconnected young child patient, enabling young children the possibility to show their inner world in a very graphic, 'embodied', and alive way.

His treatment started online when he was 5 years old. He lives with his mother, stepfather, and a 2-and-a-half-year-old half-sibling. His parents separated during pregnancy, but he sees his father regularly. His parents were concerned about his constant disconnected attitude in lessons, especially during virtual lessons. The teachers saw him as somewhat melancholic, and his mother could notice this as well at home. This was sometimes related to issues around the early separation, wondering why his father wasn't with him and his mother in the photos of him as a baby. He would also wonder if he would be missed if he separated from one of his parents. He is a sweet boy but was also described as a demanding child that would want to control much of his mother's movements. In general, he wanted things to be as he pleased. Otherwise, he would throw a tantrum. In the first meeting with him and his parents, he struggled very much to remain in the video call, and I thought he wanted to constantly leave because of anxiety.

First sessions

I proposed playing *Minecraft* at the beginning of the assessment, however, the game didn't work in the first session. Even though he wanted to leave the session very soon, I managed to keep him interested and he began drawing Iron-Man pictures, his favourite character, but this didn't last for the whole session, and he left ten minutes early.

From the following session onwards, *Minecraft* worked, and we were able to play together in the *Minecraft* world. This enabled him to stay for longer, but most times he would play by himself and leave me far behind in the game. During this period, I thought that he seemed to keep a safe distance from me and therefore instead of turning to me for help, he would, at times, leave the room and ask things to his mother. Even though we were in a shared virtual space, he seemed to try to keep a cool physical-virtual distance, where he didn't feel the heat of the closeness, as this seemed to contain the fear of a potential rejection on my part.

During the early stage of the treatment, there were some brief moments of interaction until at one point he stopped playing *Minecraft* and started playing other video games just by himself, keeping me completely out. At times, I could only see his hair and wouldn't get any answer from him. Getting through to him was very difficult, especially around the time of the first summer break approaching. As said previously, I think that with children that tend to disconnect emotionally, online treatments can be more challenging and as a psychotherapist one can feel more easily nullified by the child. With the parents, we thought that face-to-face sessions may be the best for Mario. However, when we came back from the break, the second wave of the pandemic started and we remained online.

Some changes after the first long break

After some weeks back from the summer break, Mario started to be more interactive with me and more willing to play *Minecraft* with me. Maybe this was enabled by us working on some of his fears of rejection around the break and that my coming back implied I didn't abandon him. The following session is when he started to show some interest in playing together with me, however, he would put some pressure on me to keep the pace up and follow him. I thought that even though he wanted to be close to me, at the same time, he seemed ambivalent about it as well.

Session (seven months)

He demanded in a slightly bossy way to follow him.

Therapist: Ah, I see, there you are. (He was flying and going fast. I could barely see him from time to time and the feeling was of having to keep up so I wouldn't lose him.)

Patient: I'd like to move to the beach now. Let's go and find a beach. (He continued flying very fast, seemingly looking for the beach. Every so often,

I would get left a bit behind and he would stop, look at me and then say) Come on Carlos! where are you?! Come!

Therapist: Ooh! There you are! You're going very fast. (And sort of mirroring his demanding and diminishing voice I said) Carlos, come on! You need to follow me closely!

Later into the session, he once again demanded me to come close to him.

Therapist: You seem to want to be far away from me, but at the same time when you're far away, then you don't like that and want to be close.

He kept on flying and talked to me about wanting to find the ocean.
   [...]

Patient: (He continued flying) Look, Carlos, a golem!
Therapist: What's a golem? (I could see what he was referring to and it was like a big-foot-type character).
Patient: It's the village keeper.

He killed him and then celebrated that it had given him iron and something else as well, which I wasn't able to hear.[5]

Therapist: You're very happy that it gave you iron.

He continued flying and then he found a spear.

Patient: Carlos! Who has thrown this spear?! It wasn't me!
Therapist: You feel someone else has done it. You're wondering if it may have been me or otherwise there may be someone else in this *Minecraft* world. Or someone may have been here before.
Patient: Who may have thrown it?!
Therapist: You're suspecting there may be someone else that has been or is here.

He moved on and then suddenly the game logged him out. He got a little bit annoyed, but not too much, and then he went out to look for his stepdad. He remained calm. (His stepdad had asked him to remain calm if that happened, as he could become very frustrated).

Once he came back, he decided to play without me, in a world of his own. His stepdad left. He became immersed in the game and very disconnected from me, as he tends to become. I felt frustrated as I'd noticed him somewhat more willing to play with me just a bit before, after such a long time of not showing much desire for interaction.

Therapist: Mario, something came to my mind. I think that just now you wanted to play with me and be with me. However, you got very disappointed when that didn't work. And when it doesn't work, and you become disappointed I think you say 'you know what?! I'm not gonna be hurt anymore! I wanted to play with Carlos, however, it wasn't possible, so I won't want to look for him anymore, because it hurts me when I can't play with him, so I prefer just to play with myself. In that way, I won't get hurt. My heart won't get hurt'.

He continued playing by himself, very focused. There was silence. [...] He remained silent and then I decided to be more inquisitive as he seemed absolutely disconnected.

Therapist: Hey Mario, and what are you playing now?
Patient: I'm looking for something. I'm here. (He showed me where he was).
Therapist: Oh, that looks like a waterfall.
Patient: Yes, and I'm looking for something, but I won't tell you what it is.
Therapist: Oh! I see! Oh my god! There's something interesting Mario is looking for, however, I'm unable to know! I need to really know how it feels to feel left out. I won't let you know Carlos and you'll have to know how that feels!
Patient: (A bit triumphantly, but playful) Yes.

He continued playing. After a while in which he wasn't reacting I said:

Therapist: You know what Mario, I think that you feel that when *Minecraft* doesn't work and we can't play together and it takes you out of the world, I think you feel I am the one doing that and saying, 'I don't want to play with Mario, so I'm kicking him out of the world'. And I think that's when you say 'well, if Carlos doesn't want to be with me and play with me, then I won't play with him and I won't tell him what I'm looking for. I'll do the same as I think he's doing to me!'

He continued playing very much on his own for the last part of the session until it finished. I attempted a few other times to ask him what he was playing and he responded briefly then, but then immediately would get once again immersed in the game.

With this vignette, I'd like to show how, after the emotional experience of having gone through the first prolonged separation that was the summer break, Mario seemed a bit more eager to relate closer to me and play together with me. He seemed to trust a bit more that I was really interested in him. He wasn't so interested anymore in keeping me out, playing other games by himself, but was interested in playing together within a shared virtual space.

However, when coming closer to me, his anxiety increased and he therefore had to keep me at a safe distance. Calling me, but it was me who ended up following him and carrying the desire for closeness, something that I think is very important for the development of healthy narcissism. That is, to be able to feel that one is interesting for the object (Alvarez, 2012).

He, on the contrary, was searching for a nice place, but I was the one who ended up wanting to be close and not left behind. I think the projection of that feeling has been very important for Mario, i.e. that someone bears that difficult position to be the one desiring closeness, the one left out, even the forgotten and unimportant one. This is a challenge for a child with parents that separated during pregnancy. Fantasies around their reason for separating and the feeling of being unwanted can emerge easily, as one is the living link with a partner who isn't desired anymore. The child carries aspects of the undesired former partner and this can make the child wonder about his value to others. This aspect of the family configuration is something I think Mario was carrying and therefore his fears of being undesirable and forgettable seemed to be pronounced.

There is then a fight with a big-foot-type character that could be seen as an oedipal clash and after taking away big-foot's belongings, he suddenly becomes worried someone else may have been around, or I may have thrown the spear at him. It seems that there could be, at least, two possibilities: one, in which I may have wanted to retaliate, as a revengeful father-figure, throwing a spear at him because of taking away my resources (iron) or the other possibility could be that someone else, maybe another patient, has been in this *Minecraft* world, whilst he wasn't able to be with me, in the time between sessions. And, in that precise moment, the game fails, and he is kicked out of it. So, either his fantasies about me, a father-figure not wanting to be with him, preferring to be with others, or retaliating because of him taking away my iron seemed to have been confirmed by the electronic glitch. And he had to go through the distress of that experience.

These glitches are one of the most unhelpful things that can happen in online treatments. One relies on electronic devices and on the internet. And both can be very inaccurate devices to carry important, emotionally loaded communications. In face-to-face therapy, there are two people with their bodies. The interaction depends only on what the pair conveys to each other, and a device isn't necessary to pass on the communications. Therefore, I think unconscious communication can happen more straightforwardly and less affected than in online treatments. In the vignette above, one can see how Mario withdraws after the glitch in the game and then the connection to me is more difficult to sustain. As a psychotherapist one has to dedicate time to work hard around these 'missteps in the dance' that are caused by the communication being mediated by electronic devices.

Being more connected and using the game in a more interactive and playful way

Even though there was a problem with the device in this session, in the following sessions the emotional connection with Mario continued to increase and he started owning his desire for interacting with me each time a bit more. This process was interesting, as I could notice that he wanted to interact with me, however, to do that, he needed to be in control of me and assure himself I wouldn't go away from him. He would do this by building a room made from stone and no windows. He placed a bed inside and encouraged me to get inside. Once I was in, he would imprison me, and celebrate with joy I was a prisoner. He would keep me in there for a while, whilst I dramatized voicing my distress for being trapped. I would actually feel claustrophobic because of the embodiment phenomena I've described.

I thought he needed to trap me as I thought he was more eager to own his desire to relate to me, however, he was so anxious that I could leave him at any point and not want to be with him, that he had to control where I was and therefore imprison me, as he tried to imprison and control his mother who felt controlled by him in a minute way. In that way, he could come closer, but he didn't risk the possibility of being rejected, as even though his father was still in touch with him, Mario seemed to feel that he could lose someone easily. He grew up noticing that his father had parted from him and therefore Mario seems to feel he can't risk relating to someone in a non-controlling way, in case they leave. In relation to his control, these are also features present in some family members, as well, and he seems to have identified with these.

This new development in the playing led us to a new, more interactive phase within the video game. He started building a house with me: a more stable place where we settled. He made a swimming pool with a slide outside the house and planted some crops. He proposed to play hide and seek with me, within the game. He enjoyed me looking for him and beating me in the game. I thought this more enjoyable interaction, which contained issues around separation, reunion, and competition, amongst others, led him to ask me to join him in building a pen for animals, at the end of a session. He kept horses, chickens, and other types of animals in there. He seemed to be creating a containing space that could store alive beings. If one thinks of it in terms of a metaphor for the mind, one could see how Mario seemed to feel able to experience his mind as a container in which he could store alive things experienced in his relationship with me in therapy, whilst we didn't see each other.

Through the playing of hide and seek he seemed to be processing the going away and coming closer to me and therefore seemed to feel safer when faced with separation anxieties. He built a sign outside the house that said, 'Mario and Carlos house', seeming to be more willing to claim his desire of closeness to me without being too defended and frightened of being left.

Closer to the Easter break, he started playing (in *Minecraft*) an adventure where we had to get ourselves ready to leave the area surrounding the house, as if we were almost going exploring. He said that if we got lost, we would build another house, but had the expectancy to explore and come back. He seemed more flexible about leaving the place and even more aware of the implications of separation, but willing to explore, without so much fear of losing something. Maybe he relied a bit more on his container-mind to keep important experiences alive in his mind. We found a village and he decided that we should stay to live there 'but only for a while'. I thought this seemed related to the therapy break. There was a place that could contain him whilst his therapy sessions weren't available. I think that now that he was a bit less defensive in relation to experiences of separation, he could use the shared playground that Minecraft provides to explore, through play, his transforming feelings around separation.

Even though around the Easter break he became more disconnected, after the break he continued to be more and more willing to make sure I would connect to the games he was playing. He even, in a very tender way, blew me a kiss goodbye by the end of one of the sessions. At this stage he wanted us to play another online game called *Roblox*. In this game, one can choose different types of games. It is more structured than *Minecraft*, as it has tasks. Many of the games he chose were games in which he could play to compete against me, i.e. who was the quickest and strongest, for example, however, at other moments he also wanted to play in a team with me and would even get angry if someone attacked me. He showed much more eagerly how much he wanted to play closely to me.

I think that these last games have shown how Mario needs not only to measure his strength against mine, in a sort of playful oedipal rivalry with a father-figure, which could allow him to grow and make use of his capacities. It has also become clear how much he needs me celebrating his strength and abilities as a boy who could become a capable man in the future. He currently wants to play a game called 'Adopt Me!' and I think that in that he seems to be playing his experience of being also adopted (in a figurative way) by his stepfather and desired by the father figures in his life, as they have become very important for him. I think this important developmental need is being played out currently in the treatment and he seems to be wondering as to whether he is a capable boy or not.

I think that even though Mario is a boy who can be very effective at distancing himself from close contact and therefore in online therapy he can be more effective at nullifying me, with the passing of time and the working through of some of his fears around rejection and valuelessness, he has been able to engage in a less anxious way and feels freer to interact now. I do think that the possibility to play in a shared space, where he could display effectively his fantasies and anxieties in relation to the distance and control of the object, such as trapping me, being close or far away from me, collaborate with me, but also hit me in a physical-virtual way, amongst other things, has enabled the progress and the feeling that he can actually connect with me in a deep and relevant way, to play with me, if he wishes so. And this has enabled us to work on his inner world, making him less defensive about approaching relationships, as I think he has developed a more reliable capacity to use his mind as a container, somewhat more able to bear frustration and able to display his rivalrous fantasies as well, through play. This has enabled Mario to remain connected with me, to play *Minecraft* during his last session before the last winter break and to ask me to store some of his resources, trusting that a containing space exists, that it exists in my mind and that it is able to store representations of himself when he isn't around. This has eased his need to reject when separations are due.

Conclusion

I have tried to exemplify how I think that online treatments with children curtail the possibility to communicate with the therapist in comparison to face-to-face treatments. The way in which children unconsciously use projective identification as a way of communicating gets affected, because of the absence of the body. However, the fact that it is affected doesn't mean that it is totally impeded. I do think that if, on top of a video call, one uses a virtual game that allows free play and the possibility for patient and therapist to share a 'physical' space, albeit virtual, where patient and therapist can identify with their virtual characters, a shared space gets created where communication of psychophysical states can be more effective. An important aspect of this is how an online video game can include the phenomena of embodiment in relation to one's character and therefore some aspects related to the body in the relationship get recovered, when unable to meet in person.

I have been surprised to read about the process of embodiment in virtual reality games, in which, for example, if the virtual character has a tail and the player needs to move their hips to move the character's tail, then one ends up feeling one has a tail, through a phenomenon named *embodiment illusion* (Steptoe, Steed, and Slater, 2013). Even though it isn't the same as meeting an embodied other face-to-face, it adds to a virtual experience and allows for some body-related phenomena, such as distance and body sensations, to be somewhat recovered. I think this is particularly important when considering remote treatments for children living in areas where there aren't psychotherapists or analysts around.

I think that the *Minecraft* game allows children that are able to play to display their fantasies and therefore makes the work with children during a pandemic more feasible and helpful and it can bring the possibility of remote psychoanalytic treatment where there isn't the possibility of doing it face-to-face, such as Widdershoven (2017) has exemplified.

Notes

1 I'll use 'child psychotherapy' to refer also to 'child psychoanalysis', to make it less confusing for the readers.
2 Duncan (2021) has recently presented an unpublished paper on working with a boy using *Minecraft*, in which he touches on how using a video game such as *Minecraft* allows for the possibility of working in a deep way with children. In his paper he also notes on how virtual treatment allows for the rhythm of comings and goings from the sessions to be maintained in the therapy process.
3 https://dkofva0t6jnyn.cloudfront.net/sites/default/files/styles/amp_blog_image_large/public/consumer/blog/csm-blog/minecraft-glossary2-blog-569x329.jpg
4 See Reid (1990) for an example of this.
5 In *Minecraft*, when you kill a monster or animal, you get some of their belongings or meat, in the case of animals. This golem had iron as one of his belongings.

References

Alvarez, A. (2012). *The Thinking Heart: Three Levels of Psychoanalytic Therapy With Disturbed Children*. East Sussex: Routledge.

Bailey, J., Bailenson, J. and Casasanto, D. (2016). When does virtual embodiment change our minds? *Presence*, 25(3): 1–12.

Bion, W. (1959). Attacks on linking. In *Second Thoughts*. London: Karnac.

Duncan, A. (2021). Unpublished paper. Presented at the Squiggle Foundation.

Glasser, M. (1992). Problems in the psychoanalysis of certain narcissistic disorders. In *The International Journal of Psychoanalysis*, 73(3): 493–503.

Harrison, A.M. and Tronick, E. (2011). The noise monitor: A developmental perspective on verbal and non-verbal meaning-making in psychoanalysis. *Journal of the American Psychoanalytic Association,* 59(5): 961–982.

Music, G. (2011). *Nurturing Natures: Attachment and Children's Emotional, Sociocultural and Brain Development.* East Sussex: Psychology Press.

Music, G. (2001). *Affect and Emotion.* Cambridge: Icon.

Pozzi, M. and Micotti, S. (2020). 'Making the best of a bad job': A literature review on digital psychoanalytic psychotherapy with children, adolescents and families at the time of the COVID-19 pandemic. *Journal of Child Psychotherapy*, 46(3): 273–280.

Reid, S. (1990). The importance of beauty in the psychoanalytic experience. *Journal of Child Psychotherapy*, 16(1): 29–52.

Rey, H. (1994). *Universals of Psychoanalysis in the Treatment of Psychotic and Borderline States: Factors Of Space-Time and Language.* Magagna, J. (ed.). London: Free Association Books.

Salomonsson, B. (2007). 'Talk to me baby, tell me what's the matter now'. Semiotic and developmental perspectives on communication in psychoanalytic infant treatment. *International Journal of Psychoanalysis.* 88(1): 127–146.

Sehon, C. (2015). Teleanalysis and teletherapy for children and adolescents. In *Digital Psychoanalysis 2.* Oxon and New York: Routledge.

Steptoe, W., Steed, A. & Slater, M. (2013). Human tails: Ownership and control of extended humanoid avatars. *IEEE Transaction on Visualization and Computer Graphics*, 19(4): 583–590.

Stern, D. (2009). *The First Relationship: Infant and Mother.* Cambridge: Harvard University Press.

Taylor, T. L. (2002). Living digitally: embodiment in virtual worlds. In Schroeder, R. (ed.) *The social life of avatars: presence and interaction in shared virtual environments*, pp. 40–62. London: Springer-Verlag.

Widdershoven, M.A. (2017). Clinical interventions via skype with parents and their young children. *Infant Observation: International Journal of Infant Observation and its Applications.* 20(1): 72–88.

11

Primitive anxieties about intrusions

Imaginative conjectures about "no-entry" defences and COVID-19

Gianna Williams and Leontine Brameijer

Introduction

In this chapter, we are going to share some imaginative "conjectures" (Bion, 1970) about possible links between a pathological "no-entry system of defences" and the current pandemic.

Many years ago I (GW) suggested that "no-entry" patients may defend themselves from emotional toxicity, such as parental projections experienced as "foreign bodies", by concretely blocking access to their body orifices.

In the pandemic we all had to protect ourselves with masks covering our nose and mouth, even fearing access of the concrete foreign body, the virus, to our eyes.[1]

Has this global objective fear of intrusion into some of our body orifices coalesced with the dread caused by unconscious phantasies in "no-entry patients"?

It is difficult to talk about current patients and we are not in a post-traumatic predicament but living *in* a traumatic predicament.

I started to think about patients I saw in the past who would have been, I imagine, particularly vulnerable in the present climate. I returned to think of two of them in particular: Natasha and Sally.

Clinical cases from the past

I saw, many years ago, a young, prepubescent girl whom I called Natasha (Williams, 1997a). She was severely psychotic and I saw her five times a week for quite a long time. At the beginning of treatment, Natasha was terrified that insects, particularly fleas, would enter her orifices, and this included all her orifices; her mouth, her nose, her ears, the pores of her skin and her genitals. She kept the same clothes on for quite a long time. It was momentous when she allowed her parents to take her clothes off.

Natasha so feared that the fleas might enter any possible access in her body, that during the sessions, when the anxiety was very high, she covered her nose with one hand, and with one finger of that hand she closed one of her ears (she had very long fingers). She put a pillow on the other ear, and she spoke hardly

DOI: 10.4324/9781003216360-14

opening her mouth. It was at times really difficult to hear what she was saying, but generally, in that state of mind, she would just repeat a sort of litany containing the words "go away", and the litany had very few variations. On one occasion she addressed with "go away" the minute particles of dust held in a ray of sunshine.

Natasha was also very frightened of opening her mouth to let food in, and for a long time she mainly ate her food during her five sessions. She also drank with a straw, hardly opening her mouth, and she ate a large number of little triangles of cheese. She opened with her fingers the top of the triangle and then she squashed it and sucked the content. Those symptoms lessened during the treatment, but only very gradually.

My voice was experienced at times as a threatening foreign body.

I understood only retrospectively that the experience of being a receptacle of parental projections had been a significant trigger of Natasha's "no-entry" symptoms. Hence her fear that I might project toxicity into her with my words.

I was supervised on this case by Esther Bick and she did not focus so much on body portals as opening access to damage or to toxicity. She mainly focussed on Natasha's primitive anxiety about leaking out of her body.

I have found detailed notes of a supervision of Esther Bick in March 1972:

> the experience of the end of the week bites Natasha like fleas that make holes in her skin. That is what the fear of fleas is about. Every hole in her body is like a mouth, all those holes must be covered all the time or she will leak out of those holes. That is why she must cover all her orifices and she cannot take her clothes off ... When the separation takes place, the experience is an experience of liquefying, of laceration, of bleeding ... If you don't feel held you fall and you continue to fall and you never touch the ground.

The supervisions of Esther Bick and Frances Tustin have helped me enormously to understand the nature of primitive anxieties concerning body orifices.

What I have learned from their perceptiveness of terrors attached to body portals both in some autistic and some psychotic children (Tustin, 1972; Bick, 1986) helped my further exploration of the anxieties related to body portals from a different perspective, that is as terrifying portals of *entry*.

I developed this particular interest once I started assessing, treating, and supervising a large number of eating disorder cases.[2]

One such patient, the one who helped me to formulate the hypothesis of a "no-entry system of defences", the one I called Sally when I wrote about her (Williams, 1997a, 1997b), was an anorexic girl, terrified like Natasha of giving access to her body, and in this case all orifices were involved. (This would be very evident in the following drawing.) In Sally's fantasy, tadpoles would eat the inside of her body, so they were very dangerous. Sally was, as I said, anorexic, but she was also frightened of loud sounds, for instance, she could not bear the sound of an alarm clock or the sound of the phone. She could not be touched by a doctor except very lightly,

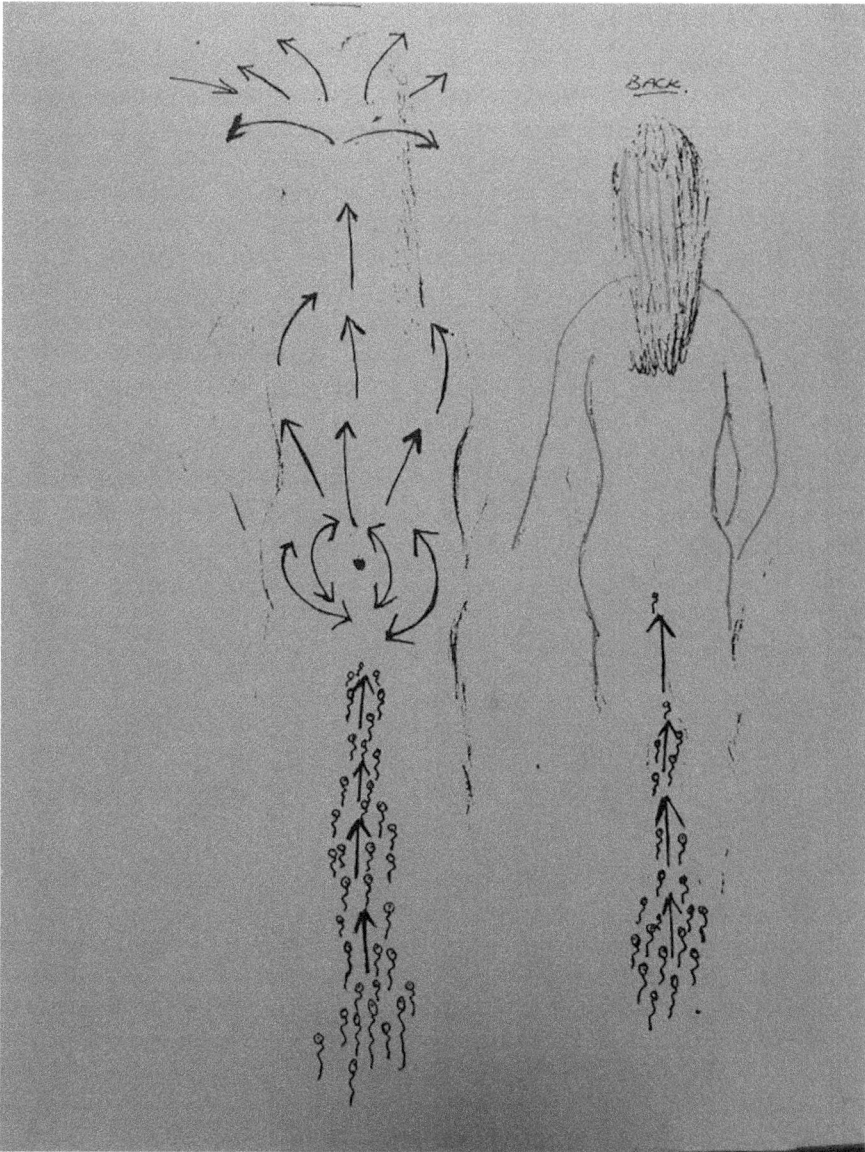

and not on intimate parts, and she was terrified of penetration. It is interesting that she was not a severely sexually abused child.

It has occurred to me that patients with terrifying fantasies about access to their body orifices, like Sally and Natasha, could be prone to excessive fear of the virus during the pandemic. I have in fact noticed in supervisions that some patients with eating disorders have increased their "no-entry" defences.

Brief notes about a current case

A little boy whose treatment I'm currently supervising developed anorexia after his family was tragically affected by the virus in the early days of the pandemic. Massimo is a 9-year-old Italian boy. It is well known that some parts of Italy were massively affected in the spring of 2020 by the pandemic. Many villages were decimated, and the people affected were mainly older people. Massimo lost two of his grandparents, a maternal one and a paternal one, both very close and very dear to him. Massimo became at first terrified of the virus entering through his eyes, because he had heard that this was also a portal of entry. Gradually this "no-entry" anxiety spread over other parts of his body, and it seems to be a component factor of the eating disorder he currently is being treated for. Massimo also suffered from projections of psychic pain from his parents in mourning: an example of projecting parents not being mentally ill but working through traumatic experiences.

I have been talking with a colleague (LB), who is familiar with the cases of Natasha and Sally, and she thought that the hypothesis about a possible link between "no-entry" defences and the pandemic was worth exploring. We spoke about some of her current adolescent cases and felt that they could provide food for thought.

She will describe two of those cases. We discussed them in the context of the hypothesis that there may be a link between the pandemic and the increase in "no-entry" defences.

*****

Notes on current cases

Claire

Claire, a 19-year-old student, was referred to me (LB) by her case manager at the in-patient unit where she had stayed for three months for treatment of severe anxiety. She had left home that year to start university but had soon suffered a breakdown. During her time in the psychiatric hospital, her symptoms had become worse. When I met her for the first time in my waiting room, I was struck by how extremely frightened and vulnerable she looked. I slowed my pace, avoiding sudden movements, and I spoke much softer than I normally do. A rather circumspect approach was required to enable her to establish a trusting relationship with me, as had been the case with Sally. Only after some time, I learned that Claire had been born prematurely and had spent the first six weeks of her life in an incubator.

Claire's anxiety centred around intrusion. She couldn't bear sudden or loud sounds. She had not been to the dentist for two years and was worried about tooth decay, but the thought of having to open her mouth for inspection made her rigid with fear. She had had no sexual relationships up to the age of 18. Since then, she had tried to have sex only once, with a fellow student, but had perceived that experience mainly as an attack. Only later she realized that her partner had not been aggressive but merely confused by her mixed messages. She had in any case totally "clammed up" and was now convinced that she suffered from vaginism. It seemed her sexuality was strongly repressed, due to a much earlier stagnation in her development. I could not diagnose an eating disorder, but Claire confessed to occasional binges and kept a close watch on her weight.

Claire needed to keep her eyes on me during our sessions and agreed to a face-to-face twice-weekly psychotherapy – my minimum. Initially, most of our sessions passed in silence. I often had images of Claire as a miniature baby in a transparent box with holes through which gloved hands frequently entered, inserting probes into her tiny body while she was surrounded by nothingness, not held securely by a mother and reassured by her voice and heartbeat. I interpreted very little and in an open, tentative way. Nevertheless, Claire frequently withdrew into a dissociative state following my attempts to reach out to her. I became more reticent at such moments until she was able to tell me she needed me to keep talking while she was trying to come back into contact with me. Perhaps she needed the reassuring sound of my voice, having missed the reassuring sound of the voice and heartbeat of her mother in the incubator.

After nine months, COVID-19 put an end to our live sessions. Claire, however, did not mind speaking to me over the telephone, on the contrary. She could now stay where she felt most safe: in her small studio with her cat on her lap. She started to use the telephone for all her contacts. She ordered her groceries and paid for them over the internet and carried them inside long after they had been delivered to her doorstep, to make sure all the viruses possibly present on the surface of the products had died. She washed and disinfected her hands religiously. In spite of these obsessive measures, Claire became convinced that she had been infected, interpreting even the slightest cough or sneeze as a symptom of the disease. She attempted to reassure herself by undergoing many COVID-19 tests performed at a local clinic, always getting a negative result, but this provided only temporary relief. After I had to undergo a COVID-19 test myself, I started to wonder how Claire underwent this highly intrusive and uncomfortable procedure of having a swab inserted into the nose and mouth, again and again. There seemed to be an addictive quality to her behaviour and in my discussions with GW, we wondered if this might have derived from a need to repeat and work through traumatic experiences, such as the intrusions into her body in the Intensive Care Baby Unit. There were clearly masochistic aspects in her behaviour too, and this could perhaps be understood as the acting out of a sexual phantasy involving a sadistically penetrating object.

Gradually, I became more fully aware of the significance of Claire's earliest, unmetabolized experiences in the incubator, first enacted by her in the transference as a longing to hear my voice as a reassuring container, and by me in the countertransference as a feeling that she needed to hear a mother's voice and heartbeat. Later, traumatic experiences seemed to be repeated by her physical withdrawal into her incubator/flat, including the invitation to repeated intrusions of the COVID-19 tests in nose and mouth.

In our relationship, there has been a gradual lessening of Claire's need to monitor the sound of my words to ensure there was nothing dangerously penetrating her, and I am feeling freer in the modulation of my voice when speaking to her. Both could be understood as a diminution of her anxiety of something breaking and entering into her. Also, since she has received two vaccinations, she is still aware of the risk of contracting the virus but in a more realistic way.

Lynn

Lynn was the only child of parents who were running a business at the time she was born, and she was often, from the start, looked after by different relatives. When she was 8 months old she suffered from recurrent ear infections. She was admitted to hospital for observation and was left there all by herself. This had caused her extreme panic and her screaming had been heard in all the wards, as she was later told. In addition to this early trauma, Lynn had been the "receptacle" (Williams, 1997a, 1997b) of the projections of her mother's youngest sister, who suffered from a progressive illness and died when Lynn was 12. She remembered how this young aunt rang her on her mobile at all hours of the night, sharing her despair with her niece and expressing a strong wish to die. Lynn was described by her mother as a hyperactive child, jumping on the trampoline for hours on end. As a 3-year-old she started at ballet and was soon identified as a talent so that she, at the age of 12, was accepted by a renowned ballet academy with a view of becoming a professional dancer. Lynn's obsessive trampoline jumping and dancing, which developed into a strict regime, reminded me of Bick's muscular hyperkinetic self-containment, a defensive second skin formation (Bick, 1964).

When Lynn was 14 her parents separated, to her "out of the blue". Her father left the area and her contact with him became sporadic. Her mother could no longer afford her expensive ballet school and she had to abandon her ballet career after 11 years to continue in mainstream education. The disintegration of her family and the loss of a rigid but containing training schedule seems to have dramatically interfered with her adolescent development. She started to suffer from migraines and quickly became addicted to the painkillers (opiates) her doctor prescribed. Now able to anaesthetize herself, she began to relentlessly attack her body, which had been such a source of attention and admiration only a short time previously. She started cutting muscles and blood vessels where she could clearly see them, on her hands and feet, sometimes damaging nerves in the process. She watched the results of these actions with a detached, almost academic interest. She swallowed small items too, like her stepfather's razorblades, and buttonhole batteries, which apparently cause small shock sensations in the oesophagus. She would then panic and raise the alarm, and was rushed to the A&E department of her local hospital where she had the swallowed items removed and the damage repaired, as far as possible. Stitches on the surface of her skin she would often remove at home, reopening her wounds. Her oesophagus was left permanently damaged so that she could only swallow liquidized food. At 20, Lynn was in and out of psychiatric and medical wards. She was on the verge of being given up when I was asked to see her for assessment, with a view of taking her on as an analytic patient, as a last resort.

On our first meeting, she was wearing tracksuit bottoms and a wide jumper, having wrapped herself in a scarf, in an attempt not only to hide her scars but also her emaciated body. Perhaps the more openly violent symptoms had distracted her previous therapists away from the fact that she was also an anorexic, as this was not mentioned in their reports. Perhaps afraid that I would turn her down, Lynn gave me some hope by telling me that, in spite of it all, she had been able to keep up with a volunteer job at a local dance school, serving coffee and tea one afternoon per week in exchange for a modern dance class free of charge, which she enjoyed very much.

Admittedly to my surprise, Lynn responded reasonably well to the routine of five-times-per-week analysis, even though my interpretations were often met with disbelief and ridicule. Apart from a few more incidents of self-harm her general condition improved and after six months she was discharged from the hospital into the care of a psychiatrist at an out-patient facility. She moved into a tiny apartment her mother had found and paid for her. Initially, she lost some weight but regained it too without much effort. She filled her days with her volunteer job and household chores, walking her mother's dog and doing odd jobs for relatives. At weekends she met up with her old school friends. As an out-patient, her attendance became somewhat less regular but she managed to come to most of her sessions, a 30-minute cycle ride away from her new home, and further analytic work could be done.

Then Covid struck. I had to stop seeing patients in my consulting room and Lynn found it too hard to speak to me over the telephone. Was it reminding her of the sinister calls from her aunt about suffering and dying? Of being left by her parents at the children's ward when she was still much smaller? I think she was angry too that I stopped the live sessions, interpreting this not as a measure also to protect *her* from possible contagion by *me*, but just as a way of protecting *myself* against *her* destructiveness. She telephoned me irregularly and our contact became more fragmented. She continued to be seen by her psychiatrist.

When the number of cases of COVID-19 increased, Lynn became convinced that she too had been infected with the virus, and this caused her great panic. She had numerous tests done (all negative) and was even seen by her GP, in full PPE, [3] at her home. When the infection rate went down a little and I resumed seeing her in my practice, she complained that she was not able to sleep at night, feeling either hungry or nauseous. She confessed that she ate almost nothing during the day but at night binged on defrosted meals her mother had prepared for her, without heating them up first. Also, she said that she was hearing continuous noises, probably made by mosquitoes "out to bite her". She began to stay away from her sessions again, telephoning me occasionally, saying that she felt too tired to cycle the distance to my practice and was now almost permanently suffering from nausea, headaches, and itchy skin. It was as if she felt that something invisible was attacking her relentlessly, rendering her exhausted and desperate. I think the state Lynn was in was many decades earlier aptly captured by Sally in her drawing of herself and the tadpoles trying to enter her body through all orifices, and by Natasha when she attempted to protect herself from the fleas by covering all of her body openings.

There was a hallucinatory quality to the way she described her nightly ordeal, and it occurred to me more than once that she was possibly again experiencing the dread caused by the telephone calls from her dying aunt (the "buzzing" in her ears) and the much earlier violation of her auditory channel by a piercing pain, experienced as an internal persecutor. Eventually, I became aware of Lynn spraying huge quantities of insect repellent around in her small flat, keeping the windows shut for fear of a break-in, effectively poisoning herself, as she did with her mother's cold casseroles.

In our discussions, we felt that Lynn had been quite dramatically affected by the pandemic. Her self-destructive acts could be seen as enactments of being intruded upon, as a small child, particularly via her auditory system, by foreign bodies both from inside (the ear infection), aggravated perhaps by the return of her own desperate cries in her attempt to get through to a deaf object, and from outside (her aunt's deathly projections). We also felt that there was a psychotic quality to these enactments, which distinguished them from the more benign enactments of Claire such as her projections into her analyst and her object-seeking behaviour. Initially, Lynn seemed to be able to benefit from psychoanalysis. Her acts of self-harm returned, presumably as a response to the sudden and real deadly threats caused by the virus, while at the same time live contact with her analyst became impossible and she could not bear just hearing a voice through the telephone. Lynn is currently only seeing her psychiatrist, but there is some hope that she will return to her psychoanalytic sessions.

Conclusion

In this chapter, we referred to some cases of young patients seen in the past, whose difficulties included a "no-entry" system of defences (Williams, 1997a). We wondered what effect the COVID-19 pandemic might have had on their symptoms had they been exposed to it. We also looked at two contemporary cases of adolescents in which a fear of intruders entering the body dominated the clinical picture. In these last two cases, the virus became one of the foreign bodies. The similarities in symptoms in all four patients are quite striking, centring around the intense fear of small entities, tiny living creatures like insects, tadpoles or spermatozoa and of course the virus, getting "inside" from "outside", through the orifices of the body, even as narrow as the pores of the skin. These symptoms can be seen as a consequence of having been projected into by a real object, having been used as a "receptacle" (ibid.) at a very young age, or as a return in the shape of "nameless dread" (Bion, 1962) of early unreceived projections of murderous rage and anguish (Lynn's screams as a child in hospital), something akin to Bion's minute fragments of beta elements (Bion, ibid.). We would imagine in many cases that the patient may defend against a combination of both.

The COVID-19 pandemic affected us all in many ways. Some of us lost loved ones, and we were all surrounded by anxiety and fear, and deprived of live social contact. We were also exposed to a bombardment of media coverage reporting on the risks, the infection rates, protective gear, vaccines, severe illness, death, loss, and grief. We saw endless images of patients in ICUs, [4] deserted streets, and of rows of coffins and graves. For many children and adolescents who, previous to the COVID-19 outbreak, were suffering from a "no-entry" system of defences, it is likely to have caused a dramatic increase in their symptoms. This certainly was the case with Claire and Lynn. External events may reinforce existing internal dynamics.

We were reminded of Melanie Klein, who wrote in her book about her young patient Richard, whom she saw in the summer of 1941, that the bombs and the threat of an invasion by the German army had not caused his difficulties, but had greatly aggravated the frightening destructive unconscious phantasies already present in his internal world (Klein, 1961).

Notes

1 In this chapter we focus on disturbed patients when talking about the link between "no entry" and the pandemic, but the media confront us with evidence that the pandemic has triggered mental health problems in people who were previously reasonably healthy.
2 I was for a long period assessing all ED cases referred to the adolescent department of the Tavistock Clinic.
3 Personal Protective Equipment.
4 Intensive Care Units.

References

Bick, E. (1964) The experience of second skin in early object-relations. In: Briggs, A. (ed) *Surviving Space. Papers on Infant Observation*. London: Karnac, 2005.
Bick, E. (1986) Further considerations on the function of the skin in early object. *British Journal of Psychotherapy*, 2(4), 292–299.
Bion, W. (1962) *Learning from Experience*. London: Karnac, 1984.
Bion, W. (1970) *Attention and Interpretation*, London: Karnac, 1984.
Klein, M. (1961) *Narrative of a Child Analysis. The Collected Works of Melanie Klein Vol IV*. London: Karnac, 2017.
Tustin, F. (1972) *Autism and Childhood Psychosis*. London: Hogarth.
Williams, G. (1997a) *Internal Landscapes and Foreign Bodies*. London: Duckworth.
Williams, G. (1997b) Reflections on some dynamics of eating disorders: No-entry defences and foreign bodies. *Int. J. Psycho-Anal.*, 78: 927–942.

Index

Ablow, J. 51
abused/neglected children: case study
        (Cassie) 74–81; construction
        of mind 88; defending against
        terrifying dread 74; developmental
        delays 85–87; gang state of mind
        74; 'multiple families in mind'
        of 82; progress measurement
        82–83; psychoanalytic intimacy for
        99–104; self-blame 101; therapist's
        survival 72–73, 76
Acquarone, S. 7
acting in-out xiv, 47, 140, 153
actions (all have an effect) 68–69
Adamson, L. B. 51
addressing the infant 1–2, 50–53, 57, 58,
        60–61
adolescence: challenge of 111–112;
        external reality today xii–xiii,
        xv; narcissistic vulnerability in
        111–112; paranoid mother (case
        study) 116–117; task of 108, 111;
        transference interpretations (in case
        study) 119–120, 123; transgender
        discourse attractive during 112–115
adolescent breakdown 116, 117, 120–121
affective-blindness 23
aggression (repression of) 39
Alexander, F. 91, 97
Almeida, Mendes de xxiv
Alvarez, A. xxiii, 5, 22, 143
anal/anality 36, 38, 94, 129
analyst: assets of xvii–xviii; capacity to
        bear induced affects 91–92; identity
        feeling as xvii; survival of 72–73,
        76, 130
analytic object 93

analytic office (transitional space in)
        xxiv–xxv, 42–43
Antinucci, G. xxv
anxiety: depressive 21; detecting deepest
        22; as a double-edged sword 21;
        mantling of 22, 31; movement
        between various levels of 22, 24;
        paranoid-schizoid 21, 73; from
        parents' detachment 37; psychotic/
        autistic fluctuation 22; separation
        anxiety 41, 46, 145
Anzieu, D. 44, 111
Anzieu-Premmereur, C. 7, 37, 41, 44, 52
assisted reproduction: and child's origins
        36; egg donorship 36, 37–38; IVF
        38, 39
Association of Child Psychotherapists 72
attachment disorder 40–41
Aulagnier, Piera 115, 119, 120, 122
autism: biologically based view of 5;
        changes and ASD child 23–25;
        Checklist for Autism in Toddlers
        (CHAT) 9; damaged mouth
        anxieties 10; despair when
        defences fall 4; development
        of understanding of xxii–xxiii;
        individual sessions 14–16; long-
        term analysis (case study) 24–30;
        more prevalent in transgender
        population 115; mother's
        identification with sibling figures
        17; optimal responders 5; parents'
        interactional style and 6, 7;
        resentment towards "cure" 4, 23,
        29; vocabulary development 11;
        see also observationally based
        interventions

For Product Safety Concerns and Information please contact our EU
representative GPSR@taylorandfrancis.com
Taylor & Francis Verlag GmbH, Kaufingerstraße 24, 80331 München, Germany

www.ingramcontent.com/pod-product-compliance
Lightning Source LLC
Chambersburg PA
CBHW050654280326
41932CB00015B/2909

9 781032 106458